Heroes, Villains
& Velodromes

Heroes, Villains & Velodromes

Chris Hoy and Britain's Track Cycling Revolution

Richard Moore

HarperSport
An Imprint of HarperCollins*Publishers*

HarperSport
an imprint of HarperCollins*Publishers*
77–85 Fulham Palace Road
Hammersmith, London W6 8JB

www.harpercollins.co.uk

First published in 2008
Re-issued in 2008
This updated edition published in 2012

1 3 5 7 9 10 8 6 4 2

A catalogue record of this book is
available from the British Library

ISBN 978-0-00-726532-9

Printed and bound in Great Britain by
Clays Ltd, St Ives plc

MIX
Paper from
responsible sources
FSC   **FSC® C007454**
www.fsc.org

Photographic credits
All photographs supplied courtesy of Getty Images with the exception
of the following: Chris Hoy family collection (plates page 1),
PA Photos (2bl, 2br), Action Images (4, 6c), Rex Features (8c),
Popperfoto/Getty Images (8b).

Thank you to Chris Hoy, whose cooperation and support for this book has been – a bit like Chris himself – exemplary. *Heroes, Villains & Velodromes* is not Chris's story, but Chris is the principal character, and, as he has so often been in the last decade, the star of the show.

Contents

PART 3: Bolivia to Beijing

'Excellence is an art won by training and habituation … we are what we repeatedly do. Excellence, then, is not an act but a habit.'

Aristotle

INTRODUCTION

A Righteous Kick up the Arse

Palma de Mallorca, March 2007

The scent of drying concrete fills the air; scaffolding is everywhere; workmen go about their business with a sense of urgency, adding bits to the Palma de Mallorca Arena here, painting bits there. The impression is unmistakable, and not in the least encouraging. The 2007 Track Cycling World Championships begin here tomorrow, in a place that currently has the atmosphere, smell, appearance, sound, and ubiquitous dust, of an unfinished building.

However, deep in the centre of the arena, in what feels like its core, far from the madding construction, there is a rather surreal spectacle: a perfect oval of varnished wooden boards, glistening and shining as they reflect the bright spotlights – a bit like crashing through a waterfall and entering a peaceful, serene hideaway. In the case of the Palma Arena, the sight is that of a beautifully finished, brand new cycling track: 250 metres all the way round, with steep, wall-of-death-style banking at each end, sweeping into short straights, then quickly curling into the next banked bend.

And in this oval, burling around the bends, thundering along the brief straights, the British team, comprising eighteen riders – with twenty-eight support staff looking on – are going through their final training session before the championships. They are slick, organized and thoroughly impressive to watch; they also present a neat juxtaposition to the chaos outside, the only reminder of which is the occasional sound of a drill or some piece of machinery wafting in when a door opens.

But … hang on. Twenty-eight support staff to eighteen riders: did I hear that right? Are twenty-eight people really necessary? I suggest to Dave Brailsford, the British Cycling performance director, that this seems 'a healthy ratio'. 'It's a winning ratio,' smiles Brailsford, a man who manages, somehow, to appear simultaneously intense and relaxed as he watches his men and women whirl around the velodrome in a blur of red, white and blue.

I am here in particular to see one of Brailsford's 'blue-chip' athletes, and a man regularly described as the ultimate athlete – the Olympic and world champion Chris Hoy. Chris and I were team-mates once. We were in the same Scotland team at the Commonwealth Games in Kuala Lumpur in 1998, but in many ways we belonged to different eras. For him, the Commonwealth Games were the start – they provided a springboard. For me, they were the end, the Commonwealth Games being as high as the bar of my ambition – I use the word advisedly – was set. In my case, a springboard with a malfunctioning spring – more like a trapdoor, really.

Back then, Hoy tended to be a little in the shadow of another rider, slightly older than him – Craig MacLean. The two of them came as a package: they were both blond, they were similar in appearance, they seemed inseparable and were constantly mistaken for each other. Craig used to sit in the apartment in the games village strumming his guitar. Chris didn't play the guitar but he was, in other respects, Craig's mini-me. There was something that set these two apart from the rest of the team, though. It was clear they were going places. The bar of their ambition was set fairly high; precisely how high, no one – not even them – could have imagined.

I was at those games, if I am honest, for the T-shirt (and three polo shirts, tracksuit, sweatshirt, shirt, tie, smart trousers, kilt and sporran, brogues, kit bag, racing and training kit … and yes, it says it all that I can reel that list off without really thinking about it).

'That [Kuala Lumpur] Commonwealth Games,' Hoy said to me on one occasion, 'was the last games where the Scotland team had the attitude of being second-class citizens, and of thinking, "We're gonna get humped here, but at least we've got the clothing."'

Our team returned from these games, according to one report, 'burdened by highly embarrassing statistics'. Which could be translated as: no medals. Again. Not that such humiliating return journeys were restricted to Scottish teams; at UK level, Britain's cyclists repeatedly travelled to the Olympics, and returned – one or two notable exceptions notwithstanding – similarly 'burdened by highly embarrassing statistics'. We were British: that was what we did. We got humped, as Hoy might put it.

Oh, but how times change. In Palma a new era is upon us – but more on Palma in a moment. This is the story of how that has happened: how the British team reinvented itself, and how Chris Hoy – who has been at the vanguard of this revolution, and is the central character in this story – is the embodiment of this new era in British cycling.

In one sense, Hoy was fortunate to find himself in the right place at the right time. In another, he is the perfect athlete to act as flag-bearer – because Hoy epitomizes all that is successful about British cycling. His finest hour up to that point was on a stifling hot evening in Athens in August 2004. The kilometre time trial at the Athens Olympics: Hoy's event. As reigning world champion, he was last man to go – a mixed blessing. As he awaited his turn, he was forced to watch no fewer than three riders break the existing world record, knowing that he would have to step up and go faster than all of them – and faster, of course, than he had ever gone before.

Each new world record inevitably made Hoy's task appear more and more difficult – impossible, even. Watching it unfold on TV, I found myself making excuses for him. Whatever happened in the next few minutes, he had done well to be crowned world champion. He, however, was not thinking along such lines. Finally, it was his turn to step up to the plate, as they say, and Hoy, looking like a man about to face the gallows – albeit clad in his unlikely 'death suit' of lycra – stood up, and walked awkwardly to the track in his cleated cycling shoes. And hurriedly, since a mistake with the timing device meant the countdown began early.

That technical glitch – possibly even more than the three world records he had just witnessed – was the moment when panic should have taken over. But if he was rattled, it didn't show. Instead, he sat on the wooden boards, looking confident rather than pensive, while the mechanics fitted his bike into the starting gate. Then he climbed aboard, took several deep breaths, as if inflating his body down to his ankles, and settled forward, wrapping his fingers carefully around the handlebars, standing up on the pedals, waiting for the clock to finish its countdown. And when the last five seconds had cranked up the tension to an almost unbearable degree, he went off like a bomb, releasing enough power to illuminate a small village.

As Hoy started his ride, cheeks puffed out, legs pumping, I watched in a pub in Edinburgh, where the atmosphere was close to that of a football match. We roared at the TV, and when, after four laps, he flashed across the line in a world record time, we cheered, and I turned to a friend and said, 'Did I mention that he and I were team mates …?'

Something else that happened in the build-up to Hoy's ride in Athens was telling. While he was warming up, a medal presentation from another event got underway; but when it came to the national anthem, while many continued what they were doing, Hoy stopped, dismounted, and stood in respectful silence for the duration of the anthem, before remounting his bike and resuming his warm-up for the biggest race of his life.

Back to Palma. The stakes are high as we near the end of another four-year Olympic cycle and the 2008 Beijing games loom on the horizon. Hoy is in action on the first night of the world championships, in the team sprint, a thrilling three-man race that, like many of the track racing disciplines, can appear utterly bamboozling to the outsider. But it is actually very simple. In a nutshell: three men start, one finishes. Opening that nutshell and examining the contents: the trio line up together on the start line, side-by-side-by-side. On the opposite side of the track their opponents do the same. On the inside is the lead-out man, who rides the first lap flat out and then swings up the banking; next to him is the rider who, having followed an inch behind him on the first lap, will hit the front on lap two; and on the outside is the rider who will finish off the job, completing the third and final lap alone. For Team GB, the experienced – that sporting euphemism for 'old' – Craig MacLean is the lead-out man; the young pretender Ross Edgar is number two; the dependable Chris Hoy is the anchor. Hoy makes a comparison with athletics to explain their specific roles: 'Man one needs the pure speed of a 100 m sprinter; man two has the speed and staying power of a 200 m specialist; man three needs the speed and endurance of a 400 m runner.'

The British trio qualifies fastest. It puts them into the final, against the French, where MacLean – billed as 'the world's fastest man over one lap' – explodes out of the start gate, all popping eyes and pumping arms and then, after a lap, swings up the banking, allowing Edgar to come past, with Hoy remaining in Edgar's slipstream. They are 0.290 seconds down on the French after a lap; Edgar reduces it to 0.281 after two, then swings up the banking as they approach the line. Hoy hits the front.

And now, not for the first time, we are treated to a head-to-head between Hoy and his old rival Arnaud Tournant. Hoy puts in a stunning lap, or perhaps Tournant slows down – it is difficult to tell. They are neck-and-neck on opposite sides of the track, and as they cross the line it is impossible for one pair of eyes to separate them.

The clock can, however. Just. The French have completed the three laps in 43.830 seconds – a world record; the British in 43.832 – also a world record, had the French not gone two-thousandths of a second quicker. So it's silver for Hoy, Edgar and MacLean.

'There wasn't much else we could do,' says MacLean. 'But I'm sure when we look at the video we'll pick a few things out. There's always room for improvement.' 'Tonight the French were outstanding,' adds Hoy, 'but at least we got that ride out the way before Beijing. We'll be better then.'

The following evening in Palma is the keirin, a discipline with its origins in Japan, where it forms a betting industry worth $7.5 billion a year; 'kei' means bet in Japanese, 'rin' means wheel. Many seem to be under the impression that 'keirin' means fight – which it doesn't, though it would be fitting if it did.

The keirin is a sprinters' event where six of them fall into line behind a motorcycle-mounted pacer, who over several laps gradually winds up the pace. There can be jostling for position, but generally the cyclists form an orderly line behind the motorcycle pacer and remain in order until, with two-and-a-half laps remaining, he swings off. Then, with the speed up to around 30 mph, it becomes a straight fight for the line, or as straight a fight as you can expect with six sprinters – who by definition are muscle-bound, (naturally produced) testosterone-fuelled alpha-males – competing with each other for the most advantageous position, which is generally held to be third or fourth man in line, where you have the benefit of shelter plus the advantage of surprise should you choose to launch an early attack.

But in Palma, Hoy doesn't ride the keirin like this. He opts for a different tactic altogether. In the semi-final he tucks in behind the pacer, as first man in the string of six riders. When the pacer disappears Hoy stays there, ramping up the speed with deceptive ease, and effectively making it impossible for his opponents to come past him. His is a victory based on sheer power rather than tactical acumen.

In the other semi-final his team-mate Ross Edgar takes the opposite approach. With a lap to go he is last man, placed sixth and seemingly out of it. Yet, despite the fact they're now travelling at around 40 mph, the compact, stocky Edgar manages an extraordinary surge, injecting enough speed to propel himself around the outside of the five flying bodies, to cross the line first. More of a pure sprinter than the powerful Hoy, Edgar has just demonstrated why, at twenty-four, he is tipped as one of the world's hottest prospects. It is a performance that is destined to become a YouTube classic.

So to the final, and a fascinating contrast in styles – but it is not just about Hoy and Edgar. There are another four riders, most notably Theo Bos, the rapid Dutchman. Bos – or 'The Boss' – is the fastest man in the world, the undisputed king of the sprint –

up to this championship, at least. Is he still the same awesome force? There are whispers and murmurs that he might not be – that chinks have been spotted in his previously impenetrable armour. Since being voted Holland's sports personality of the year there are even rumours that fame might have gone to his head, that he might have been afflicted by the potentially fatal condition for a sportsman – that of believing that he really is as good as everybody is saying.

Thinking about Bos, and speculating about his form, I am reminded of something Dave Brailsford has told me. 'We've banned the C-word,' said the British performance director. 'That's something we insist on.' But I wasn't looking at Bos and thinking that he was the most offensive word in the English language. 'Complacency' Brailsford had elaborated. 'We've banned it.'

As in his semi-final, Hoy tucks in behind the pacer. Bos sits behind Hoy. Edgar sits behind Bos. It is a good tactic: a British sandwich with a Dutch filling. When the pacer swings off, all hell breaks loose, as it always does in the keirin. As they hit 40 mph there is jostling, bumping, barging, but, as in the semi-final, Hoy appears quite serene at the head of affairs – all the frenetic stuff is happening behind him. Bos, try as he might, cannot quite find the strength or the speed to come round him: Hoy is too fast, too powerful. Holland's golden boy and defending world champion crosses the line second, with, emerging from the melee behind, Edgar holding off the challenge of Mickaël Bourgain of France to claim bronze.

'I had no pressure on me today,' says Hoy, who couldn't have been more imperious in winning the gold medal, but for whom it was, nevertheless, an unexpected bonus. 'Jan [van Eijden, the GB sprint coach] told me to relax, and in the final I used my kilo strength to lead out from a long way. It couldn't have gone any better. But it's a big surprise.'

And still to come, on the final night of the championships, is Hoy's main event – the kilo, in which he is Olympic champion, three-time world champion and sea-level world record holder. In six weeks, at the altitude of La Paz in Bolivia, he will go for the absolute world kilometre record, currently held by his great rival Tournant.

As reigning world champion, Hoy is once again the last man to go. The kilo – he insists this will be the last time he will contest this event in a major championship – also gives him the chance to draw level with the two kilo kings, both of whom have four world titles to their name. Ahead of him in the table are Lothar Thoms and – who else? – Tournant.

Another British rider, Jamie Staff, the second man to start, is the early pacesetter. He tops the leader board for the best part of an hour, until the penultimate rider – another Frenchman, the youthful François Pervis. In Manchester, just a few weeks earlier, Pervis placed second to Hoy in the World Cup kilo – and gave him a real fright in finishing just thirty-five-thousandths of a second slower. Now, in Palma, it all comes down to Hoy and the clock. He races through the first of the four laps marginally up on Pervis, but down on the time set by fast starter Staff. Hoy has to lift it and he does; at half distance he is a tenth of a second ahead but it is in the second half that he makes the difference, accelerating to cross the line in 1.00.999, almost a full second quicker than Pervis. It is Hoy's second fastest kilo and the second fastest time ever recorded at sea level.

It puts the icing on a generous cake: the championships have been an astonishing success for Hoy and for Team GB. In fact, Hoy's haul here in Palma means that he is now the most success-ful British cyclist of all time in terms of gold medals won at world championships, with seven golds, one silver, three bronze, to add to Olympic gold and silver, not to mention two golds and two bronzes at the Commonwealth Games He can now be hailed as Britain's most successful track cyclist ever. The debate over whether he is the best ever can rage in internet chat rooms.

Yet there is a sour taste in his mouth. It had been his final championship kilo, but not out of choice. The decision had been effectively forced on him by cycling's world governing body, the UCI, who, in an act as bizarre as it seemed perverse, responded to the most exciting kilo of all time – at the Athens Olympics in 2004 – by dropping the event from the Olympic programme.

'I'd love to do the kilo at the world championships in Manchester next year and go for a fifth title,' Hoy tells the press in Palma, 'and obviously I'd have loved to go to Beijing and defend my Olympic title, but I really have to draw a line under this event now and focus on an Olympic event. But it's frustrating because I don't think the powers-that-be really understand certain facets of the sport. I don't think they realize the implications of what they've done.'

The challenge now for Hoy is to try his hand at new disciplines – the sprint and the keirin. His surprise victory in the keirin in Palma gives him confidence but Hoy is under no illusions: he knows he has much to learn. He also knows that, at thirty-one, he doesn't have much time. He is a (comparatively) old dog having to learn new tricks if he is to have any chance at all of fulfilling his ambition of a second Olympic gold medal. Imagine Michael Johnson, at his peak, being told the 400 m was being scrapped; or Ed Moses being told to switch to flat racing. This is the scenario Hoy has been presented with thanks to the scrapping of the kilo. The next twelve months will tell him if such a transition is possible – he is acutely aware that it might not be.

But otherwise the taste in Palma is of sweet success. 'Being here at the world championships with the British team has been great,' says Hoy after his kilo victory. 'We're really unified. There are no cliques, no divides. We go into every event thinking we can win medals. We have a winning mentality.'

As he is talking, the opening bars of 'God Save the Queen' fill the Palma Arena (again), and Brailsford can be seen deep in conversation with a member of his four-strong senior management team – Britain's 1992 Olympic pursuit champion Chris Boardman. Both are standing with their arms crossed. They uncross them and cease their conversation for the national anthem, then immediately recross their arms and renew the discussion. It looks like they're plotting something.

They are. But eventually they part and Brailsford offers a review of the championships. Or, rather, he doesn't. Instead, he looks forward. 'Tomorrow,' he says, 'I will be at my desk in the Manchester Velodrome, relentlessly planning our pursuit of medals in Beijing.'

In the final reckoning, the British team has claimed eleven medals in Palma, including seven gold: 41 per cent of all the available world titles. The other squads retreat from the arena licking their wounds. 'We've just had a righteous kick up the arse,' admits the Australian coach, Martin Barras. 'That was the best performance by a track team, period,' he elaborates. 'It's as simple as that. And Chris? What can you say? His win in the keirin was something else, and I'd put his kilo here in Palma above his performance at the Olympics. It was phenomenal. As a professional coach, never mind the coach of a rival team, you just have to go: "Wow."'

Brailsford can well afford to be satisfied, then. The Olympics are the overriding goal, as he keeps stressing, but with every medal his stock – and that of the British team – rises. The unprecedented success in Palma means it has never been higher, and it was already pretty high before Palma, when it was reported that various performance directors from other sports had been beating a path to his door, to pick his brains and learn from Britain's most successful team. Apparently, the people charged with running athletics, rugby and rowing had all been to visit Brailsford in recent weeks. Brailsford is coy on this.

In talking to Brailsford, however, there is one subject that looms ominously and lurks malevolently in the shadows. This being cycling, there has been a gathering cloud of suspicion, rumour and innuendo, whispered in the past, but inevitably set to be more explicitly stated the more successful they become. In the Italian camp there have been accusations that the secret to the British team's success must be doping – organized, systematic doping.

When asked about this, Brailsford doesn't sigh in exasperation. He doesn't fix you with a withering stare. He doesn't point out that it is impossible to prove a negative. In short, he doesn't dodge the subject. And what he says, though it may look almost naive, contains an irresistible logic. 'We create an environment in which athletes don't want to dope,' he says. Ah. Okay, then. But how? 'Come and have a look at what we do,' shrugs Brailsford. 'We have nothing to hide. We look at aspects of performance that have nothing to do with doping. But anyone who wants to check us out can come and have a look at our anti-doping programme and draw their own conclusions.'

But if it isn't a highly sophisticated and organized doping programme, then what is the secret? Is there one? Still hanging around the track centre is Boardman, whose remit, as director of coaching, includes 'research and development'. The man who was once famous for winning the Olympics on a machine christened 'Superbike' is now – appropriately enough – charged with sourcing and developing the latest, most cutting edge equipment, from clothing to bikes. Boardman is leaning over one of the barriers that segregate the teams, in their 'pens', when I approach him. He looks furtive. Nothing to hide, eh? Yeah, right – not according to Boardman. While Brailsford stresses that the anti-doping programme is open for inspection, Boardman makes it clear that the equipment bunker – the 'Secret Squirrel Club' he calls it – is strictly off-limits. So the implication is clear. Effectively, what they seem to be saying is: 'You can come and watch our athletes piss into a bottle; just don't ask them about the fancy saddles they use in training.'

'We have kit we've been using in training but we haven't used it here,' confirms Boardman. 'We produced some really sexy handlebars for the sprinters last year, but at last year's world championships the Germans came along and took some pictures of our handlebars, and now they've got them.' It is easy to see how this could happen. At a track meeting, where the teams occupy their pens in the centre, separated from each other only by metal fencing, equipment is easily visible. All kinds of people are sniffing around. And some, says Boardman, are spies. 'If you leave stuff lying around the track centre,' he points out, 'then people will see it.' It is fairly important, then, to keep the top Secret Squirrel 'stuff' hidden – and note, incidentally, the deliberately frivolous, almost Orwellian sounding, moniker assigned to Boardman's 'club'. 'We're paying a lot of money to develop this stuff,' he points out, 'so next year we'll use it in competition, but it'll be too late for anybody to copy.

'And a lot of it you won't even be able to see,' he adds, looking satisfied. As well he might. He knows that, if nothing else, such talk will score points in the psychological war. Consider this: if it is frustrating for the opposition to look enviously at the state-of-the-art machines belonging to their rivals, then how frustrating must it be to know that you can't even see half of what makes it state-of-the-art? It is the sporting equivalent of Donald Rumsfeld's infamous 'known unknowns' argument. 'There are known knowns,' said the then US secretary of state for defense, speaking of the War on Terror. 'Then there are known unknowns. But there are also unknown unknowns.' Some of the stuff in Boardman's Secret Squirrel Club comes into this category. As far as the opposition is concerned, it is an unknown unknown. How much of a mind-fuck is that?

This, mind you, is a game that goes on between all the teams, with psychological warfare a big part of track cycling for all kinds of reasons – the riders rub shoulders in the track centre, they warm up in full view of each other, the racing itself is gladiatorial; there are no hiding places; image and appearance is (almost) everything. Boardman doesn't criticize other teams for 'sniffing around.' Far from it.

'Oh, we do it,' he says. 'I don't do it myself, because that would be too obvious. I have somebody doing it for me, and I can assure you they're not wearing a GB T-shirt. I heard about one bike manufacturer sending guys who looked like cycling groupies in long hair and long shorts. They'd look daft and ask stupid questions and the mechanics would just stand there and tell them everything.' Boardman shakes his head. 'You have to be clever.'

What is remarkable about all of this – the confidence, the gold medals, the ample resources, the subterfuge, the aura of invincibility, the sheer ebullience – is that this is a British team we're talking about. A British *cycling* team. Ten years ago British cycling teams were the designated whipping boys, and girls: that was their role. To other nations it must have seemed their raison d'etre. Yet now it is they who do the whipping, kicking the collective arse of the once dominant Australians. *The Australians!*

To fully understand how far the British track cycling team has come you must first understand where it was. It was nowhere. Over the decades there have been exceptions – outstanding individuals such as Reg Harris, Beryl Burton, Hugh Porter, Graeme Obree and indeed Boardman himself – but each succeeded despite the system, not because of it. Because there was no system.

In 1997, when Hoy began to be a regular member of the British team, he was given a racing outfit, 'told to feel grateful for it', and lent a bike, 'a state-of-the-art bike – from the 1960s', and told to feel grateful for that, too. In 1996, when he was selected for his first international event – the European Under-23 championships in Moscow – he was one of three riders, with no support staff. They could only afford to send three people, so they decided not to bother with a mechanic or a team manager. Compare and contrast that to the twenty-eight support staff in Palma.

Perhaps the most surprising aspect of what has happened over the last decade – the development of a system every bit as efficient and effective as the old East German system, without the systematic doping – is that it just seems so unBritish. We don't really do success – or not systematic success, at any rate. According to the December 2007 issue of the *Observer Sports Monthly* magazine, we are, in fact, 'ritually accustomed to defeat'. According to Simon Barnes of *The Times*, we 'have no contingency plan for excellence, no strategy for dealing with the calamity of victory'. When we win, we go off the rails. Whatever it takes to build on success, or even sustain it, we just don't seem to possess it.

That *Observer* article (entitled 'Born to Lose') concluded by claiming that is not that we do not want to win: 'We want to win as much if not more than anyone else. We just do not want to do what is necessary to win.' *We do not want to do what is necessary to win*. Which raises the question: what *is* necessary to win? Well, if anyone knows the answer to this question it is Chris Hoy. And the British cycling team. How has this happened? And why in track cycling?

What struck me in Palma, as the British team dominated event after event, and my old – ahem – team-mate Chris Hoy confirmed himself as one of the all-time greats, was the realization that there was something – beyond winning – that was very special, and very unusual, about this team. There was planning, and attention to detail, and athletic talent – all these things, of course. But there was something else – a unique and very potent chemistry. And there were secrets – intriguing, closely-guarded secrets, from Boardman's Secret Squirrel Club to the team's employment of a clinical psychiatrist – someone whose previous work had been with inmates of a high-security hospital, but who, in 2002, had made the surprise career switch to work with Britain's top cyclists. The success of his work with certain members of the team prompts Brailsford to say that he is 'the best person I've hired – and I've hired some great people'.

Sporting success, skulduggery, psychiatry, suspicions of systematic doping, in a world of heroes, villains and velodromes … there could be a hell of a story here, I thought.

A couple of weeks after Palma, a month before he was to travel to Bolivia to try and set a new world kilometre record, I sat down with Hoy in a bar in Edinburgh and gave him my spiel: 'I'd like to write a book – about you, and about this incredible year you have in front of you, taking in Bolivia, the World Cups, the crazy keirin circuit in Japan, the madness of six-day racing, the world championships in Manchester … and looking ahead to Beijing. Only, it won't really be *about* you, as such, well it will, and it won't – it'll be part your story, your BMX-ing as a kid, that sort of thing, but it'll also be the story of the British team – the revolution there's been over the last ten years. I mean, it's an incredible story, really, when you think about it … what do you think?

'Okay,' said Hoy.

PART 1

*Portrait of the Athlete
as a Young Man*

CHAPTER 1

BMX Bandits

Ile de Ré, France, August 1992

Though he wasn't to know it at the time, a seminal moment in Chris Hoy's career occurred while he was on a family holiday on Ile de Ré, La Rochelle, western France, in August 1992. He was sixteen. And he had hired a bike for the holiday – a mountain bike.

At the same time, several hundred miles south of Ile de Ré, in the Spanish city of Barcelona, the Olympics were taking place, and a remarkable thing was happening there. It was remarkable if you were British, and a cyclist. Because a British cyclist by the name of Chris Boardman had reached the final of the men's pursuit, and appeared to be on the verge of winning Britain's first cycling gold medal in eighty-four years, when the quartet of Leonard Meredith, Ernest Payne, Charles Kingsbury and Benjamin Jones were victorious in the 1,810.5 metre team pursuit at the 1908 London Olympics. Boardman's breakthrough was like Eddie the Eagle winning the ski jump – or seemed like it to many people.

And the British media responded accordingly – which is to say that, rather than focus on the athletic achievement, or any physical talent that Boardman may have possessed, they discovered a quirky angle: the fact that Boardman was riding a space-age Lotus bike, promptly christened 'Superbike'. Super*man*, meanwhile, was all but ignored.

Boardman says now that he didn't mind – that in fact it worked in his favour. 'It was part of the package; it was a ploy if you like,' he says, hinting that he was as devious – or clever – then as he is now, in his current role as the man who holds the keys to the Secret Squirrel Club. 'That bike had actually been to more than one World Cup before the Olympics,' reveals Boardman. 'But I hadn't ridden it – Bryan Steel had. But because Bryan only finished eighth on it, nobody really noticed. In the end, yes, the bike got lots of publicity, probably more than me, but people still remember it and talk about it today. So I don't regret that at all.'

In Ile de Ré, meanwhile, the sixteen-year-old Hoy, fanatical about cycling, and by now becoming interested in track cycling, genuinely was interested in the fact that a British rider – and not just a space-age bike – was in the final. 'I remember being so excited about the Olympics,' recalls Hoy. 'The final was in the evening. We didn't have a television where we were staying so I'd been listening to Boardman's progress on the radio thanks to the BBC World Service. I remember calling my dad to come, because the final was on. And I remember listening to the final, hearing Boardman win, and being so inspired that I went straight out on the mountain bike I'd hired. I did ten miles flat out on that bike every day, and I'd already been out earlier in the day. But I went out and did it again.

'It's funny, I've watched that Olympic pursuit final since then, and it bears no relation to my memory of it. The images don't remind me of how I felt at the time.

'After that holiday we went straight to the British track championships in Leicester. I'd just started riding the track. But Boardman was there with his Lotus bike. I rode round behind him for a few laps and sneaked into a photo. I remember being completely in awe.'

Boardman's Barcelona success acted as the launch pad not only for Boardman, who was propelled into a professional career on the continent, but also for his coach, Peter Keen, and, ultimately, you could argue, for the sport in the UK. What Keen did with Boardman he eventually replicated, on a far bigger scale, with the British team. In 1997 he was appointed by the British Cycling Federation to devise a 'World Class Performance Plan', which – in a revolutionary development – would receive millions in National Lottery funding. For the sport of cycling, things were about to change, and Hoy would be one of the main beneficiaries – indeed, he would be integral to the programme that Keen established. But no one – perhaps not even Keen – could have foreseen how dramatic the change would be.

Back in 1992, although Hoy had only just started riding on the track, he had actually been a competitive cyclist since the age of seven. Like so many children of the Eighties – he was born on 23 March 1976 – it was BMX-ing that provided the introduction.

The BMX bike was a child of the 1980s, just as Wham! or *Grange Hill* were. (Indeed, to emphasize how closely associated with the Eighties it was, the first official BMX race in Britain was staged in August 1980, and the international body set up in 1981.) But the sport was also treated as a child by the sporting authorities, being so far outside the mainstream that you would have thought it was a different sport: a BMX might as well have been a horse as far as cycling organizations were concerned. While thousands of kids competed up and down the country, and millions were inspired by the film *BMX Bandits*, not to mention the BMX chase scene in *E.T.*, the conservative bodies that ran cycling ignored it, and them.

It was *E.T.* that snared Hoy. As he told his school magazine in 2004: 'I saw the film *E.T.* and became hooked on the BMX craze.' The film's famous BMX scene, with Elliot and friends smuggling E.T., wrapped in a blanket and sitting in a handlebar-mounted basket, epitomized the appeal of the BMX. The scene, in which the kids evade their adult pursuers, summed up what the BMX represented: namely, freedom and escape – escape from adults, that is.

The adults are made to look silly, relegated as they are to the role of car-imprisoned spectators while the kids flee over what looks suspiciously like a purpose-built BMX race track. And then, of course, comes the serious 'air' – they take off. It provides the most famous image from the film: BMXs being ridden by a gang of kids (accompanied by an extraterrestrial creature) into the night, silhouetted against the moon. 'This video makes me wanna' ride my BMX again,' is one comment below 'E.T. the chase scene', which inevitably features on YouTube. 'Anybody who says they don't hum the theme [to *E.T.*] while riding their bike is lying,' says another. Absolutely.

But for Hoy it wasn't all fun and games. The BMX racing scene was deadly serious and furiously competitive. So was he. 'My first bike was one I got at a jumble sale,' says Hoy, though his mother, Carol, corrects this. '*I* got him his first BMX at a jumble sale,' she says. 'I'd gone on the bus, so I couldn't take it home – I had to get a friend to put it in her boot. It cost £5, I think.' Hoy remembers that the first bike was 'stripped down by my dad, who sprayed it black and put BMX stickers and handlebars on it. I snapped the frame after a month or so, doing jumps off planks of wood on bricks. I then got another bike, which was a neighbour's daughter's old bike. My dad gave it the same spray treatment and put on the same bars. But I bent the frame of that one.'

When he started racing – 'I was second in my first race,' says Hoy – a better bike became a priority. He spotted the machine he wanted in the window of an Edinburgh bike shop: a black and gold Raleigh Super Burner. It cost £99. 'Too much,' said his mother. She explains: 'I said, "When you've saved up half the money, your dad and I will pay the rest." He did it in no time. He was very clever. If we had people round for dinner, then Christopher would come in to show face, and then he'd talk about his BMX-ing, and how well he was doing, and he'd say, "There's a bike I want but I have to pay half myself ..." and the uncles and aunts would feel sympathetic and slip him a fiver.'

'I waited until they'd had a drink or two,' reveals Hoy, with evident pride.

Hoy's father, David, was a great supporter of his son's first outings as a BMX racer with Edinburgh club Danderhall Wolves. 'He had a great start in Scotland, but then we went on holiday to the south of England and all these kids turned up on their £500 bikes,' says David. 'Chris was still on his Raleigh Super Burner. He got hammered. He was really pissed off. I thought, well, if he's going to be serious about this then he should be on a better bike. The Burner was a toy, really.'

With a serious bike – a 'SilverFox' – he decided to join a 'serious' team. David Hoy explains: 'There was a shop in Edinburgh, Scotia BMX, which had a wee team which Chris joined, and they contested races all over the country – in England too. With Chris at first it was the case that the further he travelled the more he got beaten and the harder he worked.'

David says he wasn't a pushy parent, just a supportive one. It would be difficult to imagine him as a pushy parent – his enthusiasm is tempered by a zen-like calm. 'I learnt a lot about child psychology from travelling with him and seeing other kids and their parents,' he muses. 'The Italians were especially interesting. If their kids came over the line and they hadn't won, they got beaten – literally. I didn't think that was the way to get the best out of them.

'I didn't put any pressure on. BMX was just a wonderful sport for kids. He did the cycling bit and my hobby was to look after the bike. On a Wednesday night I'd have the bike on the kitchen table, stripped, bearings out, the works, and then rebuild it for the weekend. I always loved taking bikes to bits.'

Carol Hoy, a bubbly woman with a sparky sense of humour, was sanguine about the weekly transformation of the kitchen table into a workbench. 'I just thought that it was a lovely thing for a father and son to do. They spent whole weekends together, travelling mainly, and I used to only get involved in the local races, when I did the catering. I made burgers – BMX burgers, I called them. I told them they'd make them go faster. They were very popular.'

George Swanson, whose son raced with Hoy, was the man in charge of the Scotia BMX team. 'We must have been one of the most hated teams in the history of cycling,' he laughs. 'I mean, Christ, talk about parochial! We were accused of signing up all the good kids – cherry picking. We sponsored riders from all over Scotland – Craig MacLean was one of our riders – and we took them down south to race. But when they raced in Scotland they rode for their local track. The idea was not to concentrate on the Scottish scene but to venture further afield, set our sights a wee bit higher. We had a yellow Bedford minibus and every weekend we had them away racing: Preston, Crewe, Bristol, you name it.'

'People used to say, "You're mad, how can you possibly take a kid 1000 miles at the weekend?"' says David Hoy. 'But actually

Chris used to get more sleep on a race weekend. If I was taking him, we had a big Citroen estate car. I had a bit of foam cut out, and we laid that in the back of the car. What happened then was that he'd go to bed at 8 p.m., just like normal, then I'd wake him at 1 a.m., and carry him into the car. He'd go back to sleep and sleep all the way, while I drove. The furthest we went in a day was Bristol. We'd get there about 6 o'clock on the Sunday morning and he'd go out and practise for a couple of hours – the other kids would have been practising on the track on the Saturday. He would race all day. Then we'd leave about five; stop for a meal; he'd get in the back and go to sleep – and when we got home I'd carry him up to bed. So he used to get two twelve-hour sleeps.'

'I didn't get any. I was usually pretty tired on a Monday,' David adds.

Swanson is interesting on the young Hoy-as-competitor. 'The Chris you see now is nothing like the Chris we saw back then,' he says, smiling. 'He seems very calm now, totally in control and great in the high-pressure situations, but back then there was a kid from Musselburgh [near Edinburgh] who put the fear of God into him.

'His name was Steven McNeil. McNeil always beat Chris in Scotland, though he never went south of the border. But I remember on one occasion we turned up at Chorley, after leaving about three in the morning. Chris and my son Neil went to register and Chris came back almost in tears. "Dad, Dad, Dad!" he said. "What?" says David. "He's here." "Who's here?" "Steven McNeil's here!"'

Swanson laughs: 'He'd seen a red helmet – McNeil always wore a red helmet. But we went and checked – it wasn't McNeil. It was strange, because Chris didn't get involved in the mind games or worrying about his other competitors – apart from one: Steven McNeil. He was his nemesis. If he was there he cracked up. That time at Chorley, Chris didn't want to race. But as soon as we told him he wasn't there he was okay.

'I saw Steven McNeil a couple of years ago,' continues Swanson, 'and I said to him: "If you ever run into Chris, tell him you're thinking about making a comeback and taking up track racing, and watch his face go white."'

Swanson had first spotted Hoy on a BMX when he was seven, and still on his Raleigh Burner. 'He was out of place; everyone else was on proper BMXs, but you're looking at this kid, and he stood out because he was actually keeping up with kids older than him. I went over and spoke to Dave and said, "Do you mind if we try him on a proper BMX bike?"' He became a regular member of the Scotia party that travelled down south. 'They were long weekends,' says Swanson, 'but bloody enjoyable.'

Hoy's competitiveness was apparent to Swanson, which didn't make him unique, but Hoy did stand out in one respect. 'He was a ferocious competitor,' says Swanson, 'they all were. There were lots of tears, tantrums, but what made it worse was you had a van load of kids aged from about seven to ten, and it was fine and dandy if they all won, but if only one or two of them won, then you had a problem. You're trying to be happy for the ones that have won and at the same time not go overboard because of the poor buggers who are sitting there with their noses out of joint. It was a difficult balance.

'Chris's reaction to defeats was interesting, though, because he was different to the others. If my son won, he was hyper. If he was beaten, he wouldn't talk to anybody, especially not me, and he wouldn't be in a mood to listen. Like most kids, it was one extreme or the other. But if Chris was beaten he would have a discussion with his dad about *why* he was beaten: whether he'd made a mistake in the start gate, or Dave geared him wrongly, or he got the line wrong going into the corner – whatever it was, there was always a rational conversation with his dad on the way back up the road, even at eight or nine years old, about why he was beaten. I remember being struck by it at the time. His reaction to getting beaten, or indeed winning, wasn't the reaction you'd get out of other kids of that age. I think some of it was down to Dave. He's not your pushy parent. You'd see a lot of parents getting torn into their kids, shouting, "What happened? I've driven 200 miles to bring you here and you made a complete arse of it!" Dave was always very calm and rational. He's quite technical and logical. He's also one of these great theorists, which could be more a hindrance than a help – sometimes he got carried away with his theories about gear ratios and so on.'

Swanson can only recall one occasion when Hoy became upset and emotional. On the occasion in question they were returning to Scotland following a triumph: Hoy had won, and the handsome gold trophy sat in pride of place on the dashboard of the van. Slowly, though, as they travelled north, the trophy's shape became distorted – it melted. 'The heater was on,' explains Swanson. 'It was plastic, of course, with a BMX rider on top. Chris was crestfallen when he saw this piece of molten plastic. He was eight and it was like the bottom had dropped out of his world.'

While in Scotland Hoy was 'head and shoulders above every-one' – apart from McNeil – in England it was a different story. There was another nemesis there: Matt Boyle, British champion an incredible twelve years in a row, European champion, and a silver medallist in the world championships. Younger still, and an even bigger player in the BMX scene, was the prodigious David Maw.

Everyone I talked to about BMX-ing mentioned Maw. He was a big star, and a three-time world champion, with an eight-year-old ego – it seems – to match. 'In one race they were all at the start gate, up on the pedals, ready to go, when David Maw sticks his hand up,' recalls Swanson. 'So all the riders have to come down off their pedals, and David Maw starts doing stretching exercises! He was eight years old! The other kids were looking at him, rattled – which was his intention, of course. But he knew how good he was, and it worked. He was unbeatable, huge – there was a BBC documentary made about him.'

Tragically, Maw was killed in a car crash in 2000. And it seems he wasn't the only one – a remarkable number of former BMX prodigies have met untimely deaths. 'It's quite an eerie world,' says Hoy's former rival, Matt Boyle, who continued to race BMX as a professional in America until 1999, when he was twenty-three. 'A lot of people have been and gone.'

Another top rider of the 1980s, who like Boyle went across the Atlantic to continue racing into adulthood, was Jamie Staff. Staff reckons 'you had kids who obviously liked speed, and a bit of danger, when they were young … a few of them certainly got into fast cars.' Staff, like Hoy, persisted with bikes rather than cars and eventually transferred his talents to the velodrome, becoming a mainstay of the British team, alongside Hoy, from 2002.

But the vast majority of the BMX generation were lost to cycling. 'It was booming,' says Staff, 'there were tonnes of tracks, especially in inner cities – Slough, Surbiton, Hounslow. It was a huge scene and anyone could do it. In the late Eighties the nationals at Hounslow would have thousands.'

And then, abruptly, the BMX boom ended. 'It stopped dead,' says Swanson. 'My view is that it never recovered from the recession in the early Nineties,' suggests Staff. 'It was very much a sport that depended on volunteers and families. Everyone's purse strings tightened in the early Nineties and it hit BMX-ing hard. In my age category there was so much talent. I didn't win much – there were about ten guys as good as me, but most of that talent was lost. Only the die-hards remained.

'It's a shame,' continues Staff, 'because I'll argue with anyone, all day long, about the merits of BMX. It's the hardest bike to ride. If you can race a BMX then you can jump on any other bike, in any other discipline, and it's dead easy. It's ironic because we were seen as unprofessional, as kids, to the cycling establishment, but we were very professional. I trained four or five hours a day on my BMX.'

And not only was it good at honing bike-handling skills, for 'it turned what were basically shy kids into fairly outgoing, confident kids,' according to Swanson.

But by the early 1990s there was a new bike on the mass market. The mountain bike was seen as the grown-up version of the BMX, and it threatened to force the BMX into extinction. Yet even in the face of this competition, and while sales of new BMXs plummeted, the race scene survived into the early 1990s. Hoy raced until 1991, switching teams again, trading up, joining the GT Factory Team, and enjoying personal sponsorship from Slazenger and Edinburgh-based exhaust specialists Kwik-Fit.

His sponsorship deal from Kwik-Fit offers another illustration of Hoy's entrepreneurial flair, following the successful fund-raising for his first bike. 'He wrote to Tom Farmer, the Kwik-Fit owner, asking for sponsorship,' says Carol Hoy. 'The headquarters were just down the road from the house. He got a letter back, inviting him to come and meet Mr Farmer.

'His dad went with him and they were ushered into the office. David started to speak, but Tom Farmer interrupted him with, "That's lovely Mr Hoy, but Christopher, tell me why you want this money. Sell it to me."' He did, and was rewarded with a cheque for £1,000 to assist with equipment and travelling expenses. Sir Tom Farmer, as he is now known, has kept in touch since, writing letters of congratulation to Hoy after the 2002 Commonwealth Games and 2004 Olympics. The owner of one of Edinburgh's two big football clubs – Hibernian – obviously doesn't hold it against Hoy that he is a confessed supporter of the other one, Hearts.

In his new team, Hoy cut a dash in his yellow and blue outfit, emblazoned with GT, Slazenger and Kwik-Fit. But that wasn't a universal opinion. 'I remember Chris because he had dodgy race gear,' says Boyle. 'I was reminded of how bad it was when I looked at some old pictures the other day. There aren't many with Chris in them, but he's always behind me, which is nice.'

In the end, Hoy's BMX career, which spanned 1984 to 1991, and took him from the age of seven to fourteen, saw him ranked number one in Scotland for five years; he was Scottish champion, British number two (to Boyle), European number five and world number nine. Holland, France, Germany, Denmark and Belgium were all race destinations, giving him an early taste of travel and international competition.

David Hoy believes this also helped his education, in the widest sense of the word. 'I remember standing at the Berlin Wall with him before it came down,' says David. 'In some of the big races in Europe there were teams from behind the Iron Curtain, on rubbish bikes, dressed in rags, really, and Chris used to be quite affected by that. I remember him saying, "It's a shame for them Dad, because they're good riders and if they had decent bikes they'd be really good."'

As well as BMX-ing, Hoy declares his other early interests as maths and chess. On his first day at school – George Watson's College in Edinburgh – the head teacher asked whether he had any questions. 'Do you have a chess club?' was his response. He describes maths as 'a hobby' – albeit an unusual one for a five year old. 'When we went to my auntie's I'd ask her to give me sums to do,' says Hoy. 'She'd write down a whole page of them and I'd sit there quite happily doing them. Then I got the Star Wars figures, about 130 of them altogether, and each one had a number next to the figure on the back of the packaging. I memorized the numbers. If you said "Forty-seven" I'd say "Imperial Storm Trooper!" Or you could say "Obe Wan Kanobi" and I'd say "Twenty-three!" I was about five or six at the time. I had weird little autistic tendencies.'

But it could be argued that maths and chess were compatible with BMX-ing: it, too, represented a puzzle that needed to be solved. Chiefly this concerned the start. It was the area that could be improved with thought, analysis and practice – three things that Hoy, even as a youngster, seemed to love. 'The start is what I was known for,' says Boyle. 'My dad taught me at a young age not to wait for the gate to drop – then you're using your eyes. He taught me to look ahead and use my ears – to listen to the command of the starter. And I could tell Chris started doing the same, because he was very quick out of the gate.'

'Chris went out to the track in Livingston, about twenty miles away, twice a week, just to practise his starts,' says David Hoy. 'He'd go over it again and again. It's very similar to the kilo, really. But Chris has always been into the technical side, the minutiae of it. He was always like that, looking into every little thing.'

Hoy senior agrees that BMX racing couldn't have offered a better introduction to sport, and to cycling, from 'learning to ride and race a bike, how to win and how to lose,' and so there are certainly no regrets in the Hoy family about the seven years spent driving up and down the motorways of Britain, often in the company of other kids of different ages and backgrounds, or with Chris sleeping on a piece of foam in the back of the car, while plastic trophies melted on dashboards, with a bike that would be dismantled and rebuilt by dad on the kitchen table in midweek, before the routine was repeated the next weekend.

They were good days, says David – good for Chris, good for Dad, certainly good for father–son bonding. The strength of their relationship now probably owes much to the old BMX-ing days, and their ability back then to calmly, and rationally, analyse the different aspects of performance together, and to be gracious in victory and in defeat. 'That was the deal with his BMX-ing,' states Carol Hoy unequivocally, 'that if he got beaten he didn't lie on the track and throw his bike away.'

In fact, his father admits that he has only one regret. 'It's a tough, tough life being a cyclist, for very little reward. I wish I'd given him a set of golf clubs when he was a baby.'

CHAPTER 2

The Kingcycle

Pentland Hills, Edinburgh, winter 1992

'One incident in the Pentlands has stuck in my mind forever,' says Ray Harris, 'and I've often wondered if the person concerned would ever realize that she almost killed a future Olympic champion.

'It was winter,' Harris continues, 'and we were coming off the hills after a day's mountain biking. We weren't belting along, but the weather wasn't particularly good, and there was an old dear with her green wellies, plaid skirt, Barbour jacket, and walking pole, a typical old Edinburgh woman. Chris got too close to her, so she made a jab at his front wheel, making some rather unladylike comments about cyclists being on her path. It was a steel walking pole and if she'd got him it would have been very serious. The image has stuck in my mind. But it didn't faze Chris. A lot of youngsters of that age would have been shouting back at her, swearing and all sorts. But although I've seen Chris disappointed and cross, I've never seen him out of control.'

Harris is one of the great unsung heroes of British sport. In Edinburgh and beyond, for a period spanning three decades, he was to the sport of cycling what Dr Emmett Brown, the mad scientist from *Back to the Future*, was to time travel. Even if his ideas and methods sometimes seemed loopy or eccentric, Harris, like the good doctor, made things happen, with his enthusiasm if nothing else. He was certainly a scientist, but he was also a visionary. Though he might have seemed eccentric, he did things, or tried things, that would become commonplace a few years later.

Hoy met Harris when he felt he had outgrown the sport of BMX. 'I stopped enjoying it and didn't see myself progressing any further,' he says now. Plus, as he told his old school magazine in 2004, 'BMX was no longer trendy. It was losing me crucial street-cred being associated with an un-cool pastime.'

At the grand old age of 14, it was time for a new challenge. The mountain bike had emerged – it was like a BMX for adults. This new machine was the epitome of cool, to such an extent that in the early 1990s it seemed they would take over the world and render road bikes obsolete; and then they all but disappeared themselves, before staging a comeback in the late 1990s, with technological improvements such as suspension forks, rear suspension, and disc brakes.

Hoy got involved during the first, relatively short-lived wave of popularity. Would he have remained a mountain biker had that wave been sustained throughout the 1990s? No, probably not. And it's just as well: because, as a mountain biker, Hoy was ... distinctly mediocre.

He found that his cycling skills didn't transfer seamlessly from the short BMX tracks, which rewarded sharp bursts of speed and acceleration, to the longer, more gruelling mountain biking trails, which provided a test of stamina. More particularly, the hills proved a problem.

David Hoy has joked of having to wait for hours for his son to finish endurance events. At least, I had assumed he was joking. 'Absolutely not,' he says. 'The car park would be empty at these events and I'd be thinking about going and checking with First Aid. Then, finally, he would appear over the hill.'

Hoy, notes his father, 'was just the wrong type of athlete' for such events, 'not that he knew it at the time. He enjoyed it. It started off with him heading into the Pentlands' – the range of hills that sit on the southern boundary to Edinburgh, around six miles from the family home in Murrayfield – 'and they'd be up there all day exploring the wee tracks and trails. There are miles of them; it's a terrific place. Then he'd be back for his tea.'

Mountain biking could be dangerous, of course, not least on hidden paths in remote glens. Although the Pentland Hills are close to Edinburgh, they seem miles away when you are in the middle of them. While the hills are visible from every corner of the city, the same cannot be said in reverse: the city is invisible from the remoter parts, and there is no road access. So there were obvious dangers associated with riding in the hills – especially down them. 'He told me he clocked 65 [mph] coming down one of the steep hills once,' says David in conspiratorial tones, confirming that, although he officially disapproved, he was secretly quite proud. 'We reached a compromise with him: we gave him a whistle and if he fell off he was to use it to attract attention.'

Hoy's competitive debut on a mountain bike followed the appearance of a small advert in a mountain biking magazine, announcing the start of a new Scottish Cyclists' Union (SCU) cross-country mountain bike series. David spotted the advert and called SCU headquarters – then and now a Portakabin parked beside the velodrome at Meadowbank – and spoke to their executive officer, 'boring him stupid for half an hour' about his son's glittering BMX career. The best thing, he was told, was to join a club. He recommended the Dunedin Cycling Club, run by Ray Harris. 'He's a good coach,' said the man from the SCU.

At the same time, at school, Hoy was playing rugby and also rowing. Rugby legend Gavin Hastings, a former pupil at Hoy's school, was the teenager's first sporting hero. The Scotland and British Lions captain came to the school one day to take training, though Hoy 'was very cool about it, as teenage boys are', recalls his mother, Carol. 'But later, during dinner, he was full of it: it was "Gav this, Gav that ..." as if they were best mates!' (A decade later the roles were reversed. Interviewed at the official opening of the Scottish Parliament, Hastings was asked what the Parliament should do as a matter of priority. 'It should build an indoor velodrome,' urged Hastings, 'for Chris Hoy and the Chris Hoys of the future.')

Hoy showed promise as a rugby player. He captained his school team – no mean feat at a school as renowned for producing good rugby players as George Watson's College – and he was also recognized at district level. On one occasion he even captained Edinburgh Schools against the North of Scotland at Under-15 level.

But he showed even more promise as a rower, going one better, competing for Scotland and, with his school, winning a silver medal at the British championship in the junior coxless pairs. His mother today expresses some regret that he finally opted for cycling instead of rowing, noting with a sigh, 'I quite wanted him to do the rowing ... I fancied myself at Henley, cheering him on – "Come on chaps!" – with a wee gin and tonic in my hand. The banks of the Thames seems more civilized than a sweaty velodrome. Ah well ...'

But despite his involvement and interest in the sports offered by his school, cycling remained a big interest. It occupied most of Hoy's spare time, though he continued to find the transition to mountain biking difficult. His easy superiority at BMX was forgotten as he struggled up the hills and through the mud of mountain bike courses – in fact, he seemed at the time to be showing more promise as a rugby player and rower than as a cyclist.

Yet Hoy was convinced it was just a matter of time before it clicked. It didn't seem to occur to him that it might not. He was in it to win it, says his dad: 'Oh yeah. He wanted to win; he didn't just want to take part. He kept thinking, "I need to work harder. I've stepped up to a different sport so I need to learn." If he finished five hours down one week then he'd try to finish four hours down the next! That was his attitude.'

Hoy himself gently disputes some of his father's claims. 'I realized fairly early on that I wasn't an endurance athlete, but I persevered because I do have an element of aerobic potential. At school I enjoyed cross-country running and rowing, where you needed power and endurance. It was the power-to-weight ratio that was a problem. It meant that anything that involved going uphill was a struggle.'

Old school mates – and teachers – may dispute this claim, however. In the interview he gave to his school magazine, after returning from Athens as the Olympic champion in 2004, he recalled a third-year school cycling trip: 'My lasting memory from those ten days of riding around the north of Scotland had to be the day I spent riding alongside Mrs Wylie, fifteen minutes behind the main group, as punishment for overtaking Mr Strachan on the hill the previous day.'

Road cycling became something he also pursued, especially as he became involved with the Dunedin Cycling Club, which was run by someone with the enthusiasm of a teenager: Ray Harris. A well-known figure in the Scottish cycling scene, Harris had greying hair, combed in a side-parting, and a strong English accent, betraying his Midlands roots. He wore small half-moon-shaped spectacles, perched halfway down his nose, giving him a professorial look. He always seemed to be peering down into them, in a 'let-me-see-what-we've-got-here-then' kind of way. But then, he always seemed to be timing, or testing, or officiating – doing something that required his concentration.

Harris talked a lot, and fast. Still does. Visiting him at his home in Coldstream, in the Scottish Borders, is like stepping into a time warp – he doesn't seem to have aged at all since the late 1980s. Which only seems to confirm that he is indeed the Emmett Brown of Scottish cycling.

'Chris's dad came to see me,' recalls Harris, 'he was a schoolboy and he was keen to realize his potential beyond BMX, because BMX was limited at that stage. Chris had this conflict at the time, between rowing and rugby, and my first reaction was: if you really want to succeed in rowing or cycling, rugby has to go. Rugby was too risky, because of the free leg movement,' and here Harris, with the agility of a gymnast, demonstrates what he means by free leg movement. 'With no resistance, you can do tremendous damage. I'd witnessed at first hand, working as a masseur in other sports, the damage to knee joints in relatively young rugby and football players. Frightening.

'In the Dunedin we had a membership of fifty or so, a great proportion of them youngsters,' he continues, not pausing for breath. 'We hadn't entertained mountain biking' – in fact, just like BMX, though not quite to the same extent, mountain biking tended in those days to be dismissed by the 'connoisseurs' of traditional cycling, which meant road and, to a lesser extent, track cyclists.

But Harris's Dunedin Cycling Club, with its youthful membership, and, in Harris, its youthful leader, embraced the new discipline. 'We organized some short course mountain biking events,' says Harris, 'mainly because it gave us an opportunity to get youngsters involved. Initially we ran them in an old mining area in East Lothian; it was just mud, really. And that's where Chris got involved. He was dead keen. Soon after, we started our Pentlands races.'

Underpinning all of the Dunedin club's activity – on the road, in the hills and on the track – was Harris's fanatical interest in a subject that, at that time, few had heard of, and fewer still had any knowledge about: sports science. The term only entered the popular sporting lexicon some time in the 1980s. It referred, broadly speaking, to sophisticated methods of training and monitoring performance, using various 'data'. Few knew anything about this mysterious 'data', never mind how to measure it or what to do with it; and even when heart rate monitors became ubiquitous among amateur cyclists, in the early 1990s, few really knew how to utilize them. They tended to be a source of interest and entertainment rather than a training tool – the 'game' being to go out and see how high you could get your heart rate.

Harris's 'scientific' approach pre-dated pulse monitors; it also related to his methodology. As Hoy says: 'The thing I remember most about Ray was his enthusiasm. As a kid you really respond to that; it was inspiring. But, unusually I think, he backed that up with a scientific approach to training and racing. Even the circuit training classes we did had a method to them; there was method behind everything he did. Not that it was always obvious ...'

Many, perhaps most – especially among the young cyclists Harris coached – were not particularly interested in the method. Cycling – sport – is all about results; what matters is where you cross the line. But Hoy was different. Even as a fifteen year old, he was fascinated by the method, the theory behind the practice, even if he didn't always understand the finer points. 'Chris has got an interest in anything that makes sense,' says Harris slowly. 'If he can see there's a logic and an end result to it, then he becomes very interested indeed.

'A lot of competitive athletes are prima donnas when it comes to performance testing,' he continues. 'They don't treat a test any differently to a race. If they fail, they don't blame themselves or say they've had a bad day. They blame you, the equipment, the world at large … but Chris, unusually, never did that, even as a youngster.'

The performance testing he is referring to came thanks to his infamous 'Kingcycle' machine – Harris's equivalent of the *Back to the Future* time machine. When he began using this, in the late 1980s, it quickly gained a reputation as the ultimate performance-testing device; it was the holy grail of testing, in the very vanguard of sports science.

The Kingcycle: even the name could provoke fear, awe and excitement, in equal measure. In fact, to some – as Harris suggests – it seemed to assume greater importance than race results. The 'magic number' given out by the Kingcycle – and, in those days, *only* the Kingcycle – could (or so it was believed) determine ability, potential, future prospects … everything. It could provide the key that would unlock the door to the cycling equivalent of Narnia or, alternatively, confirm that you might as well just hang up your wheels and take up art, music or reading instead.

And presiding over the Kingcycle was Harris. He was the man with the secret; he held your future in his hands, on a piece of A4 paper, containing an array of graphs and numbers, spewed out of a word processor at the end of a test that was close to torture. What the Kingcycle did, in short, was to reveal a measurement that was far more significant than speed or heart rate, both of which could be easily measured by a computer or heart rate monitor, but neither of which, crucially, necessarily revealed anything of actual significance. A fast speed could be achieved with the aid of a tail-wind, or gravity; and a 'good' heart rate – well, what constituted a good heart rate?

But power: power was the key. The power that you could generate through the pedals could not be dismissed; whether you were going uphill or down, into the teeth of a gale or with the wind at your back – none of these variables affected the power you were able to transmit through the pedals. In short, what separates Lance Armstrong and Chris Hoy from mere mortals is not the speed they ride at but the power they generate.

Back then, though, 'power output' was a mystical, mythical concept. Measuring it was problematic, if not impossible. You couldn't just go into a gym, lift some weights, and measure your power – it was cycling-specific, and the only way to gauge it was through the pedals. The question remained: how?

It was Harris who came up with a solution. He may even have been the first in the UK to do so. Without being remotely boastful, he seems to suggest as much: 'I cobbled together something, a forerunner to the Kingcycle, and reprogrammed a little Spectrum 128 computer to work with it. But because it wasn't very well engineered it was very hit-and-miss. We were getting better at it, but then the actual Kingcycle came along.

'I spent a lot of time going to Manchester and Derby to attend coaching seminars organized by the British Cycling Federation, and it was at one of those that I learned about it. It had been developed by an electronic signalling company. It was a breakthrough: here was a machine that could give you the magic number – it could tell you the number of watts a cyclist was able to generate and sustain before collapsing, so to speak.

'I think I had the highest number of tests for any one machine,' he adds with obvious pride. 'I bought it myself. It was terribly expensive; the set-up was well over £2,000. And it was very labour intensive: finding a lab to use it in, setting it up, packing it away. You had to know what you were doing and try not to kill anybody.'

He isn't joking. And that phrase – 'before collapsing, so to speak' – only hints at the truth. The reason the Kingcycle provoked fear was that it was painful. Actually, painful doesn't begin to cover it. What happens is this: your bike is fixed into a rig; the front wheel removed, handlebars held in place, back wheel sitting on a roller. As you climb on the soundtrack would be Prokofiev's 'Montagues and Capulets', the 'Dance of the Knights'. Just the thought of it could set your pulse racing.

You begin pedalling. It's easy. Dum-dee-dum. There is little, if any resistance, for a minute, two minutes, three minutes. Then it starts to bite. Just a small bite – a nibble. You begin to feel a little resistance. The pedals aren't quite turning themselves any more. Still, it isn't hard. A rhythm comes easily. Seven minutes, eight minutes. Now you're pushing more; and your breathing isn't so regular. Sweat pricks at your brow, causing it to itch. You begin fidgeting, moving your hands around the handlebars, searching for a position that is comfortable. But comfort is a foreign land, a thing of the past. Now it's really starting to hurt. The sweat is running down your arms, finding its way into the crevices of your hands. You wipe your hands on your shorts and replace them. No sooner have you done so than they're soaking and uncomfortable again.

Nine minutes, ten minutes. Now you're pushing the pedals, pulling them up, really aware that you're not pedalling smoothly, but forcing them round; and it's hurting your muscles, and you're struggling to maintain the ninety revolutions a minute that the monitor attached to the Amstrad computer, perched in front of you, is telling you to maintain. If you fall below that then the game's a bogey, it's all over; and the worst thing is, you know you have at least another two minutes of this.

The seconds pass very slowly, v-e-r-y … s-l-o-o-o-w-l-y. Your heart feels like it might be close to some kind of explosion; your breathing accelerates to a point where it can accelerate no more. And, all the time, the resistance is increasing; it's getting harder, and harder, and harder to just keep pedalling. Eleven minutes. You did thirteen last time.

And now, though you are edging ever closer to the point of total exhaustion, the mind games begin – horrible mind games. You make deals with yourself. If I make it to twelve, I'll stop. I'll alter the rhythm: that'll make it easier. I'll do fifteen seconds hard, fifteen easier, fifteen hard. Oh Christ, that's not working. Maybe if I move my hands to the tops of the bars it'll be easier. Maybe if I straighten my back it'll be easier. Maybe if I straighten my arms it'll help. Focus on your breathing; focus on your breathing. And stop that song, that brain worm, playing on a loop in your head – something really irritating. Hang on, maybe if I move my hands back to the drops of the bars it'll be easier. Twelve minutes. Shit.

'And stop!'

The voice of Ray Harris, standing by his monitor with a clipboard. You collapse into a puddle of your own sweat, panting like a dog, and await the whirring of the word processor, and the sheet of paper with the magic number: the number that could wipe away the pain of the previous few minutes, or increase it tenfold.

Like a sadist, Harris chuckles now at the pain endured by his subjects, or victims. 'Oh, it was the holy grail alright! But you always got guys who thought they could beat the system. And you don't beat the system! It always gets you in the end. It's bloody painful; sheer purgatory towards the end. There's no way around that. Doesn't matter who you are: it's going to hurt. But it does give you this number at the end that tells you the kind of power you are capable of generating. And that, ultimately, tells you how good you are.

'I had Chris in for testing, like everyone else, and I must say, he was never one who wanted to steal the book to have a look at the figures. Some did. Some would blow their top when I told them the figure. They just wouldn't believe it and they'd come out with all sorts: "Your machine's rubbish! It doesn't work!"

'Chris was interested in his results to see if his training was working. And that's where it was useful, really. I said to them: use it for making comparisons with yourself. Don't ever say, "I've got to get 350 watts, or 500 watts." Because, at the end of the day, someone who didn't make 500 watts could still win the race. That's one of the curious things about cycling. Power is bloody important but it isn't the be-all and end-all. Having the power is one thing, employing it is another.'

Hoy, whose passion for training remains undimmed, remembers the Kingcycle tests with something approaching fondness – which could explain a lot. 'Cycling is one of the most advanced sports in terms of scientific development,' he says, 'and the Kingcycle was an early example of a scientific way of looking at performance. I remember going for these tests in Ray's lab at Moray House [the teacher training college in Edinburgh] and I remember just loving the measurability of it all. Getting that power read-out at the end of it, and looking at it thinking, "In April I was there; it's July now, I'm here; by October I want to be there." It appealed to my personality, this idea that if you did X it will result in Y happening to your performance.

'As a kid I wasn't the kind of person who did really well at sports that required a lot of intuition, skill, interpretation or subjectivity,' he continues. 'I wasn't good at racket sports, which required good hand–eye coordination. I did alright at rugby but I was never that great. But I loved the science behind training for cycling.'

As well as his performance testing, Harris was particularly adept at working with young people; he was the adult who took your passion for cycling – and, by extension, *you* – seriously. Clearly he knew his stuff, and, through the likes of Graeme Obree and other leading Scottish cyclists, he did work with elite adult athletes. But what he was really interested in was helping aspiring young athletes, especially those just starting out, as Hoy was in the early 1990s.

It was unusual, in these circumstances, that he was taken seriously as a coach at all. As Harris explains: 'You get your coaching credibility through coaching at the highest level. Your credibility comes from coaching someone who went to the Commonwealth Games or Olympics. But I resented this. I rebelled. I'm a bit of a reverse snob. This was really cherry picking, I thought.

'The thing is, people think that you can coach children with a limited knowledge. But you can't. You have to understand that children are not yet physically mature. You can push them too hard; I've seen this happen in swimming, with interval training for eight- and nine-year-olds. You can break them. So I thought I could really help young people.

'A lot of my coaching has been with what I'd call minority groups – juveniles, juniors and women [Harris was the Scottish women's team coach for a while]. I haven't looked for the kudos of coaching elites. That was never my ambition. Plus, there was no shortage of people wanting to coach top riders. I could see where the gaps were, and I tried to fill those gaps.'

Apart from the coaching from Harris, there were other aspects of being in the Dunedin club that were different and progressive. 'On Friday nights they did circuit training in the scout hut and then had a club meeting,' says David. 'So they were exposed to democracy, because they voted for what the club was going to do. It was good. Ray used to take the circuit training then he'd talk to the guys who really wanted to do something, and chat to them.'

Hoy says that it was Harris who taught him, early in his Dunedin career, the importance of keeping a training diary, and of setting goals. 'He gave us these sheets and told us what information to put on them – heart rate, training, that kind of thing. I took my resting heart rate every morning and filled in my sheet. I didn't really know at that age why I was doing it, but it was about getting into good habits, and learning – and I had a fascination with numbers anyway ... He also taught me the importance of goal-setting – he was the first person who explained goal-setting to me. He told me there were three types of goals: long-term, medium-term, and short-term.'

In his Coldstream home, Harris digs out one of these goal-setting sheets for me to see. In fact, it's pages: one for each of the goals. And it is with particular pride that Harris recalls what Hoy wrote on his. Beneath the heading 'Long-Term Goal,' he wrote: 'Olympic champion.'

Harris says: 'He said very early on, he wanted to be Olympic champion. Now, many kids say that, but I wasn't going to mock him for it. Why should we try and limit what somebody wants to dream about? That dream might be achievable; let's look at it, break it down.

'Targets and goal-setting should never be the criteria for a coaching plan,' he continues. 'You don't focus as a fifteen year old on being Olympic champion. The first thing to look at is, what can we do in the immediate future, to spur you on to stage two? If you can't do stage one – the short-term goals – then you can forget the rest.

'So with Chris we looked at the stages. Something that was – and still is – really important to Chris was the Commonwealth Games, because he could represent Scotland, and he's very patriotic, without being anti-the other thing. So we looked at it: when can you go to the Commonwealth Games? Nineteen ninety-eight was realistic. If he did that, the Olympics in 2000 was realistic. If he did that, then becoming Olympic champion in 2004 was realistic. And it was spot-on. It's almost a fairytale.'

David Hoy – who still, somewhere in the family home, has the goal-setting sheets, with their short-term goals: 'Scottish champion'; medium-term ambitions: 'go to the Commonwealth Games'; and long-term dreams: 'become Olympic champion' – believes that Harris's role in this fairytale can hardly be exaggerated. 'Dare to dream' might have been his motto, founded on a solid bedrock of self-belief. 'It was Ray who took away the inhibition,' says David. 'When they sat down and talked about goal-setting he let him know, "You can say whatever you like. I won't laugh at you."'

Of course, Hoy wasn't going to be an Olympic champion on a mountain bike. For all his enthusiasm, even Harris would surely have discouraged that notion. But by the time he came to writing down his goals, he had swapped the muddy courses of the mountain bike races for the smooth boards of the velodrome.

CHAPTER 3

The Wellydrome

Meadowbank velodrome, Edinburgh, 1994

Of all the ill-considered sporting arenas in the world – from the ski centre in Dubai, to the two football stadiums that back onto each other in Dundee – Edinburgh's velodrome has to be up there with the very daftest.

Not that there is anything wrong with the track at Meadowbank, which is a good, internationally-renowned wooden oval that, in its day, has hosted top class competition, producing world championship medal-winning cyclists and one Olympic champion – Chris Hoy. But there is one glaring, not to mention fundamental, glitch: one oversight; one fatal flaw; one unforgivable omission. It has no roof.

We are talking here about a velodrome in Scotland, one of the wettest and most inclement countries in the world, which is rendered unusable every time it rains. A few drops are enough, in fact, to have them postponing the action and running for the covers, à la Wimbledon.

Even more remarkably, it is a state of affairs that has existed since 1970, when the velodrome was built for the first Edinburgh Commonwealth Games. Since then there have been numerous proposals to build a roof, but the roof – unlike the rain – has consistently failed to materialize, as a consequence of which the poor wooden boards have suffered, oh how they have suffered, through their constant exposure to the elements.

Still, that the track was built at all was something of a triumph for the sport in Scotland. The country had several concrete cycling tracks – longer than a wooden velodrome, with comparatively shallow banking – and there was a proposal, popular with the spendthrift council, to hold the track cycling events of the 1970 'Edinburgh' Commonwealth Games at Grangemouth, twenty-five miles away. One man who led the fight for an Edinburgh velodrome was Arthur Campbell, then president of the Scottish Cyclists' Union and a consummate sports politician, who went on to hold high-ranking positions in the Union Cycliste Internationale (UCI) and the Commonwealth Games organization. In the end Campbell won, and hundreds, if not thousands, of Scottish cyclists have since had cause to be grateful. The facility built at Meadowbank, adjacent to the main athletics stadium, was state-of-the-art. It remains state-of-the-art – by 1970 standards, that is.

Be that as it may. There is a nice link between Campbell, the man who drove through the plans for a velodrome in Edinburgh, and Hoy, who would go on to become its most successful 'product'. Twenty-four years after its construction, and with Hoy having just made a tentative start to his track cycling career, the young cyclist attended a training camp in Majorca. It was his first overseas training camp, and it fell on his eighteenth birthday. One of the senior cyclists on the camp was Campbell, then in his mid-seventies, but still showing the youngsters a thing or two on the daily training rides. Hearing of Hoy's birthday, Campbell pedalled off to a nearby village, several kilometres away. When he returned, he had something balanced precariously on his handlebars. 'Many happy returns,' he said to Hoy. It was a birthday cake.

Hoy had started riding on the track, thanks, again, to Ray Harris. The East of Scotland Cycling Association had a fleet of around a dozen track bikes stored at the velodrome, which could be used by members of the Dunedin Cycling Club at their weekly 'track night'. It was at one of these track nights, in April 1991, that Hoy had his first outing on the boards of the Meadowbank Velodrome. 'I remember being scared and intimidated by it,' he says of the track. 'Walking through the tunnel, under the track, and then out into the track centre and realizing how steep the banking was … it was daunting. And there was an etiquette about riding there that I didn't understand.' Here Hoy slightly contradicts Harris's claim that Dunedin was a 'youthful' club. It was true that its membership was youthful as far as cycling clubs went, but it was, says Hoy, all relative. There weren't many as young as he was, which was fifteen. 'It wasn't that they weren't friendly to young riders,' he says, 'it was just that there weren't many young riders.

'I remember being given a track bike and starting riding on the track, then, eventually, being led round it by one of the older riders. We followed behind him in a string. It was really scary at first. It just didn't look physically possible to stay upright on the steep banking; I thought you'd slip down unless you were going really fast. But when you rode around on the black line [near the bottom] and realized that it was just as steep there as it was at the top, then you realized that you could ride at the top as well. So you could start to move up the banking, and that was exciting.'

It was fortunate for Hoy that there was a velodrome – still the only one in Scotland and one of only a handful in Britain – in his home city. 'Our club was officially based at the velodrome,' explains Harris, 'as much because we were trying to keep it open as anything else. The history of that track has been one of bumps along a very rocky road. After the 1970 Commonwealth Games it had quite a following, because it was such a good track. The only drawback was the everlasting weather problem. Events could be cancelled with a drop of rain. They still can, and regularly are. But it got to the stage where it was almost matchwood; there were splinters appearing of astronomic proportions; everything leaked.'

At that stage, on the brink of becoming matchwood, the velodrome was rebuilt for the 1986 Commonwealth Games, at a cost of £450,000, but still with no roof. And it rained a lot during those games, playing havoc with the cycling programme. Thus was the velodrome christened – by Prince Edward, apparently – the 'Wellydrome'.

Although the Dunedin Cycling Club was based at the Wellydrome, track racing was merely one activity. They were very active in the other disciplines – road and now mountain biking, too – and they were all encouraged. Hoy, as a consequence, did a considerable amount of time trialling and road racing, even competing in the 1994 Junior Tour of Ireland, a mini-Tour de France-style stage race and a major event for juniors, held over nine days, with stages of sixty to seventy miles a day. For juniors this was a gruelling, demanding event, in many cases providing their first experience of a proper stage race, and Hoy did reasonably well. As he says, he was never going to be a climbing specialist – though he wasn't big at the time; 'he was a wee sparrow,' says his father, David – but on the fast, flat stages he could remain safely in the 'peloton' and even get near the front in the hectic sprint finishes. He managed two top-ten finishes on road stages.

Earlier road race outings hadn't been so successful. Having travelled to the north of Scotland for a weekend of racing in and around the town of Forres, Hoy was unfortunate to puncture as the first road race was starting, within metres of having left the neutralized zone. He stopped to get a wheel change from the following 'service' car, then began to chase and appeared to be successful. But when he got within thirty metres of the rear of the peloton – almost touching distance – they began to speed up; he dropped back and never got close to them again.

He seemed to take to the track, though – or take to it as well as anyone when confronted by the steep wall-of-death-style banking, which, as Hoy says, was a daunting prospect. But he enjoyed it from the start. 'You enjoy what you're good at,' he says. 'I found that I did okay on the track and enjoyed it from day one. I started doing the weekly track league, on a Tuesday evening, and really enjoyed the 500 m handicaps. Being so young I'd start with about a lap-advantage over the big boys. I'd only be racing about half the distance they were, so it'd be flat out and I enjoyed that kind of effort – it was a bit like the start of a BMX race.

'Every week I'd hear the older riders coming up behind me – whooom! – and then sweeping past, but I found I could hold them off for a bit longer each time. I could see I was improving, which felt good. I remember the first time I won one of those races – it was a great feeling. Though it did mean that my handicap got smaller. The better I did the harder it was to win.'

But to say that Hoy took to track cycling like a duck to water would be stretching it. He did suffer teething troubles. Even at the 1994 national track championships – immediately prior to the Junior Tour of Ireland – there was an incident that Ray Harris puts down to 'inexperience'. Harris was there helping – though Hoy had joined a new club, the City of Edinburgh Racing Club, at the start of that year – and he was horrified when his protégé took to the start line of the junior kilometre with a spanking new pedal-and-shoe ensemble. He had got himself a clipless system, whereby shoes snapped into pedals, and were held there, rather than being attached by old-fashioned toe-clips and straps, which were still overwhelmingly the choice of track riders for whom reliability was the most important consideration.

'You don't try new tricks on the day of the competition!' exclaims Harris. 'Of course, he starts his effort, and in the strain of starting, he pulls his foot out of the pedal. My god! In the kilo there's a rule that if you have a mechanical problem in the first lap, or fall off, then you can start again. But a pulled foot doesn't count as a mechanical, so the commissaire [referee] is looking at me, saying "Push him over!" It's an old trick, that, the trick of falling off your bike if your foot comes out. But Chris didn't realize. It's a learning experience, but it can be costly if it's the one chance you've got as a junior. However, I think the least perturbed by all that was Chris himself. He seemed very calm. I was having kittens.'

To make matters worse, Hoy had 'previous' in this regard. At the 1992 British championship – his first, where he had the experience of riding around, awestruck, behind the new Olympic champion Chris Boardman – he had also pulled his foot out of his toe-clips and straps during his starting effort, riding the entire race with his foot resting limply on top of the pedal. Two years later, when he caused Harris to have kittens by pulling his foot out of his new pedals, he at least managed to clip his foot back in, and placed fifth in the junior kilo. But it could and should have been so much better, says Hoy, who feels that the 1994 championships – about which more later – were significant for being 'the first time I realized I had potential. I probably would have won the kilo if I hadn't pulled my foot out.'

It had been at the end of the 1993 season that Hoy felt it time to leave the club environment of the Dunedin, and the mentorship of Harris, to join a more specialist and more serious club, whose overriding focus was track racing. But he didn't forget Harris, who explains: 'I've had lots of lads come through the club and most of them move on to the next stage of their life and you never hear from them again, or see them; they become adults, get married, have kids, move on, though they probably keep a memory of it. But if I send Chris an email he always replies. It's one of the endearing things about the lad. He keeps in touch, in quite regular contact really.'

Stepping into Harris's shoes as mentor was Brian Annable: the inimitable, irascible Brian Annable – the Brian Clough of Scottish cycling. Annable ran his team – the City of Edinburgh Racing Club – with all the obsessive zeal, and occasional bursts of bad temper, of Clough. And the truly remarkable thing is that, twenty-five years on, he is still doing it. Since November 1982, when the City of Edinburgh Racing Club was established, Annable has been at the helm, skippering the good ship through some choppy waters, but invariably to success – which, in his book, means medals in British championships. Sitting in his large house in Edinburgh, behind a pile of immaculately blue-bound City of Edinburgh Racing Club annual reports – all twenty-five of them, in order – the well-spoken Annable spells it out, like an army major listing battles won: 'By 2006, seventy-six championships and two-hundred and forty-eight medals, won by club members in British championships.'

Annable has been the driving force behind those seventy-six national titles and two-hundred and forty-eight medals. He was a competitive cyclist himself, and in the British team pursuit squad for the 1952 Olympics, but his training, as an architect, got in the way of his cycling ambitions. A peripatetic career took him to Coventry, then to Manchester, 'to clear the slums of England in five years', and finally to Edinburgh, in 1970, just in time for the Commonwealth Games. 'I had been out of bike racing activity for several years,' he says, 'but I was appointed as deputy chief executive of the national building agency, based in Edinburgh.

'I went to Jenners [Edinburgh's big department store] on the first morning of the Commonwealth Games; down in the basement, where I was told I'd get tickets. But they had no plan of the track or anything,' he says with disgust and disdain. 'They didn't know where the finish line was!' Clearly this offended Annable on two fundamental levels – it showed an ignorance of sport, and an ignorance of the architecture of the arena. 'If you're in the left-hand end, where the track goes up, you can't see the finish. And I ended up with tickets there, because they didn't have a bloody clue.

'The problem,' he continues, now on a roll, 'is that the track was not done properly. For some reason the city engineer's department was involved in designing a cycle track, though they had no knowledge.' He discusses some complicated-sounding facts pertaining to cycle tracks, mentioning German designers and UCI manuals, longitudinal expansion, roof trusses, metal angle irons, and slotted holes.

So, is he saying that there were no velodrome specialists involved in the building of the Edinburgh velodrome? 'No! That's what amazes me,' he replies. 'It was a bunch of amateurs. But somebody must have known something; if someone contacted Schuermann [the renowned German architects, reputed to have built 125 velodromes worldwide] then I wouldn't be surprised.'

After the 1970 games Annable found himself down at the velodrome on an increasingly regular basis. A Scot, Brian Temple, from Edinburgh, had, surprisingly, won a medal at the games – silver in the ten-mile scratch race – and it provided evidence that Scottish cyclists could compete on such a stage, after all. There was also much in the 'build it and they will come' mantra of *Field of Dreams*, the baseball movie. The state-of-the-art Meadowbank velodrome proved quite a draw for cyclists from throughout Scotland during the 1970s.

But there was little organization to it. And there was certainly no pathway from participation to elite competition. When talented cyclists emerged, they had to make their own way. That is when mistakes tend to be made, and repeated ad nauseam.

In 1982 another talent emerged: Brian Annable's son, Tom. With Eddie Alexander – a Highlander based in Edinburgh – he enjoyed some success at that year's British championships, winning bronze in the junior points race. Two days later Alexander won bronze in the junior sprint. Incredibly, says Annable, these were the first two medals ever won by Scots in the British championships. 'And they were getting no support in Scotland!' he adds in characteristically bombastic fashion.

That winter Annable sat down with Alan Nisbet, 'Mr Track Cycling in Scotland', and discussed forming a specialist track club whose remit would be to 'bypass Scotland and target success at British level'. They talked to Arthur Campbell, who agreed that the track cyclists needed more support but felt they should do it within an existing club. Annable was having none of that. 'I got so fed up with the Scottish approach, still am, because it's more concerned with the importance of people who are office bearers than with talented young riders. Bunch of blithering idiots! They were stuck in the past, obsessed with time trialling and with no advertising, sponsorship or money. They didn't want to support people. Arthur was different, he was progressive, but he was keen we be part of a bigger club. In the end we said, "We're going to do our own thing, we've got two youngsters here [Tom Annable and Eddie Alexander] with enough talent to start it, and others who are being ignored."'

Annable wrote the constitution for a new track club, which remains, word-for-word, to this day, and appears on the first page in all twenty-five of those annual reports:

Cycle racing at the international level, including the World Championships, the Olympics and Commonwealth Games, and the British Championships, recognise champions in two road events and seven to nine track events.

In 1982 two Scottish junior riders won bronze medals on the track at the British championships. Eddie Alexander from Inverness in the Sprint and Tom Annable from Edinburgh in the Points race championship. It was clear to them and some other young Scottish track riders that they would have to concentrate their efforts and seek out specialized training and coaching and travel to competitions outside Scotland, if they were to have a chance of winning championships at the British and international levels. It also became obvious that an organisation devoted to this purpose was a prerequisite to success and that there was no such organisation in Scotland. Talks were held with an objective of winning medals at the British level, concentrating mainly, but not exclusively, on track racing and composed of young riders who were prepared to train, travel and race as necessary to reach that objective. It would be necessary to recruit expert coaching and team management and financial support.

The City of Edinburgh Racing Club was formed in November 1982. The country's top track riders were recruited, and in 1985 the club could boast its first British champions. 'Scotland has never had a British champion in track racing,' read that year's annual report. 'It now has two: 1km Eddie Alexander; 20km Steve Paulding.'

The club was not wealthy. Sponsorship was modest and numbers were kept low. 'I got sponsorship from the council, but

I only asked for £1,000,' says Annable, 'because my experience, and advice, was to never go for a big team. Keep it simple and small. We've got nineteen members now [in 2007]. It's always been a low number.' Membership was – and is – restricted. 'In terms of criteria for joining … well, I don't think we've ever had anybody we didn't know,' says Annable. 'It's a small part of a small sport, so we know the riders. And we've always gone for riders who were talented and keen to travel – ambitious.'

Other individuals and companies put money into the club. In the early days they included Joe McCann, who gave £1,000. He described himself as 'an enthusiastic optimist'. This was the kind of sponsor that clubs such as the City of Edinburgh RC tend to attract and upon whom they depend.

Within a few years, the club, by now known – and feared – as 'The City', was achieving its objectives. In fact, it was wiping the board. The City was so dominant in British track racing that in 1988 it was likened to the mafia by Kenny Pryde, a reporter for *Cycling Weekly* magazine. 'The City of Edinburgh "mafia" were to be seen sitting at trackside cheerfully exhorting their team-mates to greater efforts,' read Pryde's report, which prompted a response, published in the magazine the following week. It was a letter that appeared beneath the headline 'Message from the Edinburgh Godfather':

> Maybe your reporter Mr Pryde had little joke about the enthusiasm of members of the family encouraging the boys in the team. He calls them a 'Mafia', but the boys don't understand what this means. I have arranged for one of the boys to drop in on him one night in Glasgow to discuss the matter, and to make him a little offer I know he won't refuse.   *Brian Annable, Edinburgh*

Eddie Alexander was the club's star in its early years and in 1986, at the second Edinburgh Commonwealth Games, he won a bronze medal in the men's sprint, beating England's Paul McHugh in the ride for third. That and other successes earned him selection for the world championships in Colorado Springs, from where he sent Annable a postcard, which he still has. On one side there is a picture of the majestic San Juan mountains, and on the other, beneath the date (19 August 1986), the scrawled message: 'Dear Club. Very hot and sunny out here. Having a real good time – these BCF [British Cycling Federation] holidays sure are good value. I think we're going to fit in some racing next week at the velodrome. Wish you were here. Eddie.'

He was joking about it being a holiday but it might as well have been, because men's sprinting, the blue riband track discipline, was a closed shop. Alexander, the only British rider, had about as much chance of making an impression as Eddie the Eagle had of not embarrassing himself in a ski jump. Check the four semi-finalists: Michael Huebner, Lutz Hesslich, Ralf-Guido Kischy and Bill Huck. They had one rather significant thing in common, these four semi-finalists. They were all East German.

Now, you can speculate all you like about why the East Germans were so dominant. They were certainly awesome physical specimens – extraordinary physical specimens. There is a clip of a Huebner sprint, from 1990, that has proved popular on YouTube. Type in the words 'pumped up Huebner' and you will find it: Claudio Golinelli, the Italian, against Michael Huebner, in the final of the world sprint championship in 1990. Huebner, resembling the Incredible Hulk, is majestic, utterly impervious, while the words of the American commentator are unintentionally humorous. 'With that show of upper-body strength [from Huebner] I think Golinelli will be heading for the health club,' he muses, before suggesting: 'He is on the podium today, perhaps starring in *Rocky VI* next.'

Not to suggest that Huebner – nor indeed Hesslich, Kischy or Huck – did anything illegal. But East Germany, a country of fewer than 17 million people, was, throughout the 1970s and 1980s, the dominant Olympic force, in particular in sports such as swimming, athletics and cycling, for reasons that are now a matter of public record. Thousands of East German athletes were given perform-ance-enhancing drugs during that time; many didn't know what they were taking – some thought they were vitamins. Numerous ex-athletes have since suffered terrible health problems, includ-ing liver cancer, organ damage, psychological trauma, hormonal changes, and infertility. Eventually the German government set up a fund for doped athletes to pay medical bills arising from their years of being doped. By the March 2003 deadline 197 athletes had applied for the compensation of $10,000 each.

In 1987, Alexander's second world championship, he qualified thirteenth but, once again, all four semi-finalists were East German. But by now there was also another Scot – and a City of Edinburgh club-mate – at the championships in the form of Stewart Brydon. Brydon qualified twenty-first and told *Cycling Weekly*: 'The worlds have been an experience and it's made me realize how much work needs to be done. The Eastern Bloc countries are in front, but not by that much, and it's done me good to see them. You think they aren't human when you read what they are doing, but on the line they have fear in their eyes, the same as everyone else.'

Alexander also earned selection to the 1988 Olympics in Seoul, and it was here that he demonstrated just what a talented rider he was – and hinted at how far he might have gone had the playing field been level. Being the Olympics, there was only one rider per nation, which meant a guarantee of only one East German in the semi-finals. And Alexander, incredibly, made it that far, finally finishing in the worst place of all – just out of the medals in fourth. Lutz Hesslich, 'the man with the broadest shoulders in cycling,' was the Olympic champion, as he had been in 1980. Alexander, though, became the first British sprinter to reach the last four since Reg Harris, some forty years earlier.

The near-miss prompted Alexander, an amateur whose day job was to design power stations, to reflect on the 'Cinderella status' of British track racing: 'A lot of these guys have been in training camps or preparing in Europe. What did we get? Five days at Leicester [the outdoor track which hosted the British championships] and it rained on two of those.'

In the following years Brydon inherited Alexander's title as Britain's fastest sprinter, though he didn't make the same impact as Alexander on the international stage. At the British championships the City of Edinburgh sprinters were dominant – the East Germany, if you like, of the British scene – with Alexander, Brydon and Steve Paulding taking a clean sweep of the medals in 1989. The success in this discipline satisfied the club's 'Godfather', Annable, for it was sprinting that enthused and excited him. As far as he was concerned, it was real racing.

'You have to make a distinction between an athletic event and a race,' says Annable. 'My emotions are for racing, which for me means match sprinting. The most boring event in the world for me is the qualifying round for the women's pursuit. Riding fast against the watch doesn't excite me, whether it's the kilo, pursuit or team sprint. That's not a race! Whereas the racing from the quarter-finals of the sprint is electrifying. It appeals to my emotions.

'When I started there were two ways into the sport of cycling,' he continues. 'On the road you had the inspiration of the Tour de France, the mountains and all the rest of it. But in Britain at that time you couldn't road race – massed start racing on the roads was banned. You could time trial or ride on the track, and track racing was huge. Heavyweight boxers and sprint cyclists were superstars in those days.'

And the biggest star of all was Reg Harris, whose bronze statue now looms over the final bend of the Manchester Velodrome, the home of British cycling. Harris, born in 1920, won the amateur world sprint title in 1947, following that with two Olympic silver medals in 1948, in the sprint and tandem sprint, despite having fractured two vertebrae three months earlier, then falling and smashing his elbow just weeks before the games. But it was as a professional that he made his name: he won the world sprint title four times between 1949 and 1954. Then, perhaps even more famously, he came back twenty years later, winning the 1974 British title at the age of fifty-four.

Harris embodied the familiar traits of the star sprinter. He had panache, and, with his huge legs and puffed-out chest, the confident swagger of the sprinter. Backing up Annable's claim that the sprinters were huge stars, his feats also captured the imagination of the wider sporting public: in 1950, for example, he was named Sportsman of the Year by the Sports Journalists' Association, and he was twice named BBC Sports Personality of the Year.

Harris was colourful and controversial. He married three times, ran numerous businesses, including the Fallowfield Stadium velodrome, which he renamed the Harris Stadium, and started a 'Reg Harris' line of bikes. The man dubbed 'Britain's first cycling superstar', and known as 'Sir Reg' on account of his incongruously cut-glass accent and debonair manner, died after a stroke in 1992.

In some ways it seems strange that Harris is held up as the gentleman of British cycling and the grandfather of British sprinting. He was certainly utterly ruthless in pursuit of victory, and, according to some witnesses, not above skulduggery or dubious tactics. Tommy Godwin, the other great British track rider of the 1940s and 1950s, writes about Harris in his autobiography, *It*

Wasn't That Easy, and the picture that emerges is of a devious, scheming rider. In one race, writes Godwin, 'I passed Reg on the final bend and was into the straight when suddenly a pull on my saddle almost stopped me. My friend Harris [safe to assume he is being sarcastic here] wanted to win the final sprint in front of his home crowd, which he did. My response was to get to him as soon as possible and physically attack him.' Godwin also makes allegations of race-fixing and, at one point, tells of an exchange with a Belgian *soigneur* – a cyclist's masseur/trainer/unofficial doctor – named Louis Guerlache, who offers him 'a little help'. Writes Godwin: 'The inference of this I understood. I immediately said, "No, if I can't do it with what I have been gifted with then I don't want it." But at the mention of "No" Louis had picked up all the things laid out for the massage, threw them into his suitcase, which was packed with about half a chemist's shop, and stormed away.' Later in his book, Godwin notes wryly, and without comment, of one of Harris's world titles that: 'His trainer was Louis Guerlache, a Belgian.'

Annable's eyes light up as he remembers Tommy Godwin, his own particular favourite. He, to Annable, was a real racer. And he has seen enough of them now come through the City of Edinburgh, with the club snapping up any track cyclist with a modicum of talent and plenty of ambition. Meadowbank has always proved the testing ground; the weekly track league, on a Tuesday evening, provides a showcase, or audition, for any aspiring young rider. Arguably no other track in the UK has produced such a conveyor belt of talent, or so many British medallists.

There is no question, though, about who is the best of them all. Chris Hoy is the only individual world champion – with seven individual world titles among his nine gold medals – and, of course, the only Olympic champion to have taken his first pedal strokes at Meadowbank, and to come through the ranks of 'The City'.

Yet Annable, asked if Hoy is the most talented rider he has worked with, hesitates. 'His head wasn't good initially,' he says, eventually, and in his very matter-of-fact way. Annable is talking of the 1994 national track championships at Leicester, where a pulled foot led to Hoy finishing fifth in the junior kilo. He also placed sixth in the junior points race, but it was in the sprint – Annable's favourite – which served as a demonstration of his potential. Hoy qualified fastest, with 11.777 seconds, beating the best junior sprinter of the day, James Taylor. 'James Taylor's mother came over to me after that,' recalls Annable, 'and said, "God, you've got another one – who's he?"'

Someone else who was impressed was Doug Dailey, the national coach. He was sitting in the stand, just behind Hoy's parents. 'I overheard him saying, "That kid looks like he's got something about him,"' recalls David Hoy. 'I spoke to him later, told him I was Chris's dad, and he repeated what he'd said. Chris was over the moon to hear that.'

He progressed to the final, to meet the experienced Taylor in a race that also saw Hoy make his first TV appearance – it was broadcast by a new satellite sports channel called Sky Sports. 'He got to the final,' says Annable, 'against Taylor, and I said, "Look Chris, you may be faster, but he can stop you riding. He'll put you against the barriers and do whatever it takes to stop you." I told him exactly how to get out: "Don't chicken out!" I told him. "He can't hurt you; he can intimidate you." But Chris was outmanoeuvred, and Taylor got the better of him, beating him in two straight rides.'

This is what Annable means with his assertion that Hoy's 'head wasn't good initially'. It seems a harsh judgement on a seventeen year old. He must be surprised that Hoy became his first and only

Olympic champion. 'You have to give him his due,' says Annable, grudgingly. 'His single-mindedness has been phenomenal and so has his work rate. It took him a long, long time. He is now much bigger, physically, through specialized gym training, but it's taken him years. When he made up his mind, and had the confidence to know what to do, I mean, you can't fault him' – much as it would seem Annable would like to! – 'he has really done the work. But other riders have been better at knowing how to win a race. Craig MacLean, for example.' In MacLean Annable discovered the kind of rider he liked, almost – almost! – without qualification. 'Craig won sixteen gold medals with our club,' he says with evident pride. 'Chris won six,' he adds less effusively.

If the diplomatic Hoy has a criticism of the City it is that, although expectations were high in terms of successes, support off it, in the form of coaching and guidance, left much to be desired. Hoy says he was 'thirsty for knowledge. I knew I wasn't doing the right training, that there were pieces of the puzzle missing. I was desperate to know what I should do, and I kept asking questions, but there weren't many answers.'

It is also fair, however, to say that although Hoy's progress in his early days with The City demonstrated he had talent, there was little to indicate that he would go on to become arguably the country's most successful ever track rider. As well as his silver in the British junior sprint in 1994, he claimed two gold medals in the Scottish championships, winning the junior sprint and pursuit. Annable, typically, is dismissive. 'The Scottish championship is a fish-n-chipper,' he snorts, a 'fish-n-chipper' being one of those baffling pieces of sporting parlance – in cycling, it means inconsequential, rubbish.

October 1994 brought a significant development for the sport in the UK. The country's first indoor velodrome was built, in Manchester, as part of the city's planned bid for the 2000 Olympics.

Costing £9 million, it proved an instant hit, not least with the City
of Edinburgh Racing Club, who transferred their dominance from
the traditional home of the national championships, in Leicester,
to their new home in Manchester. In 1995, the first year the championships were held on the indoor track, the club won a new
event, the team sprint. Hoy figured in that gold-medal winning
team and also – illustrating his earlier point that he did have 'an
element of aerobic potential' – in the silver-medal winning team
pursuit team, contested over 4,000 m.

There began to be talk, already, of a 'Manchester effect' –
namely, a raising of the standards of Britain's track cyclists, who,
finally, were able to train all year round, whatever the weather.
It meant no more running for cover at the sight of rain. A
Manchester Super League was established, with races held in the
winter, traditionally the off-season, and with the riders representing cities, pitting Edinburgh against London, Birmingham, and
Manchester.

But of all the talent that was beginning to shine from the mid-
1990s, it was another Highlander – MacLean – who stood out. After
Alexander, though Brydon was successful at British level, there
had been no sprinters who made an impact on the international
stage. At the 1992 Olympics in Barcelona no British sprinters were
even selected. And four years later, at Atlanta in 1996, it was the
same again: no British sprinters were deemed good enough to
go. It was, explained the British coach, Doug Dailey, simply a case
of 'quality control. They just weren't fast enough.'

Speaking in 1997, Dailey admitted that the track sprinters had
for several years been treated like outcasts. But, he explained,
'That's about to change now. There is real progress and my feeling is there'll be a leading light who will drag sprinting along and
set the standard other sprinters have to aspire to. This boy MacLean
will set the standard and he can have a dramatic effect on sprint-

ing.' Sprinters tend to come in little groups – the Americans and Aussies have theirs. 'MacLean,' Dailey added confidently, 'can become the Guv'nor.'

CHAPTER 4

The Guv'nor

Chris Hoy's flat, Manchester, October 2007

'I've never talked about it with Craig but it must have been hard for him. He was the one breaking new ground, pushing the boundaries. He did the hard work. He was like a climber, he'd make the next foothold, and I'd follow. When someone else has forged ahead it's easy to follow because you see it's doable. But when you're the one taking the first step, that's a hard thing to do.'

Chris Hoy is sitting in his flat in Manchester, talking about Craig MacLean. It is fifteen years since the two first met – or met officially. Back then, they were finding their feet, both trying their hand at mountain biking, road cycling, a bit of track riding, both in the garish red-and-yellow of the Dunedin Cycling Club, both under the enthusiastic guidance of Ray Harris.

Like Hoy, MacLean's background was in BMX, though because they were in different age categories, their paths didn't cross. MacLean was five years older, born in 1971, hailing from the

Highland town of Grantown-on-Spey, which nestles in the pictur-
esque Spey Valley. Again like Hoy, MacLean retired from BMX-
ing – a sport with a retirement age younger than female gymnastics
– in his teens. He was fifteen when he stopped, having enjoyed
some success, though not as much as Hoy. 'My age group was
more competitive than Chris's,' says MacLean with a wry smile.
'But he'll contest that.'

MacLean didn't cycle for several years after that. He got into
music – he plays guitar and drums – grew his hair long and dressed
in AC/DC and Metallica T-shirts with the sleeves cut off. But after
starting college in Edinburgh in 1990 he began using a bike for
transport. 'Just to go back and forth to college,' he says. 'I was quite
prone to putting on weight in the winter, so I wanted to keep
myself fit. My dad had always cycled so there were always bikes
around the house, but I was more into my skiing and snowboard-
ing at that time. And music, of course.'

On taking up cycling again MacLean visited George Swanson's
bike shop in Edinburgh – no longer known as Scotia, but in prem-
ises near the original shop – and the two of them chatted. 'Chris
was working in the shop part time,' says MacLean, 'but I didn't
really know Chris. I knew his name from my BMX days. I told
George I'd got back into doing a bit of cycling and he told me
about the velodrome at Meadowbank, and the track league on a
Tuesday night. I started going down there for that, just to watch,
cycling from one side of Edinburgh to Meadowbank. But that was
the extent of my cycling, because once I got there I just sat and
watched from the stand, then cycled home.

'I didn't know anyone there and, you know … I was from
Grantown-on-Spey – you're scared to speak to people,' says
MacLean with another smile. As he points out, he was still into
his heavy rock phase, noting, deadpan, that 'I had long blond
ringlets.' And, despite his wild man of rock look, he imagined he

could sit in the stand at the velodrome and blend anonymously into the background? 'Well, yeah … I just used to sit in the stand in my cycling kit and keep out the way.'

One week, as he was making his usual journey to the velodrome, he was overtaken by a motorbike, which slowed as it passed him and then pulled in. 'This motorcyclist stopped, watched me pass, rode past me again, then stopped again – he kept doing that,' says MacLean. 'It was pretty strange.'

The motorcyclist was the father of Stewart Brydon, then Britain's top sprinter. Brydon senior rode to Edinburgh from the west of Scotland on his motorbike every Tuesday evening to help with the track league. He had spotted MacLean sitting in the stand and recognized him. The blond ringlets probably helped. That evening, when he arrived at the velodrome, and took his usual seat in the stand, MacLean was approached by Brydon. 'He talked to me and said I should come and have a go,' says MacLean. 'He encouraged me to turn up on a Friday for the Dunedin club night. So I went down on a Friday night, introduced myself, and they said, "Okay, if you want to join then you'll have to prove your worth." You had to be nominated and seconded at the monthly committee meeting. So the following month, after four weeks of me going on club runs and going to circuit training, my fate was decided.'

MacLean's recollection of the club's recruitment policy seems at odds with Ray Harris's description of the inclusive Dunedin club, though it might have something to do with MacLean's perception of himself as an outsider – as evidenced by his reluctance to get involved in the track league, other than as an observer. But he insists: 'I remember sitting in this club meeting in a Portakabin and having to go out the room while they talked about me, and assessed whether I was suitable for the club or not.' He qualifies this, though, by adding that: 'I don't think they ever rejected anyone.' And in his case, he adds, 'I think Dave Hoy put in a good word for me.'

In fact, David Hoy was a Craig MacLean admirer from the moment, at around the same time, that he first took him away to a race – a mountain bike race in the north of England. 'I remember we were travelling to a race and we had a spare seat in the car, so we asked Craig. I was really impressed. Chris and one or two of the others were just kids, but we went out for a meal on the Friday night and Craig had salad and rice, no meat. He was very particular about it. I thought, here's someone who's thinking about what he's doing; he's really thought it through. He had a very strict regime for looking after himself, and I was impressed that at that age – and that stage in his cycling career, because he was just starting out – he was so serious.'

When David Hoy's praise is put to him, MacLean winces a little, because his close attention to diet, though it might have been interpreted as a sign of his commitment to his sport, actually masked a serious problem. 'Partly because I got into cycling to lose weight, my diet was something I was into,' explains MacLean. 'But it became quite detrimental. It developed into an eating disorder. I was kind of reluctant to specialize in track cycling, to be honest – road racing was my main thing, mountain biking as well, because weight was a key thing to me. But I was fighting genetics, because I was never particularly light and I struggled to keep the weight off. It just turned into a bit of an issue for me.'

Within sport eating disorders might not be uncommon – even, or especially, at elite level. Chris Boardman has written about the subject in his book. 'Instead of the weight loss becoming a means to an end,' he wrote, 'it became the end itself. I was losing weight in order to enhance my chances in the Tour [de France], but – and those close to me will sigh heavily at this point – it became obsessive.'

Boardman is unusual, because the subject of eating disorders is rarely openly discussed. And there is a difficulty of definition, since there is an extremely fine line – some might argue no line at all – between a strict, almost obsessive diet, and what most people would interpret as an eating disorder. Certainly 'strict' or 'close to obsessive' is how you'd describe the eating habits of perhaps a majority of elite sports people; it would be difficult to find any world-class athlete who is not preoccupied by what he or she puts in their body. Perhaps, as Boardman says, the line is crossed when the primary goal becomes weight loss, or weight management, rather than sporting performance; again, though, there are problems in determining where that line is.

But MacLean, with a refreshing unwillingness to become bogged down in issues of definition, says that his problem went beyond that. 'It was a form of bulimia,' he says. 'It was never diag-nosed, and it's not something I've ever talked about; I just know myself that's what it was. I would starve myself for two or three days, not having any food whatsoever, and train at the same time. When I eventually admitted it to myself I got control of it. But it took about a year and a half.

'It was about 1993, and it was probably the worst season of my life. I was doing a little bit on the track by then. But my performance suffered. I would starve, binge eat, starve, binge eat. My form fluctuated and my weight actually increased as well. There was a point in 1994 when I realized I had a problem. I was at the British track championships, which were a week long, and because I had to cook, buying in the food I needed, I got to grips with it. I had to set myself some rules and targets, telling myself what I can and can't do. It still took a long time. I think there are always going to be some body-image issues there as well.'

One of the main problems – as MacLean recognizes – was the fact that his heart, at that time, was set on road racing and mountain biking. Athletes in these disciplines are, almost without exception, lean and lithe, or – if you prefer – just plain skinny. It must have been demoralizing and dispiriting to realize that your build might effectively disqualify you from ever succeeding in these disciplines, especially if you were putting so much into them.

The answer was staring MacLean in the face, however. At the opposite end of the scale to the whippet-like road racers were the track sprinters, who were all big, bulky and muscular: the colossuses of cycling. Not only did MacLean have the build for sprinting, he also had the physiology – the fast-twitch muscles necessary for lightning bursts of acceleration, as well as the power to sustain the effort. He was, in short, a natural. And, more or less as soon as he made the decision to focus on sprinting, he demonstrated that natural ability. He rode with the Dunedin club from 1993 to 1994, when, on finishing his studies, he moved back home to Grantown-on-Spey and joined a Highland club, Moray Firth Racing Team. The following season, 1995, was, he says, the first when he focused purely on the track. He was twenty-four that year, making him a late developer.

But he was enterprising, even entrepreneurial. In Grantown-on-Spey he managed, early in his career, to eke out a modest income from cycling. The Highland Games circuit is a big deal in the north of Scotland, and most of the summer meetings include grass track cycling, with significant cash prizes. The grass track circuit has traditionally been the most obscure yet also, paradoxically, the most lucrative form of cycle racing in the UK and for a while those that took part were deemed 'professionals', and therefore barred from more conventional forms of cycle racing. MacLean rode events sanctioned by the Scottish Cyclists' Union – that is, amateur events – but still made reasonable prize money. 'It was my summer job,' he claims.

Some of his training at the time was done in the company of a near neighbour and friend, Alain Baxter, who would go on to become Britain's greatest ever skier. Baxter, who, unfortunately, is more famous for a doping scandal at the 2002 Winter Olympics, when he lost his bronze medal after inadvertently using an American-made inhaler that contained a banned substance, was also a talented cyclist. He was a good training partner, though MacLean says that neither was as dedicated to sport in those days, and that much of their training was instigated by their respective fathers, who had competed against each other years earlier, in skiing and cycling. 'We had pushy parents,' jokes MacLean. 'I think they were using us to carry on their rivalry. Alain and I would meet up and have a bit of a blether, then tell our dads we'd been training hard.'

There is a strong possibility that MacLean is exaggerating his lack of commitment – and he is certainly joking about he and Baxter having pushy parents. In fact, both athletes went on to develop training regimes bordering on fanatical; and both became supreme athletes – as demonstrated by Baxter winning the BBC's Superstars series – as they reached the pinnacle of their respective sports.

Another influence at the time, adds MacLean, was Euan Mackenzie, an Olympic biathlete and 'formidable cyclist'. 'He really dragged me out on the bike until I was fit enough to enjoy it,' says MacLean.

MacLean also had a short stint working in a family business with his uncle, who was an undertaker. He once made the mistake of mentioning this to a journalist, prompting the description of him as the 'cycling undertaker'. Another quirky fact about MacLean that was – for journalists – irresistible was that he studied piano tuning at college. Thus he has repeatedly been labelled 'the piano-tuning-undertaker-cyclist', or a variation on this. All he can do now is roll his eyes whenever he is asked about piano tuning, or under-taking, or both – which means a lot of eye rolling. His undertak-ing, or piano tuning, or both, tend to be raised every time he is interviewed.

Although MacLean was able to make some money on the grass tracks of the Highlands, it was obvious his cycling income would never be enough to live on. More conventional track racing offered few career possibilities. For both MacLean and Hoy, in fact, the opportunities to make any kind of living through cycling appeared, at that time, to be minimal to non-existent. Track cycling was the poor relation of international cycling – the big money was in road racing, with, apart from in those countries that put money into their track programmes, only crumbs available, and to only a very few of the top performers. It didn't really matter how ambitious Hoy or MacLean were; like Eddie Alexander before them, they would in all probability have to fit cycling around jobs, and they would, as a consequence, be unlikely ever to realize their potential.

This was the reality faced by both, and so when Hoy left school, in 1994, he went to university. He says it didn't occur to him not to follow the traditional path of getting a degree and then a job. And so, only a couple of months after his breakthrough at the British track championships, when he claimed a silver medal in the junior sprint, he began a four-year honours degree in maths and physics at St Andrews University, forty miles north of Edinburgh.

He threw himself into university life. 'It was great,' says Hoy, 'a whole new experience, feeling independent even though you're living in halls, getting all your meals cooked and forty-five minutes from home … But I was going out all the time, partying, enjoy-ing a good social life. I relished it. And I didn't touch my bike.

'Then towards the end of the first term I got a call from my dad. He said he had invitations to two races. He asked me, "Do you fancy the Tour of the North in Ireland …" and I said, "Great! That would be brilliant." Then he added, "… or a track meeting in Trinidad?"

'I said, "Fantastic! Where's Trinidad?"'

The promise of two weeks in the sun at Easter 1995 gave Hoy some motivation to get back out on his bike. 'I pretty much hadn't touched my bike the entire first term. But at Christmas, when I went home, I started training again. I'd eaten a lot of junk food that term, drunk a lot, gained some weight, swapping fat for muscle. It was so hard getting back into it.'

The trip to Trinidad kick-started Hoy's first season as a student-cyclist – also his first season in the senior ranks – and, as mentioned in the previous chapter, it brought some success. At the national championships he was a member of the City of Edinburgh team that won gold in the team sprint; he was also still competing in the odd endurance event, and was a member of the quartet that claimed silver in the team pursuit.

And in the Scottish championships there was a snapshot of the future when, in the men's sprint, the two riders who made it to the final were Hoy and MacLean. It was a thrilling contest, going to three rounds; MacLean winning match A, Hoy winning match B, and then, according to his harshest critic – Brian Annable – 'going to sleep in the decider and getting jumped with 250 m to go'. The title thus went to MacLean.

But towards the end of the first term of his second year at St Andrews University, Hoy phoned home. 'He just said he was absolutely miserable,' says David Hoy. '"Give it another few weeks," I said. But he said: "I can't do this."' Then he corrects himself: 'What he actually said was, "I *can* do this, but I don't see any point in doing it."'

'I just thought, "What am I doing?"' says Hoy. 'I enjoyed St Andrews, liked the place, had a good group of friends, a great social life, but I didn't enjoy the course and I wanted to be doing something that was gong to help me. I had developed my interest in sports science. At the training camp I'd been to in Majorca, the previous year, there was a guest coach, Louis Passfield. Louis wasn't a sprint specialist but he had enough knowledge to answer the questions I had, and he was quite scientific. It gave me a taste for sports science. I had this hunger for knowledge in terms of physiology and wanting to know the best way to train – all these questions that I hoped sports science could answer for me.'

Hoy returned to Edinburgh from St Andrews in October 1995, contacted Moray House – the scene of Ray Harris's Kingcycle tests – and enquired about enrolling there to study sports science. His application was accepted, and he went straight into second year the following autumn. In the meantime, and to teach him something of 'the real world', his parents insisted that he either get a job or sign on the dole. He opted initially for the latter, though returned from the local dole office asking 'What was that all about?' and decided to get a job instead, working in the Edinburgh bookshop Thin's.

It was in 1996 that he was joined in the City of Edinburgh Racing Club by MacLean. In fact, it was a case of second time lucky for MacLean – his written application had been rejected the previous year. But he proved a more than useful signing: in the kilo at the British championships he won a bronze medal, while Hoy was fifth – having this time managed not to pull his foot out the pedal with his starting effort. But another significant episode that summer was a dreadful accident at the Meadowbank Velodrome, involving Hoy and, more seriously, another of Britain's up-and-coming riders – Jason Queally.

As Ray Harris has noted, the constant exposure of the wooden boards to the elements was making the velodrome increasingly dangerous and prone to splinter. This was borne out, horrifically, by Queally, who needed hospital treatment after coming off worst in a pile-up in the closing stages of the Meadowbank Mile. In crashing he was impaled by an eighteen-inch-long, one-and-a-half-inch-wide piece of wood. That was as much a 'splinter' as a whale is a minnow. The resulting wound needed seventy stitches, with the doctors telling Queally that the thickness of his chest muscles – developed during his earlier career as a swimmer and international water polo player – possibly saved his life. Had the splinter pierced his chest cavity, it would probably have killed him.

Hoy had a ringside seat, being the first rider to go down. 'It was the last corner, there had been a train of four or five City riders on the front, then Craig had done the big push and I was on his wheel; so we're rounding the last corner, I'm coming up on his back wheel, and Craig flicked slightly to the side. It wasn't intentional, but I caught his wheel, came crashing down, and took Jason, and everyone else, down with me. Craig was the only one who stayed upright. Jason hit me, went over the top and landed on his back, then slid down the track. He was screaming, shouting: "I've got half the fucking track in my back!" And I was lying there, pretty sore, thinking, "Aw, shut up, will you? I don't know who you are but you're making a lot of noise … it can't be *that* bad." Then I looked across, saw this bit of wood sticking into him, with the other end sticking out the other side, and I thought, "Okay, you can have the ambulance first …"'

It was Hoy's mother, Carol, a nurse, who was on first-aid duty at Meadowbank that day. She took Queally to hospital. 'I'd never met Jason, but it was absolutely devastating,' she says with a shudder. 'It was very obvious he was badly injured, and it was very worrying. Horrible, and scary. I always worry about Chris crashing but on that occasion I must admit I didn't even look at Chris, though he had lost half his skin in the crash.'

After a week in intensive care, and with a scar in his back that made it look 'as though he'd been attacked by a shark', Queally resolved never again to ride in a group race, shifting his focus to individual efforts against the clock. It was a decision, albeit an enforced one, that would later reap spectacular rewards – and provide some crucial inspiration for Hoy. But it was perhaps just as well that he wasn't a member of the City of Edinburgh Racing Club; accident or no accident, Annable would probably have told him to buck up his ideas and take part in a 'real race', not individual efforts against the clock.

Hoy and MacLean, meanwhile, confirmed their emerging talent with selection for that year's world championships – the first to be held at the Manchester Velodrome. The twenty-year-old Hoy was selected for the team sprint, while MacLean rode the individual sprint, the kilo and the team sprint, finishing twelfth in the kilo – though he was second fastest over the opening lap – and fourteenth in the sprint.

The team sprint proved a bitter experience, however. Queally, by now recovered from his crash, pulled his foot out at the start – and yes, he was using new clipless pedals (Ray Harris would not have been impressed). MacLean was angry with the British selectors, saying that it should have been the City of Edinburgh team – in other words, with Peter Jacques instead of Queally – that contested the worlds. 'We proved our point,' he told reporters afterwards, with the team not having been allowed a restart, and therefore posting no result. 'It should have been the club team in the worlds, but it wasn't our decision.'

By now MacLean was thinking that cycling could, somehow, become a career. How, he didn't exactly know. But ambition – or wishful thinking – overrode common sense. 'I was living back up north and it came to a point where I was forced to take one route or the other,' he says. 'Cycling wasn't a career path. There was no possibility of making it a career really, not at that point. But I was quite confident I could make a living. I don't know why I thought that, or how I thought I'd make a living. I was possibly a bit naive.

'The other option for me at that point was to join the armed forces. Once you were in there, and had passed the initial training, you could do well at sport. But it would have involved ten months' training. I didn't want to lose that time, so I had to make a choice. Then I heard about this new "Developing Excellence" programme being started by Edinburgh University – it was a forerunner to the Scottish Institute of Sport. It didn't give you money, but it did give you access to the university gym, to lectures on sports performance, that kind of thing. Chris and I were invited to be the representatives from cycling. That was enough of a spur for me to move back to Edinburgh.'

Around this period, from 1995 to 1997, MacLean, as Hoy says at the start of this chapter, was the one who was forging on ahead, while others, most obviously Hoy himself, followed. David Hoy also favours the climbing metaphor: 'Craig was like a climber with Chris hanging on the rope behind.'

Was MacLean aware of this? 'I was desperately aware of it,' he says with feeling. 'But Chris was a significant driving force for me as well, because he was constantly nipping at my heels. I think without each other, pushing each other on, then things would have panned out very differently for both of us.'

They were way ahead of the pack – and ahead not only of their peers but of previous generations as well. 'There was nobody else, really, and we'd gone faster, already, than the guys who'd gone before us,' says MacLean. 'So there was a void. The old generation – the likes of Eddie Alexander and Stewart Brydon – had moved on, we were coming up pretty fast, and there was no one there to help us; there wasn't the coaching structure in place at the British Cycling Federation; there was no money in it; there was nowhere to turn to get your ideas or information. You had to go by instinct and do a lot of reading and second guessing.'

In which circumstances, he adds, you make a lot of mistakes. Hoy refers to sprinting as a 'black art' and this was at the heart of the problem for MacLean. With no great tradition of sprinting in Britain – or huge gaps between Reg Harris and Eddie Alexander, whose career was always heavily compromised and whose potential was ultimately unfulfilled – there was no bank of knowledge, no ready mentors or sources of useful information. MacLean was keen to learn all he could – hence his enthusiasm for Edinburgh University's 'Developing Excellence' initiative.

But it was specialized advice he really needed – so where did MacLean turn? 'You heard snippets from people – what the Germans did, what the French did, bits and pieces. But it was hard to get that information. Even the people in Britain who did have a bit of experience, there seemed to be a reluctance to pass it on … it was like they didn't want us to be better than them. I remember asking one of our top sprinters, way back at the 1992 national championships, "What's the difference between us and the top German guys?" And he said: "Weights." That was it. "Weights." That was the extent of the advice. And it wasn't as if I posed any threat to him at the time.

'I remember overhearing conversations between Stewart Brydon and Graeme Obree,' continues MacLean. 'I was just listening in while they were discussing training. I took on some of Obree's ideas about using big gears for specific strength development. Some of his ideas were a bit too off-the-wall in practical terms but I absorbed some of them. But I think we wasted so much time and effort doing rubbish training, basically. We didn't know what worked so we did masses of volume, which probably stood us in good stead in the long term, but in the short term it meant we didn't progress. We were just tired a lot of the time.'

Hoy echoes this. 'Some of the training we did at the time was absolute nonsense. It was a case of taking two steps forward, one back. We trained very hard but a lot of it was counterproductive.' Among the 'nonsense' training, perhaps, were some highly experimental techniques tried out by MacLean. 'Like filling his bike with lead shot,' recalls Hoy. 'He had unusual ideas, mad ideas.'

MacLean says that at this time he and Hoy developed 'in tandem'. Hoy is generous in his assessment of MacLean's influence on him, even describing him as 'my coach – certainly the closest I had to a coach at that time'. If they were on a tandem then MacLean, clearly, was the one piloting it.

But following the 1996 world championships, Hoy could look forward to his first major overseas assignment – given that the worlds had been held in Manchester – at the European Under-23 championships in Moscow, in October. It was to be a strange trip. The British Cycling Federation could only afford to send three people, and they opted not to 'waste' a space on an official or mechanic, so three riders – Hoy, Alwyn McMath and Angela Hunter – were selected and told to fend for themselves.

Hoy viewed Moscow as a massive opportunity: he would ride an individual event, the kilometre time trial. It would thus be his first opportunity to lay down a marker as a rider in his own right, and to step out from MacLean's shadow. 'Training was going really well,' he recalls, 'I kept progressing after the world championships, improving all the time. It was all going well.'

Then he and a couple of others were 'roped in' to starring in a short film. A promotional video was being made to try and sell the sport of track cycling to television. 'They were trying to do something arty,' says Hoy. The velodrome was shrouded in darkness, with the only light coming from a spotlight trained on the finish line, the idea being that Hoy and his fellow riders emerge from the darkness, like ghosts, riding into the light.

'It went on for ages and ages,' says Hoy. 'It was my first experience of doing something for TV and finding out how it always drags on.' The track had been booked for two hours, from 9–11 p.m. At 1 a.m. they were still filming. In the midst of it, Hoy, on his bike, rolled down the ramp that leads from the track centre into the tunnel that emerges at the foot of a flight of stairs, which climb up to the main reception.

Unfortunately, as Hoy rolled down, a man pushing a large trolley – packed with cameras – appeared in front of him. Hoy – on his track bike, with a fixed wheel instead of brakes – pushed back hard on the pedals. At a slow speed that can be as effective as braking – you stop immediately. But on this occasion he pushed too hard: his effort stripped the rear sprocket. And so now, with his feet strapped tightly into the pedals, he was careering down the ramp, picking up speed, with no way of slowing down, far less stopping.

He squeezed past the trolley, and, like something from Benny Hill, carried on straight past him, gathering speed, out of control, and with, eventually, only the steps leading up to reception in his path. The only thought in his brain, he says, was 'Shit, what am I going to do here?' But there was no flash of inspiration and he carried on, 'going very fast by now', until he collided with the stairs, sticking his arm out to try and protect his face. The bike was a mess – it concertinaed. So was his arm – it was broken.

Initially the national track coach, Marshall Thomas, reassured him that his arm wasn't broken. 'Wait and see how it is in the morning,' he told him. But in the morning it was 'massive – like an old lady's leg', says Hoy. 'Really swollen, straight up and down. I went to the hospital, had it x-rayed and had a cast put on it. And this was two-and-a-half weeks before Moscow. I was gutted.'

But he was still 'determined to go. I thought, "What if I modify my handlebars?" I just couldn't face the idea of not going.' Neither could the BCF, who had paid for his travel and arranged a non-transferable visa. So it was agreed that Hoy would go anyway. 'If you can ride, then ride,' he was told, 'and if you can't, then help the others.'

He was determined to ride. So when he got to Moscow he visited the Dutch team's mechanic – 'because we had no tools with us', Hoy points out – and asked for a large set of clippers. With these he went to work adapting his plaster cast, removing the bit that covered his hand. That allowed him to grip the bars, though it was sore to do so. But, gingerly, he took the start line for the kilo, managed a personal best by 'four or five tenths of a second', recording 1 minute, 6 seconds, and placing twelfth of the twenty-five starters. 'I was over the moon with that,' he says. In first place, meanwhile, was an eighteen-year-old prodigy from France – Arnaud Tournant – who went three seconds faster than Hoy. When he returned, Hoy faced some awkward questions. His doctor asked, 'What on earth have you done to your plaster cast?' Hoy told him his hand had swollen up so badly that he had needed to modify it.

Meanwhile, MacLean was by now, to all intents and purposes, a full-time cyclist. Hoy was still a student, in Edinburgh, though his studies fitted around an increasingly busy racing programme. There was little structure, though; no real organization. What the two of them did, they did off their own bat. It required huge amounts of self-motivation coupled with large doses of inspiration and also initiative. Both must have believed – or just blindly hoped – that somewhere along the line an opportunity would appear for them.

MacLean confirms that, from early 1996, there was a vague realization that something might be on the horizon, that the new National Lottery would provide the sport, and the athletes, with something. How much, he didn't have a clue. 'We knew something was coming and that was quite motivating,' says MacLean. 'But there was quite a long period where I had no income; two-and-a-half to three years when I survived on unemployment benefit. I was part of the British team, going away to races, and then going into the dole office to sign on in between races. I think I sort of told them what I was doing, but they didn't really get it at the signing-on office ...'

Pre-Lottery, unemployment benefit existed for many top British cyclists as an unofficial grant. It wasn't as if being part of the British team conferred many benefits. It was more likely, in fact, to leave you out of pocket. 'You were given one skinsuit for the whole year,' says MacLean, 'and you were to be immensely proud of having that, because so few had it. You had to supply your own track bike. They lent you a state-of-the-art road bike, from the 1960s. There were two coaches, Doug Dailey and Marshall Thomas, but a lot of what they did was voluntary – and all the other officials were volunteers. We used to get some expenses, but all the trips up and down to Manchester for training or racing came out of our own pocket. That reflected the level of commitment and belief, I think, the fact we paid, effectively, to be part of the British team.'

The following year, MacLean would confirm the beginning of a new era in British sprinting – an era he would dominate for the next decade. He won the 1997 national sprint championship, beating Craig Percival, for the first of his seven titles; and for good measure he claimed another three gold medals, including the kilometre title – with twenty-one-year-old Hoy signalling his potential by taking bronze. MacLean also established three new British records. It was this, coupled with promising results on the international stage, that filled Doug Dailey with such optimism and encouraged him to hail MacLean as 'the Guv'nor'. He also began to receive some attention from the media, telling *Cycling* magazine: 'I needed a direction and music wasn't going to be it. There's no guarantee of success, no matter how hard you work. Cycling is measurable. You work hard, you see results. I got motivated by that.'

An even bigger motivation was still to come, though. British cycling – especially track cycling – was on the brink of revolution.

PART 2

The Plan

CHAPTER 5

Sliding Doors

A dingy office in the bowels of the Manchester
Velodrome, 1997

In the film *Sliding Doors* the destinies of several people are affected by the timing of a closing door. A half-second later and there would have been different outcomes all round; their fates would have been radically altered; their lives would have followed alternative courses. However exaggerated certain aspects of the film, the premise is completely realistic. The sliding doors hypothesis is plausible and intriguing, and it can arguably be applied to the sport of cycling in Britain.

The man in the right place at the right moment, or jumping through the sliding door in the nick of time, was Peter Keen. You may recall him from Chapter One; he coached Chris Boardman to Britain's first Olympic gold medal in eighty-four years at the Barcelona games in 1992. But his relationship with Boardman, and with top-level sport, pre-dated that by several years, even though he was not much older than Boardman.

As a coach, Keen, quite apart from the fact that he possessed radically original ideas, was an anomaly: he had been a decent amateur cyclist, who, at an unusually young age, found his niche in coaching. Then again, it doesn't seem right to describe him simply as a coach. He coached, but he was more than a coach. He was a sports scientist whose coaching involved the application of scientific principles and practices to all aspects of training and racing.

I knew about Keen's work with Boardman, or, rather, I knew all about the results of their partnership. But I hadn't realized, until I read an out-of-print biography of Tony Doyle, the successful British track rider of the 1980s, that Keen had worked with him, too. These days, Keen, still blond-haired and boyish in appearance, has one of the most important jobs in British sport – he is Head of Performance at UK Sport. But when I visit him at the UK Sport headquarters in London, and ask him about his involvement with Doyle, he appears momentarily, and uncharacteristically, flummoxed. 'Gosh,' he says. 'Wow,' he adds, raising his eyebrows and emitting a short, almost nervous, laugh before becoming thoughtful. 'That is … well, it is a very, very significant part of my story.'

In the book – *Tony Doyle: Six-Day Rider*, by the late and esteemed writer Geoffrey Nicholson – Keen's role in Doyle's entourage is described as sports physiologist, though his actual responsibilities are vague. Indeed, the impression from reading the book is that he was a marginal member of the team; that he wasn't permitted access to the rider's inner sanctum, or not to the same extent as others. In Doyle's dressing room, for example, only three people were allowed: Doyle's manager, Mick Bennett, his psychologist, and his long-standing Belgian *soigneur*. Others were shut out, which created resentment. As Nicholson writes: 'The physiologist [that is, Keen] wanted a wider involvement, and asked why he should be excluded from the dressing room.'

In cycling, certainly back then, a *soigneur* – who, as previously explained in connection with British sprinting legend Reg Harris, is part masseur, part helper, part unofficial doctor – would have commanded infinitely more respect than some newfangled physiologist or sports scientist. So to some extent the apparent ostracizing of Keen was understandable: he was only twenty-two, and just out of university, while Doyle was an experienced rider on the winter six-day circuit and a two-time world professional pursuit champion.

But I'm curious: was there another explanation – one that is absent from Nicholson's book? 'I worked with Tony from 1986 to 1988,' explains Keen. 'It was my first experience of working with a world-class athlete and I learned a hell of a lot and had to grow up very quickly. One of the most valuable aspects of it was that I – at a very young age as a coach or sports scientist – had to get my head around some of the choices that you have to make about the way you want to work.'

A pause, and then Keen elaborates: 'Tony is a larger than life character. I had very little direct experience of the traditional, continental style of training and preparation. I spent those two years asking many questions of him and of the people who worked with him, and trying to be creative with the thoughts I had at the time. Some of my ideas worked very well … some didn't work at all. It was a baptism of fire. The whole approach that most riders of that era took was that the only way to win was to immerse yourself in the continental way, which covered everything from the volume of training you did, to the way you rubbed your legs, to … a lot else besides. It was a hell of an insight into a world I knew nothing about.'

In the book, Keen's relationship with Doyle and others in his entourage is depicted – as much as it is depicted at all; it is more of a subtext, really – as fractious. 'There were a few dark weeks, yes,' he laughs. In particular, there is an incident at the world championships in 1987 – when Doyle's start time was changed and no one told him – that seems to have led to a bit of a fall-out, though again this is really only hinted at in the book. Keen laughs at the euphemistic description of what happened as 'a bit of a fall-out'. 'It went nuclear!'

'The value of working with Tony,' he continues, more soberly, 'was that he was the first person I worked with who had a completely clear ambition and approach. He wanted to be the best in the world, he was prepared to do what he felt was necessary – and that commitment wasn't commonplace in British riders. It's what made him the outstanding athlete he was, for sure.

'But I saw so many things in the way he and others approached the sport that simply made no sense to me. The frustration for me was that most of what they were doing was bloody nonsense. What I learned from it was that you have to be true to what you believe in, but you also have to be prepared to adapt and change; because if you only follow religiously what everyone else has done then you can only be as good as them – not better.'

Still, Keen's work with Doyle helped establish him as a coach with new, even avant-garde, ideas. He flickered across the radar of Doug Dailey, the long-serving British national coach – and a stalwart during years of turmoil at the cash-starved British Cycling Federation. Dailey has occasionally been depicted as a member of the old guard, and certainly as one of the principal figures of an era best forgotten, but this seems grossly unfair. As Keen says: 'It amazes me that there are so many critical views of Doug. What he did for ten years, with virtually nothing, is just absolutely astonishing.'

It is certainly no bad reflection on Dailey that he sought to involve a young, ambitious and innovative – but still unproven – coach such as Keen. It was late 1986 when he contacted Keen and said he wanted to bring some riders to his lab, at Chichester College in Brighton, to be tested.

To be tested for what? 'All the usual stuff,' says Keen, shrugging his shoulders, almost embarrassed at the tests he carried out back then, in what now seems to him a prehistoric era. 'There was stuff you did, feedback you were able to get, which at the time seemed the thing to do,' he says. 'The Kingcycle came a little bit later, but the basic principles were the same. We would take some measurements that we believed might tell us a bit more about what was going on inside somebody … and that could form the basis of a more rational training programme.'

Though Keen scoffs now at some of the testing he carried out then, he adds that, 'I fervently believed at the time that it was the right thing to do. And if nothing else, it was a tremendous vehicle for getting people to talk and look at what they were doing. I could dig out the lab book now and you'd see a staggering array of names. They all came – because there was absolutely nothing else going on.

'In early 1987 Doug brought a car down to my college from Liverpool, and one of the people in the car was Chris Boardman. He had this profile as a child prodigy. He'd ridden the world championships at sixteen – he came last, mind. But he was one of [renowned Liverpool coach] Eddie Soen's boys, a junior prodigy at time trialling and on the track, something a bit special.

'So I tested him. And … he was nothing special … at all. At least, he was nothing special in the way I would have read the data at the time. If you just looked at the power output, he was pretty average. He was surprised; I was surprised; Doug was surprised. My inevitable question to him was, "What does your winter look like?" This was January, after all. And he replied: "Well, in winter I stop. I play squash, I ride my bike a bit, I dick around. That's what we do, isn't it?"

'I thought, "That's interesting." So I said, "Here's a heart rate monitor, here are the kinds of things I think will help you." And vintage Chris, he locked onto it. The car from Liverpool comes back in three months, and the percentage change in this guy is staggering. I was like, "What the bloody hell happened there?"

'Whether that is trainability in a physiological sense, I couldn't say. But it's certainly trainability in a psychological, behavioural sense.' Which to Keen, you suspect, was almost everything. After trying and largely failing to convince Doyle to adopt his ideas, here was an athlete – a raw, potentially talented eighteen-year-old athlete – who would soak them up like a sponge – and fire back some interesting, thought-provoking questions himself. 'I thought,' says Keen, 'that here is a guy who will listen and try and examine. He had heard some things back in January that obviously resonated with him. He thinks: that makes sense to me. He tries it, and boom! He immediately gets some very positive reinforcements, and he's locked in.'

It was the beginning of a coach-athlete marriage made in heaven. 'The next time,' continues Keen, 'he doesn't come in a car full of others, driven by Doug Dailey; he drives himself down in a beaten up Renault 11. He's only eighteen, but as far as he's concerned it's worth a 300-mile journey when he's broke, and in a car that's probably not legal – that's commitment!'

Interestingly, Keen didn't detect in Boardman – at least not yet – the burning desire to be an Olympic champion, or a top professional. It wasn't as straightforward as that; significantly, his desire and ambition was focused instead on improving. 'Ambition,' claims Keen, 'tends to evolve in an athlete.' (When I later ask Boardman about ambition, though, he makes an interesting, and revealing, claim: 'Ambition didn't come into it. Pete and I were similarly fascinated, not ambitious. We were fascinated with the process, of trying things, finding potential solutions … that process excited us more than performance.')

Keen talks about 'dreams' rather than 'ambitions' – a seemingly woollier concept – and he uses a climbing analogy, a particularly evocative one: 'We all dream, but the extent to which the dream translates into a daily reality, as you get further up the mountain, and the mist clears so you can see the top … and what might be involved in getting there, that's when many think, that's it, that's enough for me; only a few think, I'll push on for the summit.'

Keen's analysis highlights the lesson also taught by Ray Harris in his goal-setting sessions, the underlying message being: don't focus on the summit, but instead select points on the way up the mountain that appear reachable – short-term and medium-term goals, in other words. And Keen's line – 'The extent to which the dream translates into a daily reality' – brings into sharp focus the most sobering reality for any athlete: that hard, hard work is the only daily reality for someone who dreams of one day pushing on to an invisible summit.

But few can pursue their dreams alone, with no support. 'If I draw on my own experiences,' says Keen, 'I was vaguely ambitious, and reasonably talented as a bike rider, but by the time I hit the buffers no one had sat me down and systematically told me, "You must do this, you mustn't do that." I didn't know what to do, and there was no system there, no support.

'One of the things I take most pleasure in now,' he continues, 'when I look at what's in place at British Cycling, is that it's a hell of a lot closer to the system that I know would have got the best out of me. Now, whether that's been a drive for me to do all the things I've done, I don't know … but it's a very tempting hypothesis.'

* * *

Keen's working relationship with Boardman became 'very close, very quickly. We're not dissimilar individuals, so there's possibility that chemistry there,' he says. And although their sights were not trained, yet, on the Olympics, it soon became apparent that Boardman's best chance of making a breakthrough, in an international sense, was on the track, riding the 4,000 m pursuit. It was a discipline that his talent was well suited to, though Keen was convinced, at first, that he was the wrong size; that he was too skinny and didn't have the muscular build of the traditional pursuiter. 'I had this naive view in the mid- to late-Eighties that the size of an athlete was more important than it probably is,' he laughs. 'I wasn't convinced he was the right shape.'

Ironically, there was, says Keen, 'another measurement that I would have done on Chris on the very first day which could have told me quite a lot about his potential'. At the time, however, he didn't study this measurement – of his lung function – or at least not for any indication of his capabilities as an athlete. 'It was a test that all trainee sports scientists did,' explains Keen, 'but you did it, printed it off and put it in a file somewhere and never looked at it again. You were looking for an abnormality, checking someone's not weirdly asthmatic or something.

'Now, I would interpret those figures differently. And in Chris's case, I would see that the guy is completely off the scale in terms of some potentially fundamental characteristics, namely size and function of lungs, which is completely un-trainable; it doesn't change. It's not that he has particularly huge lungs; it's the efficiency with which he can open and close them, and the energy cost of doing that – which in Chris's case is staggeringly high. If I'd known what I was looking for, I could have seen that on day one.'

The first sliding doors moment: had Boardman not shown an interest in what Keen had to say, then he might have drifted off, back to his squash, occasional cycling and dicking around, and – exceptional lungs notwithstanding – perhaps never realized his potential.

Boardman's progress towards the Barcelona Olympics wasn't linear. There were setbacks. He went to the 1988 Olympics in Seoul as 'an average rider', in Keen's assessment. The following year he was tenth in the pursuit at the world championship; and in 1990 major abdominal surgery, in the middle of the season, seemed to end his year in June. 'But he limped back onto the bike, ended up going to the worlds and came sixth. It was an amazing performance.' But the following year 'he was crap' says Keen, before adding, more charitably, 'He'd picked up a virus.'

The real breakthrough came in Olympic year itself, just six weeks before the games. This, says Keen, is when he switched from thinking 'It'll be nice if this happens' to 'We believe it will.' It was a session with a psychologist, John Syer, that led to this epiphany. 'He made Chris and me do a session where in effect he got us to talk in a way that brought out the deeper stuff that we just didn't talk about. It was all around what do we actually want to happen here … what is it that we're trying to rehearse in our minds as we look forward to Barcelona? Because it was obvious: he was in amazing form. So we looked at each stage of the pursuit series, and how to manage it, working back from the gold medal.'

This, Keen acknowledges, was an unusual approach. 'Most Brits would be saying, "You can't be doing that – you've just got to hope it'll all happen!" But the approach we took was interesting; the whole way you think as a consequence of a conversation like that is different: it gives you an absolute belief that this is possible; you start to see the genuine obstacles.'

And added to their confident mental attitudes, there was, of course, something else – a secret weapon. 'The Lotus bike,' smiles Keen, 'which, for one thing, was a hell of a lot better than anything we'd ever had, but psychologically it was even more important. It was massive.'

Following Barcelona Keen and Boardman went on to – arguably – even better things: three hour records, three world titles, three Tour de France prologue time trials. Keen also worked successfully with other riders, including Yvonne McGregor and Paul Manning, but cycling couldn't fully satisfy his ambitions – not least because there were so few coaching opportunities in the sport, certainly in the UK.

He was keen to apply his ideas in other areas, to other sports, and by the mid-1990s he was acting as a consultant to the UK Sports Council – the forerunner to his current employer, UK Sport – and advising governing bodies in other sports. His work with Boardman established him, in any case, as one of the country's top coaches. Other sports were keen to learn. So Keen, who was also still working in academia, earned himself a contract as an 'expert adviser' to other sports, with a brief to 'review various sports' performance programmes'.

By 1996 and 1997 the landscape in Britain was beginning to change – Keen could see that at the Sports Council meetings he attended. 'These were giving me an insight into what was going on,' he explains. 'I was attending these meetings, where briefings were happening about how this [Lottery] money was going to roll out, and I wasn't even seeing cycling represented at them. So I was thinking, "Bloody hell, we're going to miss the boat here." Millions of pounds are about to be dished out and cycling was not even on the starting line.'

Another sliding door moment: had Keen not attended these briefings, realized what was going on, and taken the message back to the British Cycling Federation, urging them to get involved, then cycling might indeed have missed the boat, or at least missed the generously funded boat in which the sport would eventually set sail.

But a major problem was that the BCF was at that time, and in the words of Keen, 'in meltdown'. It is not an exaggeration. Apart from Dailey, who provided stability as well as outstanding commitment to a cause that lesser men would have given up on, the organization was being driven to destruction by infighting. At the heart of it was a power struggle between two factions, representing the old and the new: on the one side the existing board, on the other a new presidential candidate, a recently retired rider. The man being touted as the leader of a brave new era in British cycling was Keen's old friend, Tony Doyle.

In November 1996, at the height – or depth – of the meltdown, the BCF affair was even raised in the House of Commons by Jon Trickett MP. Trickett observed that while the sport was booming overseas, with television coverage and sponsorship at record levels, Britain, despite the individual successes of Boardman, Graeme Obree and Yvonne McGregor, lagged behind. The reason, he suggested, was the performance of the BCF. 'I understand,' Trickett told the House, 'that eyebrows have been raised outside this country, at the highest levels in the cycling world – by the Union Cycliste Internationale [UCI], for instance – about the way in which the BCF has managed the sport in this country.' He quoted an interview with the UCI president Hein Verbruggen, on BBC Radio Five, in which he described 'Great Britain [as] a completely black spot in the international cycling market.'

The charge sheet against the BCF was lengthy. It included poor marketing, frightening away race organizers and failing to find a replacement for its flagship stage race, the Milk Race. More sinisterly, there were also, in Trickett's words, 'serious questions ... to be asked about the relationship between the BCF and private companies with close links with BCF board members'. In Trickett's opinion, 'the BCF board stands guilty of, at best, a lack of vision and a timorous failure to realize the full potential of this beautiful and undeveloped sport, despite the fact that it receives £500,000 a year of public money ...'.

Some of these issues formed the backdrop to the dispute, in which Doyle was cast as the White Knight, riding to the rescue. Doyle was in fact elected as president, and it seemed, briefly, that he would lead in the new dawn. But, as Trickett told the House, turmoil had ensued upon the former world champion's election and his subsequent removal 'in what can only be described as a coup by board members'.

A subsequent Sports Council audit had exposed, said Trickett, 'a grave state of affairs in relation to which the BCF has been and is being managed. The audit reveals ... concerns about the financial position of the BCF, British Cycling Promotions Ltd and the [Manchester] velodrome, which is the jewel in the crown of British cycling.' The audit also referred to 'actual, potential or perceived conflicts of interest involving some board members – some companies are supplying goods and services to the BCF; the principals of those companies have been BCF board members for years'. It was, concluded Trickett, 'probably the most damning audit report that I have ever read'.

The BCF crisis dragged on. Doyle threatened legal action, which might have proved ruinous. But eventually, from the wreckage, there emerged two new men – Peter King as chief executive, and Brian Cookson as president.

Cookson, who had served on the BCF Racing Committee for nine years, recalls it vividly. By the end of 1996, with 'all the nonsense' – as he calls it – at its peak, he attended a BCF National Council meeting at the Post House Hotel in Doncaster. Peter King, an accountant from Surrey, was also there, and, speaking from the floor, he 'destroyed the financial credibility' of the old board. At the meeting, King and Cookson, a mild-mannered and eminently likeable Lancastrian, were two of the eleven people elected to an 'emergency committee' formed to take over the running of the governing body. 'We deliberately called it that rather than a new board,' says Cookson. 'It was horrendous. People were suing each other for libel; there were lots of nasty little things going on.'

As well as all the personality clashes, the most pressing matter concerned the running of the Manchester Velodrome. More than ten years on, Cookson, sitting in his office in the velodrome, can afford a wry smile as he notes, 'People don't realize how close this place came to being bankrupt and closed down. Within a few weeks of Peter [King] and myself and the new board taking over, it became apparent that this place – which was being run as Manchester Velodrome Limited, a wholly owned subsidiary of the BCF – was not washing its face. There was a big outstanding bill for gas and electricity – about £130,000 – which Manchester City Council agreed to cover for us. If that hadn't been covered then we'd have been bankrupt. The padlocks would have been on. I'd say we were within ten days of that happening. This place would probably have been turned into a B&Q warehouse.'

It was UK Sport and Manchester City Council who ensured that didn't happen. But even with the velodrome's immediate future secured, 'It was difficult to get the right formula to make this place work,' admits Cookson. 'There were all sorts of things going on, such as cat shows. We had to cancel cycling events for cat shows!'

It gets even more surreal. 'We had a Conservative party manifesto launch!' adds Cookson. 'We had to lay down guidelines, where everyone understood what this place was for; cycling had to be the priority, and our funders – UK Sport and Manchester City Council – understood that. But it was difficult, because every other day there was an article in the press about it being a white elephant.'

Against such a chaotic backdrop, the Cookson-led emergency committee – which ultimately became the new board – succeeded in uniting some, if not all, of the factions. Eventually, symbolically, they approved a re-christening of the organization: 'Federation' was dropped, in favour of a more simple, streamlined, 'British Cycling'. King, who took on an executive responsibility 'to kick the finances into order' before being appointed chief executive, and Cookson, as president, did an essential job at a time of massive strife and unrest. The dynamic King and the unassuming but quietly effective Cookson gave the organization the kiss of life, and helped nurse it back to health. More than ten years on, it is enormously significant that both are still in their respective posts.

It is perhaps also significant that Doyle's presidency was so short-lived. Keen admits that he isn't sure whether the door at a Doyle-led BCF would have remained closed to him, but he suspects that it would. 'Well, there were some interesting person-alities involved at that time,' he acknowledges, 'and some I prob-ably wouldn't have been working for, let's face it ...'

A little like that old Yellow Pages advert, when a young man frantically tries to repair the damage from a rampant party before his parents return home, and completes the task as the door swings open, the BCF seemed to get its house in order just in time. In cycling's case, the opening door was marked 'Lottery'. When it came to applying for this new source of funding, cycling made its submission with a performance plan pulled together largely by Dailey and another BCF stalwart, Jim Hendry, with some input from Keen. But the sport, like others, wasn't too sure what to expect. All they knew was that hitherto unimagined sums of money would flow in – not that it needed to be very much. As Keen explains: 'The environment at the time, even in 1996, was one where people like Yvonne [McGregor], [Paul] Manning and of course Craig MacLean and Chris Hoy were desperately trying to fulfil their ambitions, but there was no money, no real structure, and what we could do for them was very limited. We were doing okay [McGregor was a regular world championship medallist] but with such finite resources it was very frustrating. It was never going to go anywhere.'

When British Cycling then received an initial award of around £2.5 million it meant, among other things, that the governing body would have to make an important appointment. 'I knew there'd be a performance director job,' says Keen, 'and I had to think: "Do I apply?" And … it honestly felt like, if not me, then who? Which probably sounds spectacularly arrogant. But you look at the experiences I had: some teaching skills, some experience of running a department, coaching experience, sports science experience; I knew what was happening within the Sports Council; I knew the game that would need to be played. And I thought, "Why not?"'

Cookson reveals that, although Keen is correct to present himself as the best candidate, his appointment wasn't exactly a fait accompli. 'We interviewed three candidates. One was an ex-pro' road rider; the other was a more specialist coach. Peter was quite clearly the man for the job; I think his vision and commitment were right, but it was a risk for us as well. He was a good coach, a good sports scientist, but he had no management experience. And we were asking him to manage something absolutely new. It was a risk.'

Keen, however, was appointed. He moved to Manchester. What then? 'Let me paint a picture,' Keen laughs, spreading his hands and edging forward in his chair. 'First, there was huge enthusiasm on my part. Here was a once-in-a-lifetime opportunity to work with a multimillion pound budget, although I had virtually no budget to start with. In fact, I didn't even have a bank account. We were starting from scratch. For me there was trepidation about selling up and moving, leaving academia, not really having a clue what I was going to do … and here's me arriving at BCF headquarters, the Manchester Velodrome, and being taken down this dingy corridor to an underground cavern and into a dingy room. I go out to a second-hand furniture warehouse in Manchester to buy a desk. And I come back to a note from the BCF's only paid official, which says, "You've got to do this, do that, I want all these things sorted …" I'm thinking, "My god, what have I got myself into?" It was very sobering. There was nothing there. Nothing except the legacy of Doug [Dailey]'s splendid work, a legacy of files of what races we went to, and roughly how we got there.

'Then I'm going to the [BCF] National Council meeting that autumn,' Keen continues, 'and I'm standing up there with a PowerPoint presentation – it's probably the first time they'd seen a PowerPoint presentation – and saying, "This is a vision for the future, which looks an awful lot different to what it looks like now … and this is how we're gonna do it …"' The vision, he states, 'was to create a professional team, membership of which would be the aspiration of every ambitious athlete and coach in the country. I wasn't specific in terms of reaching world number one or two; there was a business plan behind it in terms of progression and events we were going to target and medals I thought we could win, but the aspirational vision was to create a professional national team system that anybody – *anybody* – with ambition and talent would want to find their way into, because they were convinced that, if they were in there, that it was the best place they could be … like Sandhurst or the Royal Academy. People who are any good, they want to be in there; they think, "That's where I *have* to be." It's a magnet for ambition.'

road racing. It was an area of the sport that – he had good reason to believe – had a deeply ingrained culture of doping. Although Keen was drawing up his plans more than twelve months before the 1998 Festina scandal, which began to lift the lid on some of the practices of the top continental road teams, he already had more than an inkling that drugs were rife. His continuing work with Boardman, by now riding as a road professional on the continent, offered some evidence, even if much of it was circumstantial. Even before the Festina scandal, for instance, Boardman was widely hailed and commended as a 'clean' athlete. The implication – though rarely explicitly stated pre-Festina – was that the rest of the sport, or a majority of the teams and athletes, were not.

How confident was Keen, then, that it would even be possible to create his top professional team, which would become a 'magnet for ambition'? 'Chris [Boardman] said it was possible,' he responds. 'Yvonne [McGregor] said it was possible. You start from that principle. To be frank – and this certainly wasn't in the written document – but my view at the time was absolutely clear. Men's professional road cycling was, and may still be, almost completely dominated by an underlying drug culture. And almost regardless of whether I think that's right or wrong, in the context of the programme I was charged with creating, having a drug system, or even a tolerance of a drug system, was just not an option.'

It was not an option because the Lottery money was regarded as public money, and Keen's view was that any doping scandal would bring it all shuddering to a halt. The stakes were high, then. And, in Keen's view, they meant almost forgetting about road cycling. 'The idea that you could plan for men's road racing success at world level … to me it couldn't be done,' he says. 'It seemed to me that the furthest we could go with road racing for men was to create a development programme where we could take promising young riders to that line in the sand, of what I'd call performance credibility, and then say, "If that is the world you want, as far as we understand it, then off you go and good luck."' In other words, assist these young riders to reach a standard where a professional team might be interested in signing them, and then leave them to their own devices, or choices.

But there was another reason for focusing on the track, and it bore an uncanny resemblance to the founding principle of the City of Edinburgh Racing Club. Quite simply, there were more medals to be won at the Olympics and world championship on the track than on the road. And, conveniently enough, the UK paymasters would not be very interested in stages of the Tour de France, for all that the Tour garnered so much media attention worldwide. The currency of success, as far as those charged with distributing Lottery funds were concerned, was in Olympic and world medals.

Plus, 'the track doesn't have the depth of competition,' as Keen points out. 'There are twenty on the start line – okay you've got to qualify to be there. But there are 200 at the start of a road race, and there are tactics, there are deals done, and all sorts of other factors, which mean your odds are very, very long … unless you're Italian, it seems. If you're being objective about it, in women's road racing there isn't the culture of endemic drug taking; in sprint and endurance track cycling there isn't the culture of endemic drug taking … I mean, I'm sure people do it, but I'm pretty damn confident that we're winning with people who don't. So for me, in a sense, my original faith has been confirmed: that it is possible.'

Hoy attended the National Council meeting in which Keen, with his PowerPoint presentation, outlined his vision. By now he had switched St Andrews for a sports science course in Edinburgh, and after his blip at the end of the 1995 season, when he lived the lifestyle of a student rather than an athlete, he was focusing again – and more intensely – on his sport. He was still, he says, 'hungry for knowledge'.

It was no wonder that what Keen said enthused him. Yet even Hoy was a little sceptical. 'The national squad were invited to sit in, and this guy stepped up and gave this presentation and the first thing that struck you was that it looked really professional; there was no flip chart and markers, and you could see people think-ing, "My goodness, this is really good …" There were a lot of cyni-cal people around, but even the anti-Peter Keen people, against their will, were probably a little bit impressed by the ambition, if nothing else.

'I was like, "Wow this is brilliant!" But it just seemed almost, I don't know … too ambitious. I remember thinking, "I'd love to believe this, but is it really going to happen?" We just seemed so far off the pace. The only way I could see it happening was if they brought in coaches who'd worked in other countries. The optimist in me was encouraged. But the realist in me thought, "We're so off the mark, is it possible?"

'It was a generic presentation; it didn't focus on individual targets. But it was the first time someone had the vision to make it a professional set-up instead of operating from a Portakabin with a secretary and one guy running all the squads. For the first time selection was going to be based on performance, not on who you knew or what part of the country you lived in … it was about having clear guidelines, finding the talent and nurturing it.'

In the context of what was happening, and the Keen revolu-tion, Hoy and MacLean could not have selected a better year than 1997 in which to make their breakthrough on the international stage. Hoy opened his season with his Easter racing trip to Barbados, though he crashed heavily two days before his twenty-first birthday and ended up in a neck brace. Showing the same resolve as in Moscow the previous year, though, he only sat out one day's racing, removing the neck brace to return to the track for the third and final session.

The sprinters' season really caught fire in the summer, with three World Cups in quick succession: in Milan, Sardinia and Athens. In Milan, Hoy was called in to the team pursuit foursome after one of its members, Rob Hayles, was withdrawn with a heart murmur. It was proof of Hoy's versatility: the team pursuit was over 4,000 m, certainly an endurance rather than a sprint event (this would be like Usain Bolt running the 1500 m). 'My job was to do three spells [turns on the front of the string] and then get the hell out of there,' says Hoy of his ride with the experienced trio of Matt Illingworth, Jon Clay and Bryan Steel. 'But we got to the bronze medal ride-off, against the Italians, who were the world record holders. It was really exciting to be part of it; I was just hoping I didn't let them down – that was the stressful part. But I did okay; I did 3,000 m. We lost out on bronze, but fourth was a good result.'

The team sprinters would have killed for fourth place in a World Cup, and next day they had their chance. 'We were just trying to get top ten, which would have given us a World Cup point and helped us to qualify for the world championships in Perth [Australia] later in the year,' says Hoy, who lined up with MacLean and Craig Percival for the team sprint, with him first man, Percival second, MacLean last. 'We were so far down the seeding that we were one of the first teams to go, and it was a 400 m track, so we had no idea, really, of whether our time was good or bad [the team sprint not being over a set distance but three laps, whatever the size of the track].

'Then we waited, and one by one, teams went up, were up on us, and then cracked on the last lap – because it was such a long track. When the tenth last team went and didn't beat us we were like, "Yes!" and exchanging high-fives, because we'd got our point. But still the teams were slower, until the Poles beat us. There were still four to go, all the big teams, but we weren't studying the times too closely by now. We actually thought we were third. Then Marshall [Thomas] came over and said, "Boys, I've got some good news and some bad news for you. The bad news is that you didn't qualify third ... the good news is that you qualified second!!" And he started doing this little dance – in the track centre, with all the coaches and riders from other teams watching. But we couldn't believe it – we were in the final. A World Cup medal was way beyond our wildest expectations.' In the event it was silver, with the Poles living up to their seeding by beating them in the final.

They followed it with a 'solid' fifth the following week at the Sardinia World Cup, where MacLean won bronze in the kilo. From there to Athens, and further confirmation that they had arrived: another medal, this one bronze, after they beat Denmark in the race for third. But what gave Hoy as much satisfaction was their result at the world championships in Perth. There was no medal but sixth represented, for him, a performance as encouraging as any of the World Cups, since this included all the teams, all at full strength.

They were earning rave reviews in the press, too, and not only for their performance, but also their approach. 'Our team sprinters have both ability and confidence,' reported *Cycling* magazine. 'The trio exhibited an attitude nearest to the sort of dedication seen daily among the Australians.' The French, however, were all-conquering, with Arnaud Tournant one of the stars of the championships. 'The French appear to have found another man in [multiple world champion Florian Rousseau's] mould: Arnaud Tournant, who at only 18 has already collected a world junior team sprint gold and match sprint silver.'

It was while they were in Perth, at the world championships, that a letter was dispatched to some of the cyclists. It confirmed that they would get Lottery funding, £12,000 a year in the cases of Hoy and MacLean. The cheque followed in October: a pro rata payment of £3,000, to be spent between then and the end of the year. But it wasn't money they could fritter away: they had to spend it on training- and racing-related expenditure and then claim it back. But given that the first quarter – October to December – was the off-season, that proved a challenge. 'I didn't manage to spend all mine,' admits MacLean. 'I'd lived off three grand for about the last three years, so it was a bit of a shock to have to spend all that money.'

For Hoy it bought peace of mind. 'I thought, well, if I graduate in 1999 and can get Lottery funding for a few years then I should be able to do this for a few years without having to get a job. That was the biggest deal, to be able to train without having to work even part-time. Rest and recovery is the biggest thing about being a full-time athlete, because working isn't resting. When you're full-time you can recover properly, put your feet up so you're fully recovered for the next session.'

It wasn't all positive, though. For all that Keen's World Class Performance Plan (WCPP) was beginning to take shape, that Lottery funding was now confirmed, and that the sprinters were beginning to prove themselves at world level, there were problems. Hoy and MacLean wondered where they actually fitted into the plan, which seemed to focus overwhelmingly on the endurance track riders. At times they felt ignored.

Keen acknowledges that they had a point. 'My earliest memory of Chris,' he says, 'and it'll bug the hell out of him, but there was the Craig and Chris phenomenon. They came as a pair, and people who weren't paying attention often got them confused. Chris was slightly in Craig's shadow.

'The honest truth is that in the early days I spent far less time with the athletes than I could and should have done. The perspective on start-up day was that we had some interesting sprint athletes. There was a view around the sport at the time that they were a marginalized group who never got any recognition or support. And to be honest, in the first year, that was probably where we were; we didn't move on from that perception. They were a group who felt offside; there was a bit of tension; and I was probably seen in their eyes as an endurance-focused guy. But my position was that I was desperately trying to put this programme together, while also still coaching Chris [Boardman] and Yvonne [McGregor], because we sure as hell needed them to keep winning medals.

'It was a huge dilemma. It created huge resentment, because people didn't know what I was up to. I'd pop into the track, take a session, then clear off, and the riders didn't know what I was doing. From my perspective it was perfectly reasonable – I was fighting for all this money for them, trying to build a programme … but I suspect that from Chris and Craig's perspective the thought was, "Hey, when's he going to talk to me?"' In fact, Hoy says that what he was actually thinking at the time was, 'When are we going to get a coach?' – because he was still anxiously seeking specialist guidance. 'We were just desperate for a coach, desperate,' he adds.

By the end of 1997 they had a track team manager, though still not a coach. The man appointed by Keen was Steve Paulding, a founding member of the City of Edinburgh Racing team and a former British sprint champion, though Hoy says he 'shied away from being sprint coach, because Craig and the rest of us were ahead of where he'd got to. I think he thought he didn't have anything to offer. If I asked him what I should do, he said "Do lots of training," and we'd have a good laugh, then I'd say, "Yeah, but really … Just give me a programme and I'll follow it." Thing is, I'm not blaming him – he was our manager, not our coach, and he was as keen as anyone to get us a coach. He worked hard to try and get us one.'

It was at the end of 1997 that Keen, by now confirmed as performance director, with his ideas approved and his staff appointed, was able to tell the wider world something of his plans. 'My immediate concern now,' he told *Cycling* magazine, 'is to start our World Class Performance Plan next year [1998] and to complete the blueprint for the next six years.'

CHAPTER 6

The Future's Bright, The Future's Lime Green

A fridge filled with Magnum ice creams, Kuala Lumpur, 1998

Peter Keen's blueprint was initially green – lime green, to be precise. Because in one of his first moves as performance director, at the outset of what promised to be a dramatically new era for the sport in Great Britain, Keen took the radical step of replacing the national colours – the familiar red, white and blue – with the very much less familiar lime green.

When the new team jerseys appeared they provoked outrage. The reaction – universal, it seemed – was of anger, incandescence, apoplexy, and other shades of anger, but, outweighing all that rage, there was puzzlement, like a giant question mark floating in a thought bubble above Britain's cycling community. Letters appeared in *Cycling* magazine – always a reliable barometer of opinion – demanding Keen's head. But most were confused. After the shambles of the BCF under the old regime, what the hell was going on now?

I confess that I never fully understood – far less appreciated – the lime green design. In fact, I had all but forgotten it – the mind is clever like that, blocking out unpleasant memories. So I ask Keen, precisely ten years later, the obvious question: what on earth was that all about?

'A deliberate attempt to provoke!' he replies, with relish. 'It was one way of screaming and shouting, at whoever would listen, that we're going to be different, that nothing is necessarily sacred.

'We had a dire national jersey before that anyway, I would argue,' he adds. Which might be true, but it wasn't lime green. 'Well, the original was a fantastic bright lime green,' he argues. 'We had some support from the Lottery's design company. I told them I wanted something radical, and they came back and said: "You wanted radical, how about this?" It was a wonderful combination of deep blue with green. I looked at it and thought: "Why not?" You could certainly see it in the peloton. It was hugely visible. It stood out! Plus, of course, I thought it was a great statement, a great way of saying: "We're gonna be different."'

Was there, I wonder, any opposition to the proposed design from within the British Cycling Federation? 'They went berserk! I had a stand-off with the board over it which, I now realize on reflection, was something of a test case. My view was, "You either allow me to do this or I'm out." I was testing, I suppose, what they'd let me get away with. I couldn't work to a board who wouldn't let me do what I wanted when I knew what I wanted to do.' Keen looks thoughtful, then adds, 'Not that dictatorship is necessarily the answer … though it has its appeal.'

In the ensuing stand-off over the proposed jersey, Keen's strategy was to be 'incredibly irritating and very bloody-minded', and in the end he won a partial victory, which, given the universal opposition to the lime green, was quite a testament to Keen's bargaining skills, or irritability. There was, though, 'a degree of compromise'. The green remained but it was toned down.

So the design could have been even worse? 'No!' responds Keen. 'It ended up this really yucky thing, which I hated along with everyone else. But if you see the original, with this really dramatic and powerful lime green, I still maintain it's pretty sound.'

Hoy was one of the riders to model the lime green – which, in its final design (the lime green remained for a couple of seasons) was a swirling melange of green, red and blue. Already doing 'a bit of kilo work' by now, Hoy's times were consistently improving, especially over the first lap of the team sprint. At the World Cup meeting in France in 1998 he led the British team to another medal, this time bronze. The most encouraging statistic, however, was that his time for the standing start lap over twelve months went from 18.6 seconds to 18.3 – a significant improvement.

The European championships in Poland presented him with a final opportunity to ride an individual championship at Under-23 level. The team sprint yielded another bronze medal, and fifth in the kilo augured well – better, in fact, than the result looks on paper. 'I missed a medal by nothing,' says Hoy. 'It was a hundredth of a second or something between third and fifth.'

The world championship in Bordeaux that year, though, provided a setback. Hoy was there only to ride the team sprint, with the three-man team coming from a squad of four, completed by Craig MacLean, Craig Percival and Jason Queally. In the qualifying round, the trio of Hoy, Percival and MacLean suffered the cycling equivalent of an own goal from kick-off. The second rider, Percival, misjudged the countdown, and when Hoy – the lead-out man – sprinted out the start gate, Percival was left behind. In cycling parlance he couldn't 'get on the wheel' in front – and once that gap opens it is usually impossible to close. Hoy sprinted into a fifteen-metre lead while Percival, with the third man MacLean safely tucked in behind him, chased in vain. Finally their time was enough only for tenth place. A place in the top eight had been 'the minimum target' with top six the 'projected aim'.

The team manager, Steve Paulding, admitted afterwards that the omission of Jason Queally had been a mistake. 'I hold my hands up,' he said, explaining that Queally had expressed a preference to be saved for the second ride. But that was to assume that their qualifying ride earned them a second ride – which, in the event, given Percival's error, it didn't. 'It's a big disappointment,' added Paulding. 'Never for one minute did I think we wouldn't make the top six, let alone the top eight. Next year we must get it right because if we don't, we don't get the chance to go to the Olympics.'

Paulding's fear was to prove unfounded. But there is an interesting statistic buried in the team sprint squad's embarrassing failure at the 1998 world championship: it is – at the time of writing – the last in which Britain *failed* to win a world championship medal in the team sprint. Even more remarkably, Hoy has been an ever-present member of the trio – from 1999 to 2008 he has won a medal every year: ten in total.

Following the debacle at the world championships, 1998 also allowed Hoy to fulfil the 'medium-term goal' he had identified with the encouragement of Ray Harris several years earlier. His first multi-sports games took him to Kuala Lumpur in Malaysia for the Commonwealth Games, though it wasn't the success it might have been. As I mentioned in the Introduction, this Commonwealth Games brought the two of us together, as Scotland team-mates.

In Kuala Lumpur he and MacLean seemed fairly relaxed; we spent a lot of time in the village canteen, trying to catch the eye of the girls' hockey team – who in turn tried to catch the eye of the rugby team, obviously higher than cyclists in the food chain – and enjoying the novelty of a huge freezer generously stocked with Magnum ice creams. One of the big challenges of those games was to ration our daily intake of Magnums. As Hoy has pointed out, professionalism was, at that time, a foreign land to the Scottish Commonwealth Games team.

Even for the ambitious Hoy the 1998 Commonwealth Games fell flat. Looking back now he reckons he was 'a bit jaded'. 'I had been away from home a long time. And although the Commonwealth Games were probably more important to me than the world championships, and my first multi-sports games, I just didn't have a great games.

'I got knocked out in the sprint in the second round, by a guy who tested positive,' Hoy continues. The culprit was Stephen Alfred, an American who in Kuala Lumpur represented Trinidad, and who finished fourth in the sprint until a positive drugs test – for norandrosterone – saw him disqualified. (As a postscript to that, in early 2008 Alfred became only the second American athlete to be handed a lifetime ban, after refusing to submit to an out-of-competition doping test in November 2007. It was the forty year old's third offence – he also tested positive for testosterone in May 2006, and for human chorionic gonadotrophin a month later, though for some reason these two offences counted as one. When he refused a test in November 2007 he was actually serving an eight-year ban – but still subject to the anti-doping rules.)

Hoy's defeat to Alfred in Kuala Lumpur meant the best he could do in the individual sprint competition was ninth, which he duly managed, winning the race that decided ninth to twelfth places. MacLean, meanwhile, was an equally nonplussed fifth – although with Alfred's disqualification, he should, technically, be credited with fourth, and Hoy with eighth.

Hoy followed the sprint with another ninth, this time in the kilo (coincidentally MacLean repeated his fifth in this event too).

In downbeat tones, Hoy describes his kilo performance as 'a bit … nothing really. All those games did was highlight that there was a huge gulf between us and the Aussies.' And it seemed to have always been thus; Darryn Hill's sprint gold, for example, was Australia's eighth consecutive triumph in the discipline. 'They were so strong and the British riders, apart from Jason, were not even close,' Hoy continues.

'Jason' being Jason Queally, who by now was becoming a force to be reckoned with on the international stage. Apart from being a regular member of the team sprint trio, he was focusing most of his efforts on the individual kilo, and it was paying off – he won a silver medal in the discipline in Kuala Lumpur.

But for Hoy and the rest of the sprinters 1999 was to prove the big breakthrough year. Keen claims that he noticed, in Hoy in particular, a big change between the 1998 and 1999 seasons. Over a nine-month period, he says, it became obvious to him that Hoy was emerging from MacLean's shadow. And emerging as 'the new type of athlete … asking questions, really wanting to get some discipline around his training and conditioning, with a thoroughness that I really think – especially on reflection – was quite outstanding'.

There were traits in Hoy that reminded him of Boardman; Keen is even more struck by this now, and other similarities he perceives between the pair, than he was at the time, preoccupied as he was with the bigger picture. 'Chris was the first of the sprint group to genuinely want to engage,' says Keen. 'Yes, they had been marginalized as a group – it's fair to say that. To be frank, there was an unhealthy view of sprinting in the UK; the endurance guys saw them as lazy guys who didn't train; who were a bit overweight and never qualified; who never got anywhere. But Berlin changed all that. Possibly forever.'

Berlin was the venue for the 1999 world championships, when, astonishingly, the British sprint team trio won a silver medal. It was Britain's first world championship medal in a sprint event since 1960, when Dave Handley won bronze in the individual event. Perhaps of equal significance, it was also the only British medal at the championships.

Having qualified fourth, and then beaten Greece with the second fastest time of the round, the team sprint trio – Hoy, MacLean and Queally – faced France in the final. With Hoy leading, and finishing the first lap in 18.01 seconds – a personal best – before swinging up the banking, MacLean took over for lap two, before, finally, Queally took over for lap three, they recorded 45.485 seconds – just 0.637 seconds down on the all-star French trio of Gané, Rousseau and Tournant.

'We went to the worlds thinking that at best we could sneak into the top four,' says Hoy. 'That was the target. But we won our heat with the second fastest time, so we were in the final, racing for gold: us against France. It was unbelievable, unthinkable that we were going to win a world medal. France beat us – though I was faster than [their first man] Gané on the opening lap …' In fact, Hoy recorded the fastest opening lap of the competition, yet still he says that his overwhelming feeling at the conclusion to the competition was of relief, 'that I had done a good job and not been the weak link in the team; which I'd felt I had been up to that point, that I was bringing them down a bit'.

On the podium, receiving his silver medal alongside MacLean and Queally, has left Hoy with a memory that he can recall in vivid detail. 'I remember standing on the podium, looking at the flags and the crowd, hearing the noise, and thinking to myself, "Right Chris, soak it up … the chances are this is as good as it'll get. You may never be on the podium again at the world championships; I don't know how this has happened, but it has, enjoy it, this could be it." I'd have been pretty happy to retire at that point.'

MacLean also found the experience surreal, especially the ecstatic reaction of the French to their victory over the British trio. 'It was quite bizarre seeing how delighted they were when they won gold. It was nice to see how chuffed they were at beating us!' MacLean adds that it was 'pretty significant, especially to British cycling – the first medal, really, under the new regime. I think they probably hated it, because it gave us leverage.'

Keen's claim that 1999 saw a change in Hoy in terms not only of results but also in attitude and commitment owed much to a change in his personal circumstances. He finished his applied sports science degree, graduating with a 2:1, which was impressive, given that so much of the course had been, to use his father's description, 'effectively a distance learning module'. David Hoy adds: 'His lecturer told him, "If you'd turned up for one or two lectures you might have got a first." He sat exams at training camps; he even sat one at the world championships in Perth.'

But finally completing his studies meant that 1999 was, says Hoy, 'the first time I was full-time properly. I was twenty-three, starting to mature physically; I had a good winter in the gym between 1998 and '99. I'd read a lot about strength training and I was starting to put some of those principles into practice; I definitely got stronger and converted that into power on the bike.' At the end of 1999 he moved full time to Manchester, into a house in Rusholme with MacLean and three others, all racing cyclists. 'A five-bedroom house,' as he describes it, 'with five blokes, one toilet, one bathroom. It was horrific.'

MacLean's comment about the British Cycling hierarchy 'hating' the fact that they won a medal at the world championships in Berlin may be tongue-in-cheek, but there could be some truth in his claim that it gave them 'leverage' – because following Berlin the sprinters got what they had been looking for: a coach.

Nobody could question the international credentials of Martin Barras, the man appointed as coach to the sprinters. A French-Canadian retired cyclist who had lived in Australia for a number of years, Barras officially began working with the sprinters in January 2000, though he first encountered them at the 1997 world championships in Perth, where he was based. Since 1995, working for the Western Institute of Sport in Australia, he had coached Darryn Hill, the sprinter Hoy had recognized as being 'at another level' at the Commonwealth Games in Kuala Lumpur.

'The Perth world championships was the first time I became aware of these guys,' Barras says of the triumvirate of Hoy, MacLean and Queally. 'Brits in sprinting were a nonentity.' The next winter he was approached by Steve Paulding to place a British sprinter, Julie Forrester, in a training camp in Perth. Forrester returned 'raving about' Barras, and from then his links with the British set-up became stronger; he travelled to Manchester in July 1999, bringing Hill with him to train. Then he was offered a job by Keen.

Such had been their desperation for a coach that the sprinters must have welcomed him with open arms. Did he sense that desperation? 'Yes and no,' says Barras. 'They were more desperate for a kindred spirit; they were desperate for someone who saw international sprinting the way they did. They were certainly struggling to find that in the UK.'

But within the sprinters' camp there were different responses to Barras, some of which highlight the differences in their personalities, though they also have something to do with age. MacLean and Queally had more or less been self-coached for years; Hoy was younger and more receptive to being told what to do. 'We hit it off straight away,' he says of his relationship with Barras. 'We had good chemistry. I liked his philosophy.'

MacLean, meanwhile, says: 'Initially Martin created a few problems. We weren't used to working with a coach. I think the way he went about it initially was wrong. We were senior athletes in our mid- to late-twenties, and he threw down a programme and said: "This is what you're doing for the next six months." For people who'd done it off their own bat to that point, it was difficult to hand over that much control to someone else. There was a bit of a stand-off for a while.'

Barras explains: 'Their way of working was modern, they were ahead of the game – they had clearly done their homework. Within the group Jason had very well-developed ideas. When I started working with Chris, his attitude was: "You're the coach, I'm the athlete." Before I officially began working with the team I sat him down at my place in Perth and he basically said, "Show me what to do." With Craig it was more of a sparring match. It's the longest I've ever taken to work well with someone. But when we did click it worked very well. We ended up with a very good relationship – I sold my house to Craig on a handshake.

'With Queally,' continues Barras, 'at the beginning he came in and said: "I think you've got me wrong." He told me to watch him for a month. So I did; I saw what he did, and I said, "Okay, I can recognize a good idea when I see it." That's what a coach has to do. It's one thing to come in as a chef with your own recipes, but as a coach you have to look at the problems from the outside. A lot of it is understanding what makes them tick. Chris was like a sponge; he just wanted to soak up information, and he had the ability to assimilate it. Craig needed more freedom. We were sparring, sparring, sparring, but we didn't have an argument; it just needed time and trust.'

In terms of Barras integrating with Keen's regime, he says that in 2000 the set-up was far from perfect. 'What are the British good at?' he asks, a rhetorical question. 'Banking. That's what British Cycling was like. It was very hierarchical. You could feel the definite split between management and riders. It's one thing to say the athlete is at the centre, another to put that philosophy into practice. But that's one thing that's definitely changed now.'

For Hoy, the presence of Barras by his side was a bit like being given wings. 'Now we had the results to have self-belief; we had a coach we believed in; we had almost twelve months to the Olympics; and suddenly the dream of being an Olympic medallist wasn't just a dream, it was a potential reality. That was just crazy, but it was such a motivating thing, such a huge thing on the horizon.'

It was also good to have an ally on the coaching staff, since even Hoy – echoing some of MacLean's remarks – was aware that the sprinters' reputation was not entirely positive. 'I felt we were misunderstood,' Hoy says. 'We had an image of being very difficult to deal with. When a new member of staff came on board, say a massage therapist, or a new mechanic, if they were told to work with the sprinters, then you'd find that, after three or four months, you'd be having a coffee or a chat with them and they'd say: "You know what? I had this image of what it was going to be like to work with the sprint team … I was basically warned that you were a very difficult group to get on with and that you had to be very sure of what you're doing or they'll rip you apart … but you know what? This has been the easiest group to work with."'

'I don't know what it was based on,' shrugs Hoy. 'In the early days there was a lot of frustration that we had certain needs and requirements which weren't being met. They didn't require thousands of pounds, just simple things: the right bikes, a coach. Getting a coach gave us a massive boost.'

* * *

The year 1999 was a good time for the sprinters to make their breakthrough on the world stage. As well as Berlin, Hoy, MacLean and Queally won the team sprint at World Cups in Mexico and Italy, and claimed the European title in Italy. It all meant that they began Olympic year, 2000, being talked about as potential medallists. As the Sydney games drew nearer that talk became louder, with the British team's official guide reporting 'a good deal of chatter around Chris Hoy and the other members of the GB sprint squad … comparisons have been made between the current crop of sprint cyclists and the era of Coe, Ovett and Cram, when British runners dominated middle-distance running'.

Of course, the Sydney games were to provide the first sight of the Lottery-funded British teams in Olympic action, not just in cycling but in other sports, too. Naturally, it was obscenely early to judge whether or not the Lottery-funded programmes, established in most cases only as recently as 1998, were proving successful – but hey, that was hardly going to prevent anybody, especially the media, from doing precisely that.

Yet the impatience to see results – or at least to enjoy a close-up inspection of the work-in-progress – was understandable. The Atlanta games, four years earlier, had been a disaster from a British point of view, with just one gold medal. Britain was desperate for success, or at least for signs that things might be changing; desperate to think that, finally, British athletes might be adopting the kind of serious, professional approach that Australian teams, for example, had displayed for years, with huge success. And for the sports themselves the Sydney Olympics presented an opportunity to showcase themselves, to have their progress gauged – and possibly rewarded. Lottery funding, it was made clear almost from the start, was dependent on performances; put crudely, better performances meant more money.

The stakes had thus been raised, but on the eve of the Sydney games there was an episode that could have brought Peter Keen's World Class Performance Plan crashing down before the foundations had properly settled.

It is difficult to believe now, in fact, that what happened to the British cycling team on the eve of the 2000 Olympics was not bigger news; that the scandal didn't have the impact of a bomb detonating. One explanation could be that the expectations of the mainstream media lagged behind the progress the cycling team had actually been making; excited 'chatter' in cycling circles aside, Keen's team did not have a particularly high profile in the build-up to Sydney. Another explanation was that the sporting culture, then, wasn't quite as vehemently anti-doping as it would become over the next decade.

On the eve of the Sydney games, the British cycling team lost one of its number – a sprinter, Neil Campbell – to a positive drugs test. Campbell was with Hoy and the rest of the team at a training camp in Melbourne when the news broke. He'd tested positive at a World Cup track meeting in Turin in July, and then again at the British championships a fortnight later, in both cases his urine showing elevated concentrations of human chorionic gonadotrophin (HCG). Campbell was flown home, amid fears that the readings could indicate a serious health problem. 'I remember Chris phoning home,' says his mother, Carol, 'and he was very upset; they were devastated for Neil Campbell, because they genuinely thought he was seriously ill.'

In fact, and unbeknown to me until I meet Keen, Campbell was not the first doping case under the Keen regime. I ask him about Campbell – about which more later – referring to it as 'a relatively minor' case, at which Keen looks aghast. 'Well they weren't minor cases we had,' he replies. *They?* 'Yes,' says Keen, 'in 1998 we had a guy called Gary Edwards who popped up in the UK having been in South Africa. I'd never heard of him, but it was early days on the programme. Anyway, he qualified for the [1998] Commonwealth Games; the selection system was pretty open and he did 10.7 seconds [for 200 m]; he got selected; he got tested; he got busted.'

This was a revelation to me, and so I did some research on Edwards. There were a few articles at the time – and they illustrate why it was not bigger news. Because back then – unlike now – there was, if not quite a blind acceptance of the excuses typically proffered by drugs cheats, then certainly a willingness to accept that they at least might be telling the truth. The pendulum has comprehensively swung the other way now, but, in those relatively innocent days, there still seemed to exist the possibility that a 'positive' athlete really might be innocent; that their test might, as they claimed, have been caused by something they ate/something they drank/a food supplement/too much sex/not enough sex/an unidentified medical condition/a lethal combination of the above.

So it was with Edwards, judging by the small number of reports and interviews of the time. Under the headline, 'Banned rider: "I've nothing to hide"', one describes his story as one of 'thwarted ambition, of human strength and human frailty, a story of telling poignancy and stark reality ...'.

Edwards had, as Keen says, been in South Africa, though only briefly, and he was living back in the UK and in his late twenties when, in 1998, he competed in the national track championships, winning a silver medal in the team sprint. As Keen says, he achieved the qualification time for the Commonwealth Games in Kuala Lumpur. But it was at the championships that he was tested, and his sample showed elevated levels of testosterone.

The explanation, said Edwards in an interview at the time, was that he had been training at a gym near his home in Essex. Some of the gym rats had recommended Creatine – a legal supplement

– and a product he'd bought over the counter. This, he claimed, would have altered his testosterone levels. 'I was naïve,' he said. 'It was a cock-up on my part, my mistake.' He discovered his mistake, he claimed, by later reading the label on the tub, which warned: 'CAN RAISE TESTOSTERONE LEVELS.' 'I didn't check,' he said. He was banned for a year.

Edwards announced his retirement from cycling. Then he changed his mind. When his ban was up he returned, riding an international meeting, reaching the sprint final and then submitting a sample for drugs testing. It showed a trace of the in-vogue steroid of the late 1990s, nandrolone. 'I didn't even know what nandrolone was,' protested Edwards. 'After the problems with supplements the last time, I was on a strict high-protein diet.'

It was a two-year ban from the UCI this time, but before cycling's world governing body got round to determining the length of his ban, Edwards continued racing, competing in the World Masters Championships. He won two gold medals, was tested again and it came back positive – this time for another anabolic steroid, Stanozolol, which, most famously, was what did for Ben Johnson at the Seoul Olympics in 1988.

The third positive test prompted a letter from the BCF, sent by recorded delivery. It informed Edwards that he had been banned for life; it meant he couldn't be involved in any capacity with cycle sport – only as a spectator. He didn't reply to the letter. 'If we put up an appeal we have to fight,' he explained, 'and we ain't got no fight left.'

As intriguing and, frankly, bizarre as the Gary Edwards case is, the Neil Campbell case was infinitely more serious. It was potentially devastating, on various levels. As far as Keen was concerned – and for all that it wasn't front-page news at the time – it put everything at risk. 'It was absolutely massive,' he sighs. But there was also another possibility – that Campbell was seriously ill.

When he found out about Campbell's positive test, Keen arranged for the twenty-six year old to be flown home from Australia for urgent medical examinations. He had tested positive for a hormone that isn't normally detectable in healthy males and which could suggest the presence of testicular cancer.

'Five weeks before the games,' says Keen, 'and we have a positive test, for a serious drug, in a selected athlete – that was [a] doomsday scenario. And then there was the added twist, the genuine possibility that the guy had testicular cancer. That was the only reason that hormone could be in his body. So you've got to give the guy the benefit of the doubt; he could have a life-threatening tumour. We got him straight in to see the medical officer at the training camp and then on a flight home. But all the tests for cancer came back negative, negative, negative.'

The medical tests cleared Campbell of cancer, though the cyclist was adamant: 'I strongly deny that I have ever taken performance-enhancing drugs and I still maintain these anomalies are from a medical condition.' The British Cycling Federation was unsympathetic: Campbell was banned for a year and fined £1,600.

Keen, meanwhile, was left to tell the media that, in fact, his rider was not ill; and that he had tested positive for a banned substance. 'We had to deal with it with a completely straight bat,' he says. 'First, give the guy the benefit of the doubt. Then it goes to plan B …' Plan B was to reiterate the team's anti-doping policy, as spelled out in the agreements signed by all riders in 1999. 'They said no injectable medicines,' says Keen; 'we were trying to wipe out that culture – the culture of: unless you stick a needle in your bum you're not going to go fast.'

Coincidentally, David Hoy says that he had a serious conversation about doping with his son on the eve of the Sydney games, before the Campbell scandal. 'Before Sydney I asked Chris about drugs,' he says. 'We were talking about some of the other teams.

He said, "It's not something I'm going to do." I said, "Well, good, that's what I would expect you to say. But what happens if it alters your career?" And he said, "I'd rather finish fourth. If I'm beaten by guys on drugs then that's the way it goes, but as long as I'm the first clean rider."' The conversation would be repeated – but with Hoy in a far more optimistic and upbeat frame of mind – after the games. What he witnessed there changed everything as far as he was concerned.

Going into the Sydney Olympics, all Hoy's eggs were in the team sprint basket. He was the starter, the man for the first lap – all his energy was focused on that eighteen-second effort. Which meant that his entire contribution to the games was likely to extend to, at the outer limit, fifty-four seconds.

In one pre-games interview, in the *Independent*, Hoy's role in the team sprint was discussed. Hoy is memorably described, by Andrew Longmore, as follows: 'To say he is built like a brick outhouse does less than justice to the outhouse. He has an ideal sprinter's frame: 14 st 2 lb, 6 ft 1 in, legs like motorway pillars, capable of generating extraordinary forces through the mighty single gear on his brakeless carbon fibre track bike.'

Longmore finished his Olympic preview with an observation that would prove prescient: 'Unwittingly, the track cycling squad will be flag-bearers for the rest of the British Olympic team, with Queally a live medal prospect on the opening day in the 1 km time trial, and in the team sprint team, following on the second day.'

And so it was, on the first night of the Sydney games, that Queally produced his 'Boardman moment', though, in truth, his gold medal in the kilo was even more of a shock than Boardman's eight years earlier, not least to Queally himself. Whereas Boardman had prepared himself mentally for winning gold at the Barcelona Olympics in 1992, thirty-year-old Queally had targeted bronze. That was realistic, he reckoned. Others might even have reckoned it was ambitious. After winning silver at the Commonwealth Games in 1998, he placed fifth in the world championships in Berlin the following year – albeit after being hit by a car as he cycled to the stadium.

In the Dunc Gray Velodrome on the opening night of the Sydney games, Queally was thirteenth of the sixteen starters. The first shock was his time: 1 min., 1.609 seconds, a personal best by a second-and-a-half, and an Olympic record. 'I don't know where the time came from,' he said afterwards. 'I didn't feel any faster than usual but then I saw the words "Olympic Record" after my time. I thought it can't be me, but then I realized it was true. I was shocked.'

Three more riders remained, however. The first was Stefan Nimke of Germany, though he went almost a second slower than Queally. Then it was the home rider, Shane Kelly, the rider who had beaten Queally to Commonwealth gold. An enormous cheer propelled him around the track, and he was marginally up at half-distance, but he faded, and silence greeted his 750 m split – he was down, and didn't recover.

That left only Arnaud Tournant: the awesome, invincible Tournant; still just twenty-one, but world champion, and already being talked about as potentially the greatest kilo rider of all time. But what many didn't see – and what I only found out seven years later – is an extraordinary thing that Tournant did before his ride. Having witnessed Queally's ride, and having been surprised by it, he committed a fatal error. He discarded his game plan, ditching the strategy that he had established, in the cold light of the build-up to the games, as the one designed to give him the best chance of a gold medal. He went to his mechanic and requested that he change the gear on his bike.

Then, while Queally nervously circled the inside of the track on his warm-down bike, Tournant took to the start. And he began fast; he too was up on Queally after 500 metres, by more than a tenth of a second. Then, 'Inexplicably' – as one report from the time puts it – 'he tailed off badly over the last two laps.' He crossed the line a second and a half slower than his British rival, and, remarkably, out of the medals. For the Frenchman it was 'an awful shock', as Queally put it. 'I feel a bit sorry for him.'

Queally, meanwhile, 'seemed unable to comprehend the magnitude of his performance and looked blank and drained as he answered questions from reporters'. In a stroke, and on the first day of the 2000 Olympics, he had equalled Britain's gold medal tally from the Atlanta games. After the nightmare of the Neil Campbell affair, it was a dream start for Keen's team, providing early and spectacular vindication for British Cycling's World Class Performance Plan.

Brian Cookson, sitting in his office in the Manchester Velodrome eight years later, remains struck by the huge significance of Queally's ride. 'It took 61.609 seconds,' he says, 'for the perception of this place to change from white elephant to gold medal factory.'

CHAPTER 7

Zero to Hero to Zero Again

Dunc Gray Velodrome, Sydney, September 2000

The day after Jason Queally's Olympic gold medal in the kilometre time trial, the hero of the hour returned to Sydney's Dunc Gray Velodrome with Chris Hoy and Craig MacLean, to contest the team sprint. After a virtually sleepless night, Queally might not have been at his best, but the trio matched their performance at the world championships in Berlin the previous year, winning silver behind the dominant French.

Hoy had a sleepless night that night: an Olympic silver medal was undoubtedly the highlight of his career to date. Yet in talking to him there appear to be two aspects that act to qualify the undeniable truth of an Olympic medal representing the pinnacle for any athlete. One is that Berlin seemed to be not better but perhaps more significant in terms of confirming his ability to win medals at that level. The silver medal in Sydney, as wonderful as it was, was not a surprise; he had known it was within their grasp. The second aspect is that the most powerful legacy of the Sydney

Olympics, as far as Hoy is concerned, came not from his silver medal in the team sprint, but from Queally's success in the kilo.

Hoy, six years younger than Queally, watched the kilo competition unfold with disbelief and wonder, and ultimately with a sense of optimism. He was happy for Queally but also – perhaps equally – excited about what the future could hold for him. Put simply, Queally's success acted to erode Hoy's cynicism and to dismantle the barriers that he had imagined stood between a 'clean' athlete and the ultimate prize. Queally's gold medal, as stupendously surprising as it was to everyone, shattered some of Hoy's previously held ideas in one clean stroke. No pun intended.

There is something ironic about this. When athletes talk of having their eyes opened they often mean that they have come to realize the pervasiveness of drugs in sport at the highest level. When Hoy says the Sydney Olympics opened his eyes, what he means is that he realized that you could become Olympic champion without them.

He has often identified Queally's success as the moment when he realized what might be possible, and what he might be capable of. 'It was inspirational,' he says. 'That's what Jason was to me – an inspirational figure. When you turn up to the world championships and Olympics you see these guys putting in great performances. But you're only seeing the end product. You can't imagine how they got there. But if you see someone progress on a daily basis … I mean, I saw Jason progress from my level to Olympic champion: from his crash in 1996 at Meadowbank, when he was screaming and I didn't know who he was, to being in teams with him, training with him every day, getting to know him. The moment when Jason won the kilo in Sydney was the moment when I realized – because I saw it with my own eyes – that you could do it clean.

'Up to that point there had always been suspicion, and the question: am I chasing an impossible dream? Because it may not be possible to go as fast as those guys: because they may all be taking drugs. I didn't know that for a fact, I don't know if it was even fair; it was an assumption I had, based, mainly, on the information I had through the media.'

As well as Queally's gold and the team sprinters' silver, there were two other British cycling medals, both bronze, for the team pursuit team and for that stalwart of the team, Yvonne McGregor, in the women's pursuit. It was, all in all, a successful Olympics, offering tangible evidence that there would be more substance to the Keen revolution than the lime green jerseys. 'What is the secret of the cyclists' success?' mused the BBC commentator Simon Brotherton. 'Now that's a question I've never heard before.'

Keen, meanwhile, lived up to his name, appearing keen to raise interest and build momentum for his sport beyond the confines of the competitive arena, telling reporters: 'There's an important lesson here. Coming on the back of the transport crisis back home, the message is: don't lock those bikes away in the garage. We have it on good authority that people are getting out bikes they haven't ridden in twenty years. This is clearly a sport that is going somewhere.' Nobody could accuse him of a lack of ambition.

But there was inevitably some evidence of a backlash as the Lottery-funded revolution continued, including – incredibly – from within the sport of cycling. It hardly threatened Keen's plans, but Hoy detected some resentment from some of the older generation as the haul of medals at world championships – and now Olympics, too – began to accumulate. 'There was an attitude from some former riders, "When I was racing we didn't have all this ... Eddie [Alexander] was fourth at the Olympics without Lottery money,"' says Hoy. 'Well yeah, he didn't have these things but think how good he could have been if he had … why limit what we're doing now because someone in the past didn't have it?'

Hoy admits that before Sydney he felt there was a chance that he could become a little 'stale' in his role as lead-out man for the team sprint. It was a specialized role, and obviously an important one, but it was limiting, too. It meant that his sum total of competitive action in Sydney was – as predicted – less than a minute. He knew he could do more. The obvious route to follow was the one plotted by Queally; and so, post-Sydney, his focus shifted to the kilo.

First, though, there was the small matter of the 2000 world championships, which gave the successful British riders an opportunity to shine on home soil – they were staged once again at the Manchester Velodrome. There was a sense of inevitability about the team sprint competition: it ended in another silver medal – and another defeat by an unchanged French team. Team GB qualified second, beat Canada in the second round to qualify for the final, where they were beaten by the invincible trio of Gané, Rousseau and Tournant. 'In Sydney I couldn't sleep with excitement,' said Craig MacLean as he stepped off the podium, 'but now it's more like, "Oh, another silver." I'm pleased that we got faster in each round; maybe if there'd been twenty rounds we would eventually have beaten them …'

It was Tournant, the third man, who gave the French an unassailable advantage, claimed an impressed Queally. 'He's three-tenths of a second faster than me, which is a lot over one lap of the track,' said the rider whose kilo victory in Sydney provided the only evidence – so far – that there were chinks in Tournant's armour. And given Tournant's apparent superiority, it is tempting to wonder if that last-minute gear change cost him Olympic gold in Sydney.

Unfortunately Hoy's first year as a kilo rider, 2001, though it included a gold medal in the discipline at the World Cup in Cali, was hampered by a freak injury. It happened as he was preparing for the world championships in Antwerp. 'I dropped a glass on my foot,' explains Hoy. 'I was at my girlfriend's parents' house and went to get a pint glass out of the cupboard. But it slipped through my hand. It was a tiled floor, and I was worried about it shattering so I stuck my foot out to try and cushion it. But it shattered on my foot instead.

'There was only a little cut but blood began spraying out of it, and my toe was just hanging. Turned out I'd sliced through the tendon. They had to sew the tendon together. And to stop it being pulled apart I needed a plaster cast up to my knee. For a tiny cut on my toe! I had it on for a month in July and never got back to my best after that.'

A month earlier there had been another severing – one that was to have a more profound, and longer-term detrimental, effect on Hoy and the sprinters. They were disappointed and disillusioned, on the eve of the world championships, to abruptly part company with Martin Barras, the coach who'd worked with them for only eighteen months, with such positive results. Barras had intended leaving at the end of the season, since his Australian wife was keen to return Down Under. 'She was pregnant with our second child,' explains Barras, 'and she woke up one morning and said, "We're going back – you could be a taxi driver or a pizza delivery man if you don't get a job in coaching. But we're going back."'

But it turned out there was a coaching job available, and a prestigious one – national track coach at the Australian Institute of Sport, effectively the national team. Barras was interviewed in June and offered the job a day later. When British Cycling heard he was going back to work with the Australians – the opposition – they told him to clear his desk immediately. 'It was very difficult,' says Barras. 'Leaving these three guys [Hoy, MacLean and Queally] was very difficult. Dave [Brailsford, then second-in-command to Keen] cut me off very abruptly, and for a couple of years I was bitter. But I look at that now and think I'd have done the same. By that time I had a very close relationship with the guys. Still do. If I can help them I will, they know that.'

In fact, and although more than six years have passed since Barras departed, he becomes effusive when he talks about Hoy. 'I'm trying very hard to be Chris's biggest fan,' he laughs. 'Considering how his dad feels about him, that's difficult. But I'm going for number one!' Why? 'Because for a coach he's a dream come true. He's very easy to work with. I show my riders a video of Chris because I want them to copy him. There's an honesty about what he does, in training and racing. No foxing or bluffing. And he does it consistently. The guy is getting older and better, no doubt about it. And you understand why if you see him on a daily basis. It doesn't matter that we're not working together any more. As a sports professional I look at Chris – above all other athletes – with enormous respect.'

Peter Keen describes Barras's sudden departure as 'a traumatic event' in the short history of the World Class Performance Plan (by now beginning to be known simply, and perhaps fittingly, as 'World Class'). 'But we were all in agreement,' adds Keen, 'that if he wants out, he goes now.'

Hoy says it was 'a blow'. MacLean admits he found it tough. 'I struggled when he left. Over eighteen months you learn to trust someone. He sees what you need, and you develop a close working relationship. When he left there was nothing. We were back to square one, with no one to work with on a daily basis. You had to think for yourself again, which I found quite hard.

'I didn't like how it was dealt with,' continues MacLean. 'He was always leaving and we knew that, but the way he was kicked out prematurely was an issue. He was more than happy working with us, but there were personality clashes with other people in World Class. He'd decided he was going to move back to Australia, but he wanted to see the 2001 season through. But when he handed in his notice, about seven weeks before the world championships, they said: "Clear your desk. We don't want you passing on our secrets …"' MacLean laughs. 'He'd taught us all our secrets in the first place.'

Hoy recovered from his injured toe more easily than he did the departure of Barras, to go to the Antwerp world championships where he posted a respectable if unspectacular eighth in the kilo. With MacLean and Queally there was also a third consecutive team sprint medal – this one bronze rather than silver – behind France and Australia who contested the final, the French winning. The British trio beat Spain in the ride for third place, which, having 'only' qualified fourth, with an extremely rocky ride, left them satisfied.

There were mitigating factors. Apart from Hoy's toe and Barras's exit, Queally had had a difficult year, juggling his cycling career with his new status as Olympic hero, and all the demands that placed on him – or opportunities it presented, depending on which way you want to look at it. In the unsympathetic judgement of the British management, Queally had 'had the season off'. In Antwerp the usual starting order was changed as a consequence, with MacLean going first, Queally second, Hoy third. But in the qualifying round, as MacLean rocketed away, Queally appeared to be a shadow of the rider he'd been the previous year. He struggled to hold MacLean's back wheel and trailed two lengths behind him, only managing to close the gap as MacLean eased up at the end of his lap. Had the British trio ridden with their usual slick precision then another showdown with France would surely have beckoned.

All the pressures – or extra-curricular opportunities – of being Olympic champion seemed to act as a burden to Queally who, according to *Cycling* magazine, 'looked glum and preoccupied throughout the week [of the championships]'. With his bronze medal, however, he 'grinned from ear to ear'.

Queally, it seemed, had become a living example of how Olympic success can compromise performance. Through juggling extracurricular activities with his cycling career he had over-stretched himself in the twelve months after Sydney. He owed his team sprint bronze medal, he admitted, entirely to Hoy and MacLean. The juggling act wasn't quite over for him yet, either. 'Tomorrow I fly off to America to attempt the world land speed record,' he said. 'When I come back from the States in October I will become a full-time cyclist again. I've missed it a lot this year while I've tried to capitalize on my Olympic success.'

To consider the 2002 season, let us wind the clock forward, briefly, to January 2008.

I am with Chris Hoy and Arnaud Tournant in Rotterdam, where they are competing in the sprinters' grand prix at the Rottterdam Six-Day. It is the Sunday evening, four nights into the competi-tion, and they have been permitted an early finish – a night off, effectively. A meal is arranged in the hotel in which all the riders are staying, and after that, most drift into the bar. Some beer is drunk. You can see the riders checking each other out, thinking, if he's having a beer, I'll have a beer, too. It is a rare occurrence this, and one, therefore, to be savoured and enjoyed.

Hoy has a beer. Tournant has a beer. Then, with a convivial Gallic smile, Tournant buys a large round. It will be a long night. But in the midst of it Tournant tells Hoy a story that has obviously lodged itself in his brain, which in itself is highly revealing. It concerns something that happened after another night out – they are rare, honestly – in Manchester in 2006, when Tournant and two French team-mates enjoyed an evening in Hoy's adopted city, and then returned, at the end of the night, to his flat.

One of Tournant's team-mates, Francois Pervis, was – as Tournant told a slightly embarrassed Hoy in Rotterdam – 'a big admirer of Chris Hoy'. Inside his hero's flat Pervis looked in awe at some of the trophies and shirts on display, until his gaze fixed on the distinctive rainbow jersey of world champion, pressed in a glass case and hanging on the wall of the living room.

'Aaaahhhhh,' said Pervis, his eyes widening, 'this is from the world championships in 2002, Copenhagen, a beautiful race, amazing …' As he spoke, Pervis looked across to an anguished Tournant, and suddenly twigged. 'Oh shit,' he said. 'Sorry.'

It is almost impossible to overstate the significance of 2002 to Hoy's career – and also perhaps, but in a less positive sense, to Tournant's. There were signs that the balance of power might be shifting, that Tournant was no longer the invincible force he seemed as recently as the previous year. But six weeks before the Copenhagen world championships, and the 'beautiful race' recalled by Pervis, there were the Commonwealth Games in Manchester – an event of real importance to Hoy after the damp squib that was Kuala Lumpur four years earlier.

In fact, an indication of how far Hoy and Craig MacLean had come since those last Commonwealth Games was their joint election – by the rest of the Scottish team – as flag-bearers for the opening ceremony. This is a huge honour, usually conferred upon the outstanding performer in the team, across all sports. The problem here, however, was that, although Hoy and MacLean received an equal number of votes from their fellow athletes, both could not perform the honour. Magnanimously, Hoy opted to stand down, allowing his old friend MacLean to act as flag-bearer. 'That was a really nice gesture by Chris,' says MacLean. 'It's something I'll always appreciate, because it's a great honour; it goes down as one of the highlights of my career, and I really enjoyed it.' That much was obvious: MacLean made the most of it, entering the City of Manchester Stadium at the head of the Scottish team, and waving that flag with enough gusto and vigour for the entire squad as he led them around the athletics track.

As for the racing itself, there might not be the depth of competition at the Commonwealth Games, but with the presence of the Australians it is still a world-class event. For Hoy it was also a chance to challenge for a first major individual title. Yet it appeared to be a slim chance, with Queally by now back to something approaching the form that carried him to his Olympic title.

As much as the 'home' Commonwealth Games represented a huge opportunity for Hoy, the pressure told on his parents as much as on him – or more. 'Pre-Manchester I was an absolute bag of nerves,' recalls his mother, Carol. 'I was going demented waiting at home to travel there. David had to reassure me. He said, "Carol, you're a really good nurse [this being her job]. Chris is a really good cyclist. He's done his work. So there's no point you worrying about him."' That helped, she says. Briefly.

But in addition to being a 'really good cyclist', Hoy, and the rest of the British team, had a secret weapon. It wasn't quite Chris Boardman's Superbike of a decade earlier, but in Manchester the British team unveiled a machine that was christened, inevitably, Superbike MkII. It even featured, on the eve of the games, on the BBC TV show *Tomorrow's World*.

In fact it was a very early version of the bike that was being developed for the Athens Olympics two years later. It was designed by Dimitris Katsanis, a former member of the Greek national cycling team, who worked for Advanced Composites

Group, a Derbyshire-based company that produced components for the Formula One and aerospace industries, with research into the aerodynamics of the machine carried out by the Sheffield University Sports Engineering Research Group. The final version was, said Katsanis, 'four or five times as stiff as steel but a quarter of the weight'. Constructed from 158 pieces of carbon fibre, it could withstand the power of Hoy's standing start, which was, according to an article at the time, '2,200 watts'. When I ask Hoy whether that figure is still accurate, he says, '2,376 watts. Roughly.'

Peter Keen had met Katsanis in December 2001. Six months later, just in time for Manchester, the first bikes were delivered. Hoy was the first to ride one. 'It instantly felt like I'd been riding it for years,' he said. 'We used to lag behind countries such as Germany on equipment [but] now the playing field's level, or even tipped to our advantage.'

When it came to the night of the Commonwealth Games kilometre, Carol Hoy had lots of company: there was hardly a calm person within the velodrome, which was filled to capacity, 3,500 people crammed in. And in his major breakthrough as an individual rather than team athlete, her son triumphed, winning a memorable kilo in a time that seemed scarcely feasible, his 1.01.726 only a tenth of a second slower than the time Queally had recorded en route to gold in Sydney. It was Hoy's fastest time, his first 'one-one' kilo, and 'the biggest thing I'd ever done, just amazing'. What's more, the podium was completed by two other British riders, Queally claiming silver – more than three-tenths of a second slower than Hoy – and his English team-mate Jamie Staff taking bronze.

'The feeling of elation,' continues Hoy; 'I'd never done a time like that; I'd never done anything individually; to win like that, in Scottish kit, in the UK, beating the Olympic champion, hearing "Scotland the Brave" on the podium, I was very emotional …

everything about it was amazing. As I waited for [the last man] Jason to go I was over the moon to think I'd get silver. I mean, Jason not winning was unthinkable.'

After his Commonwealth Games success – which also included team sprint bronze in the company of MacLean and Marco Librizzi – Hoy says he was 'floating'. He remained so for the six weeks to the world championships in Copenhagen. 'I went to a training camp in Cottbus [in Germany] for ten days,' says Hoy. 'And every session, every day, no matter what it was – starts, speed work, in the gym, jump squats, power output – I got better and better without feeling that I was having to try that hard. I was in the zone. I felt like I was floating. I went to the worlds with no pressure, looking for a medal. I thought, if I can do a 1.01 then I can get a medal.'

And so he floated to Copenhagen, floated onto his bike, and – as quite an early starter, with only his eighth the previous year on his world championship CV – floated around the velodrome in 1.01.893, marginally down on the time he'd set in Manchester. But it might, reckons Hoy now, have been a better performance than the one that won him Commonwealth gold – it was significantly colder in Copenhagen than in Manchester, and temperature has a big effect on times in the kilo.

With his ride, he had floated like a butterfly to the top of the leader board. It was now a case of waiting, anxiously, for the top-seeded riders. They came and went. When the third man to go failed to beat his time, Hoy thought, 'Wow, an individual medal.'

In the end there was only one man left: Arnaud Tournant. Tournant had recovered from the disappointment – not to mention the shock – of being defeated by Queally in Sydney, and recovered in style. Not only had he won the world championship in Antwerp in 2001, but he had travelled from there to La Paz in Bolivia, home to the world's highest velodrome. And he had set a magical, mythical new world record for the kilometre. In the thin air of La Paz he became the first rider ever to dip below a minute: the record he established at 3,400 metres was a scarcely believable 58.875 seconds. The record put Tournant on a different level; his aura had returned. Anything other than victory for the Frenchman was inconceivable.

As Tournant burst from the start gate to begin his ride in Copenhagen, Hoy watched him, then looked down because he couldn't watch, and only looked up again at the end, as his time flashed on to the scoreboard. Hoy didn't see the time, he only saw the '+' after it, which indicated that Tournant had gone slower than the leader – than Hoy. At which point, the TV cameras zoomed in on Hoy as his mouth opened to yell the most clichéd two-word expletive in the English language, the second word of which is 'hell'. But what he hadn't noticed when he glanced at the scoreboard and saw the '+' sign was the time difference between him and Tournant. The Frenchman, who was well over a tenth of a second up with a lap to go, had recorded 1.01.894 – one thousandth of a second, the smallest margin possible, slower than Hoy. Or, if you prefer to consider the margin of Hoy's victory over Tournant in terms of distance, 1.5 cm.

Tournant was shattered. He slumped on to the track and sat there a long time, his head buried in his knees. It is customary for the vanquished champion to seek out his successor to shake hands, but Tournant didn't do that. He stayed where he was, in tears and utterly lost in his own world.

It was perhaps fortunate for Tournant that the medal presentation wasn't that evening, though the next day seemed too soon for him as well. There is a photograph of the podium and he cuts an extraordinary figure; his eyes are red and raw, his face is set in the glummest of expressions. He didn't shake Hoy's hand on the podium, either. 'He took the medal off as soon as he was presented with it,' recalls Hoy, 'and just stood there holding it, staring ahead.

It wasn't until the next day, when we were warming up for the team sprint, that he rode up behind me, and tapped me, and said "Well done."'

He would say it again a few hours later, when Hoy led the British team – completed on this occasion by MacLean and Jamie Staff – to a rare victory over the French in the final of the team sprint. That was less of a surprise than the kilo – they'd been edging closer to the French – but in some ways no less significant: it proved it could be done, that the French weren't invincible after all. For Hoy it put the cherry on his world championship.

It was the kilo defeat that most wounded Tournant. It was no wonder, then, that Pervis's eulogizing of the 'beautiful, amazing' Copenhagen kilo, in Hoy's flat several years later, was met with such a pained expression. Tournant had by then 'warmed', according to Hoy, having originally 'seemed quite distant. He was just this formidable figure.'

In Rotterdam in early 2008, with Tournant chatting amiably (in perfect English), buying large rounds, generally being the life and soul of the party, he certainly seemed a very different man to the one who stood on the podium in Copenhagen, looking as though he might burst into tears. But if Sydney dealt a blow, and exposed chinks in his armour, then Copenhagen might just have dealt a mortal blow. It is surely revealing that in Rotterdam, with the two now the best of friends – and Hoy due to attend his great rival's wedding in late 2008 – Tournant told him the story of what Pervis had said, and how it had reopened painful wounds. Six years later he was able to laugh about it – but only just.

While Hoy's star was rising, changes were afoot in the background. Peter Keen's baby was evolving, and Keen himself was preparing his exit. What he had created – 'World Class' – was more than a baby, it was a beast – in the nicest possible sense. Across the board – the sprint cyclists, endurance riders, female cyclists, even the road riders – there was evidence of a sea change in the fortunes of British cyclists.

The success raised Keen's profile. Even in Sydney, when he was still only thirty-five, he was hailed in some quarters as the brightest star of British coaching. It was inevitable that other doors would open, with UK Sport keen for him to assume a wider brief, and to try and do for other sports what he had done for cycling.

He moved on, but I wonder if he sometimes misses the day-to-day involvement. 'There are days when I a-b-s-o-l-u-t-e-l-y l-o-n-g to be back in there,' he says with real feeling. 'I watch them on the web, and I can read between the lines, or the times, and tease out what's going on, which says to me I'm probably still obsessed with it …' So that'll be a yes, then. 'But it was time to do other things …

'Technically,' he continues, 'I didn't leave British Cycling until the end of 2004.' But the transition began in 2003. 'It was the ultimate handover,' he explains. The man charged with carrying on the good work was someone Keen had appointed, but he was also someone who, had he applied cold for the position of performance director at British Cycling, might not have been an obvious candidate.

David Brailsford cuts quite an unusual figure in the higher echelons of sport. Yet the man who succeeded Keen had been involved, initially as someone who organized the supply of bikes, almost from the outset. Brailsford's background was in business – but also cycling. He grew up in north Wales, left school at sixteen and completed an HNC in civil engineering, but he was determined to go to France and become a professional cyclist. He raced there for four years, though he maintains now that 'I knew from early on I wasn't going to make it.' When he returned to the UK he went to Liverpool University to study sports science and psychology.

It was while he was studying that an old cycling acquaintance, John Herety, got in touch. Herety was a retired professional, now running a British professional team, and he needed help. 'I was absolutely broke,' says Brailsford, 'so I said I'd help him out, rubbing the riders' legs, basically. Then it progressed; I started doing a similar job with the GB team. It was quite interesting for me to be involved, because I'd ridden myself. I was only about twenty-two, but it gave me an interesting insight into how a team was run, and straight away I thought, I could do this.'

It wasn't a path he followed, though. After graduating from Liverpool University he studied for a Masters in Business Administration, at Sheffield Business School. Following that he found himself running a business in Paris. 'I got involved in a company that had problems with a subsidiary in France: a perfume company they wanted turned around. Then it went the other way; there was a big perfume company with a subsidiary in Worcester, which was really in trouble, and they wanted somebody to go there.'

Perfume to elite sport doesn't seem an obvious career path. 'I kept riding my bike,' explains Brailsford, 'and then in Worcester set up my own independent consultancy, advising four or five companies. And one of them was Planet X [an importer of cycling components and clothing]. Pete [Keen] got in touch with me through that. It was 1997, Lottery funding had just started, and he needed bikes pretty quick. He had all this money but no bikes.

'I got to know Pete. He was doing the budgets, human resources, everything; he was tearing his hair out sorting all this stuff out. I said, "Hold on, I can do the financial stuff for you, and do all these other little things for you." I could see that he needed to be freed up to concentrate on performance, because that is where his expertise was. I became his number two, or "programmes director", pretty quickly.'

But Brailsford became involved initially with some reluctance. 'To me cycling in Britain was still old school BCF, and I didn't really fancy being employed by the governing body. I didn't want to be tarnished by that brush. I was reluctant. But I really found Pete exciting. What I found exciting was his fantastic visionary thinking. He's a very, very bright, intelligent guy, and a lot of the things he was talking about excited me. I could see his vision, and it was brilliant – genius. After what he'd done with Chris [Boardman] you could see he wasn't a crazy genius. But he was willing to challenge everybody's way of thinking – and that wasn't easy. There was a set culture, but he wanted to change it; and he was quite happy to set the bar very, very high.'

For Brailsford the opportunity to become more involved was too good to pass up, mainly because it 'combined my business experience and sporting background. I still wasn't too keen on working for the BCF, I must admit, but otherwise it felt perfect. I embraced the opportunity with open arms.'

When it became clear that Keen would move on, Brailsford saw the logic in him taking over, given where the World Class project was at the time. While Keen was the man who had the vision, when it came to making it a reality, making it happen, as Brailsford puts it, 'I think that's where my strengths are. Pete is super enthusiastic and has brilliant ideas, but he'll take it so far then he'll need another massive vision. He's a very creative person. He needs to be allowed to exercise his mind; some of the drudgery of day-to-day management is not for him. I think that's where I'm slightly different.'

Brailsford admits that Keen's enthusiasm, and his unstinting focus on and belief in his 'vision', was vital in the early days, when, as Hoy has also alluded to, there was some scepticism and cynicism. As Brailsford puts it, 'Everyone's thinking wasn't aligned.' There was, he adds, 'no sharing. Some people couldn't see where it was going, so they couldn't buy into it. You'd hear comments like "It's bullshit"; "We don't know what's going on"; "They don't think about us" ... you lose people along the way.'

When the Keen-to-Brailsford handover began, the British team was becoming, in a sense, a victim of its own success. As the successes increased, so did competition, expectations, and the pressure to succeed, even within the team. As Keen's vision of creating a world-class team that ambitious athletes would feel they 'needed' to be part of began to be realized, so the stakes were raised for those who were part of it, and for those who wanted in.

Brailsford, like Keen, exudes enthusiasm, while also – and paradoxically – appearing quite laid-back. It is perhaps appropriate, then, that he is fond of apparently contradictory statements of intent, or explanations of his ethos. Some of his expressions might appear to veer dangerously close to management-speak – which is hardly surprising given his business background. There is, however, nothing dry or clichéd about his delivery, which is earnest and passionate. So, although they may share the same initials, there is nothing David Brent about David Brailsford, even if, on paper, some of his favourite expressions might appear to come straight from the mouth of Ricky Gervais's alter ego in *The Office*.

For example, 'compassionate ruthlessness' is Brailsford's creed when it comes to hiring and firing. It means, he says, 'telling people the truth all the time about where they're at, and making very tough decisions about whether riders continue on the programme, about staff continuing or not ...'.

'Compassionately ruthless,' he adds, 'is the way forward. I've let a lot of people go, but I've done it in a way that wasn't malicious, that didn't attack people, didn't belittle them. We've allowed them to retain respect and dignity, where we've said, "Okay we have to move on, get someone new in …"' Brailsford trails off, neglecting to add the final, brutal, Alan Sugaresque, 'You're Fired!'

With the stakes this high, and rising all the time, Hoy had his own brush with failure in 2003, enduring a season of such crushing disappointment that he feared he might find himself on the end of Brailsford's compassionate ruthlessness – in other words, dumped.

'Dealing with setbacks is part of being an athlete,' he says now, though he adds that it took him a few setbacks to start to appreciate that. By the start of the 2003 season there hadn't really been any, just consistent improvement, which speeded up or slowed down, but which – if plotted on a graph, which is something the methodical Hoy probably did – represented overall, steady progress. But 2003 was, says Hoy, 'a big setback psychologically', though it started well. He won the kilo at the World Cup in Cape Town by almost a second-and-a-half. 'It felt like it was coming really easily,' he says. 'Everything flowed. Then … I really don't know what happened. To this day I don't know what happened.'

At the world championships in Stuttgart he was, as defending world champion, the last man to go in the kilo. It was his first experience of being in such a position. And from the hot seat he saw Stefan Nimke, the local favourite, up the ante with a 1.01.2: a new sea-level world record. Hoy's response was to panic. 'I thought, "Right, if he's gone faster than anyone, I'm going to have to change my game plan."' It was a similar error to Tournant's in Sydney three years earlier. 'Instead of thinking, it's very warm in here, it's a very fast track – in other words thinking logically about why Nimke had gone so fast – I went out and attacked it so hard at the start that I blew to bits.' Again – perhaps – like Tournant as he tried desperately to overhaul Queally in Sydney. 'I limped home fourth. [Shane] Kelly was second, Tournant third,' says Hoy.

'To look at the scoreboard and see myself fourth – and we only got third in the team sprint as well – was terrible. From double world champion to one bronze, with less than a year to the Olympics. It was a big setback, and all kinds of doubts set in. I wondered if I'd peaked. I thought maybe that 2002 had been my peak, that it was the best I'd ever be.'

Bizarrely, Hoy had actually recorded a personal best in the kilo in which he was fourth. That offered no consolation. 'Then to add salt,' he continues, 'I went to the national championships. Craig went out and won the kilo. Jason was second. I was third. That was a really bad day. I had no desire to train, no desire to race. At that stage my thoughts were not about winning the Olympics; I didn't even know if I'd be selected. I had to go and lick my wounds. But I also had to try and find out what had gone wrong.'

CHAPTER 8

Mind Games

Another dingy office, Manchester Velodrome, October 2007

Enter the Manchester Velodrome by the main reception and, straight ahead, a flight of stairs leads down into a passage that takes you underneath the track and emerges in the track centre. To your left is a locked door; you need to tap in a security code to enter that and to enter the nerve centre of the British Cycling operation. Behind the door are the main offices and, presumably, down some corridor somewhere, an even more top secret room, probably with its very own code, which would have to be tattooed on the inside of Chris Boardman's thigh: I am talking, of course, of the Secret Squirrel Club, home to the kit that is to be unveiled at the Olympics in Beijing.

To your right, a corridor stretches and curves gently, like a banana, running parallel to – possibly beneath – the home straight of the track. It is bleak and airless in here; the shades are all grey, mainly an insipid pale grey. Actually, I'm not even sure if that's true. But it *seems* predominantly pale grey.

Have you noticed that the interiors of sporting arenas are always described as 'the bowels'? It conjures an image of an oppressive, dark place, which I don't imagine for one second is an accurate reflection of the doubtless plush rooms inside the New Wembley, for example, or Camp Nou. But in the case of the Manchester Velodrome it is perfectly accurate. In here, you really do feel as though you are deep in the bowels of the arena: in its innards. There are no windows, only artificial light; it is austere, it does feel oppressive, and of course it's always the same, no matter what the weather outside. Spend too long in here and you are likely to suffer seasonal affected disorder.

Off the corridor – the one that curves away to the right – there are doors left and right: First Aid, a canteen for officials and riders, changing rooms, press room, various officials' rooms. But the first door you come to on the left is not a public room and it is always closed. On it, a small typed label says: 'Steve Peters'. I knock on the door. 'Can you give me five minutes?' comes the voice from within, so I retreat to reception.

Five minutes later, a wiry, grey-haired man in his fifties appears in reception, wearing a pale blue British Cycling shirt and tie, smiling and sticking out his hand. 'Sorry about that,' says Steve Peters cheerfully. 'Now, what is it, exactly, that you want to talk to me about?'

Coming from a forensic psychiatrist, this could be a loaded question. But what I want to ask Peters – now a member of Dave Brailsford's four-person senior management team – is how on earth somebody such as him, who previously worked with inmates in a high-security mental institution, came to be working with the British cycling team? I want to know what he does; and of course I want to find out about his role in transforming Chris Hoy from someone racked with self-doubt at the end of the 2003 season, to Olympic and world champion a year later.

Then there is what Dave Brailsford has told me. Brailsford's aim as performance director was to 'build a team, a hand-picked team, of world experts, and give them responsibility. In any leading business now the guys at the top are similar to me,' says Brailsford. 'You're leading a team of people with more expertise than you have. My job is to create a culture, an environment, in which they can excel, in which their expertise is fully embraced – and can be delivered.'

Brailsford's motivation for wanting to find and employ someone like Peters is clear from something else he said: 'My job is to create a culture of support for the riders. To *really* support them, so they can be the best they can be. I want the best support team in the world. Not just equal to the French but across all sports, across the world – the best. If people in my team – riders and staff – don't have that enthusiasm, that drive to be the best in the world … if that doesn't *really* get you excited and get you out of bed in the morning, then this is the wrong place for you.'

The most intriguing thing about Peters is that, of all the world-class people he has appointed, Brailsford reckons he is the best. 'He was a massive find,' he says. 'I first came across him in 2001, and I thought *bloooody* hell, this guy's something special. Straight away. I really worked hard over some months to get him involved.'

The reason he wanted him involved, explains Brailsford, is because his modus operandi as performance director is not to see his athletes as machines, or performing monkeys, but as human beings with emotions and issues to deal with. 'You have to look at the whole person,' he says. 'If you've got a problem in your relationship, you're not going to be able to train properly. Some people look at us and say we go too far; we get too involved. If people have got problems we try and sort them out, in a supportive way. Some say that in dealing with athletes you should look at just one aspect of their lives – training and performance – and do X, Y and Z. I totally disagree.'

And this – in examining aspects A to W of an athlete's personality – is where the psychiatrist comes in … it explains Brailsford's obvious – and understandable – desire to involve such a person. But what about Steve Peters? Why would he swap the high-security hospital, and some of the most challenging cases in the country, for the Manchester Velodrome, and some of the best athletes in the country?

Peters opens the door to his office – his grey, drab, windowless and uninspiring office. It seems incongruous that this highly respected forensic psychiatrist works his magic in here. In fact, his reputation in the sporting field is now such that 'magician' might not be hyperbole. It has got to the stage where British Cycling even loans him out to other sports. On the day after our meeting, Peters is due to fly out to France to meet the English rugby squad, with whom he had worked in the build-up to the 2007 Rugby World Cup. 'Not sure what good it'll do,' he smiles, in reference to England's opening game in the World Cup, an abject 36–0 defeat to South Africa, just a few days earlier. He thinks he will be asked to lead a clear-the-air meeting with the players and coaching staff before their second game.

Perhaps it is a coincidence – though several players referred later to the benefits of just such a meeting – but England dramatically turned around their World Cup following Peters' visit. They even reached the final, only losing – narrowly this time – to South Africa.

Back to the beginning of his involvement with cyclists, though. 'I had two jobs at the time,' says Peters. 'I was working in the field of forensic psychiatry with people with personality disorders' – specifically those who had 'transgressed the law but have mental health issues or personality issues.' From 1993 to 2005 Peters worked at Rampton Secure Hospital, the high security psychiatric hospital in Nottinghamshire. During his time at Rampton the hospital's patients included Ian Huntley, who murdered the school girls Holly Wells and Jessica Chapman in Soham in 2002. 'Very basically,' says Peters, explaining his work at Rampton, 'it meant trying to restructure someone's outlook on life, and about themselves and their relationships with people, to the point where they would no longer be dangerous to society.'

'But I am also undergraduate dean to the medical school at Sheffield University, and one of my ex-students is the doctor here at British Cycling. He rang me one day, and said he needed help with a cyclist with mental health problems, and asked, would I do an assessment? I worked with this cyclist; it went well. Then they asked, can you see another, and another?' It 'snowballed' to the point, says Peters, where his employer asked if he wanted to take some time out to concentrate on sport. 'And I said, "Not really."'

It wasn't that the world of sport was alien or anathema to Peters. Having taken up running at the age of 41 Peters is, in fact, a World Masters champion in the over-50s category, and competes in all sprint distances from 100 m to 400 m. He has also had some involvement in athletics coaching. 'You find that your psych-y [shorthand for psychiatry] skills come into that as well,' he observes. 'So sport wasn't really new to me. But I knew nothing about cycling.'

One thing I am curious about is the distinction between psychiatry and psychology. Sports psychologists are ten-a-penny in the modern era. But I had never heard of a sports psychiatrist – and Peters admits he isn't aware of any other psychiatrists working in the sports field.

'Sports psychology uses psychological techniques in training and competition,' he says. 'And that can be very useful. But I look at the personality. I reconstruct the personality, someone's beliefs around themselves, their understanding of their own mind, how it functions. It's a medical model.' Perhaps aware that I am struggling to follow some of this – very kindly, he repeatedly asks, 'Does that make sense?' – Peters employs a neat analogy: 'A psychologist can teach you how to drive the car, but the psychiatrist lifts the bonnet, looks at the machine, takes it to pieces and reconstructs it. And *then*,' he adds with a smile, 'I teach them to drive the car.'

'My own feeling,' he continues, 'is that if you're a really balanced person then sports psychology will hit the nail on the head. You're talking there about little adjustments.

'But my experience of being with a lot of elite athletes is that they're *not* really balanced.' I laugh, but he's not joking. 'That's no indictment on them,' he stresses. 'I believe all people are nuts. That's my starting point – that we're all crazy. So I like to do the groundwork on the crazy bits, get you in control of your mind and your emotions, and, when you've got that control, then apply it to sport.'

It is not an original view this, that elite athletes are unbalanced. But coming from a forensic psychiatrist, whose previous work was with psychopaths – though he prefers 'people with personality disorders' to 'psychopaths' – it is fascinating. It also chimes with something suggested by someone else with considerable experience in the two fields (sport and psychopathic behaviour): the rower, Katherine Grainger.

Grainger, a world champion and Olympic medallist, is undertaking a PhD on homicide, and in an interview with *The Observer* in 2006 she made the headline-grabbing observation that there might be a correlation between elite sport and homicide, which was inevitably interpreted as her saying that Olympic gold medallists and homicidal maniacs are one and the same. But the point she made was more subtle.

'There are certain threads that are similar,' said Grainger. 'The same sort of extreme behaviour you get in sports people, which leads some of them to be very successful, can also be incredibly disruptive in other people if led in the wrong direction. There is a link to sport when you look into the darker parts of homicide … and examine why people do what they do.'

There is the perception, of course, that a psychiatrist is concerned with people who are – for want of a better word – nuts. When Peters began working with the team this perception must have presented a formidable challenge, I suggest. Surely the athletes would have been aware of the stigma if word got around that they were seeing a psychiatrist. A big part of the athlete's armoury, after all, is the creation of an aura: a sense that they are all-powerful, invulnerable, in control. A meeting with a psychiatrist would be perceived as an admission of weakness, would it not?

I ramble on for what feels like several minutes along these lines, until Peters abruptly sticks his hand up – literally like a policeman stopping the traffic. 'That's interesting, I'll stop you there,' he says firmly. 'I don't think that's right. I think that is the general perception. But let me tell you a story. I went to a World Cup in Moscow, very early on in my involvement with British Cycling, and I spoke to the team. Most of them didn't know me. And I said I'd put a post-it on my bedroom door. "If you want to come and see me," I said, "then come and put your name on this note, and a time you want to see me, and every thirty minutes I'll remove it. So it'll be confidential."

'Thirty minutes later I went up to my room and virtually every single name was written on the same post-it note. I said to one of the athletes, "Well, that wasn't very confidential, was it?" And he said: "Well no, because we don't see it as admitting to being vulnerable. We see that you can actually add something, that you might have techniques that can improve us." So they didn't see it as, "If you're crazy you see Steve and he sorts your head out …" – although that is something I can do! … But there's the other side:

he can get you from level A to level B. I think that's the angle they were coming from.'

And now, says Peters, the perception has turned full circle. 'As one of them said to me recently,' he says, 'the view now is not that there's something wrong with you if you see Steve, but that there's something wrong with you if you *don't* go and see Steve … One of the riders calls it a mental MOT – he comes in every so often for his mental MOT.'

Peters points out that he didn't just appear at the velodrome – or in Moscow – one day and report for duty. He had been coming on a semi-regular basis over a period of two years before he claimed the office in which we are now sitting. 'People started to get to know me, but at a distance,' he says. 'They got to know me as someone who came along and sat in the stand. I began coming one day a week. But I had to earn respect over a two-year period, which is fine; I'm happy with that.'

He says that, since those early days, there have been other sporting teams and athletes he's worked with where the process has been relatively long – that not everyone seems as eager to engage with him as the cyclists appeared to be. 'People are scared, that's normal, so there can be a barrier; but [as a psychiatrist] you don't break that barrier. What I do is reassure the person, give them the confidence that I'm not here to judge; I'm not even here to interfere. If you want to talk to me, talk to me. What has happened on a number of occasions, in teams I've worked with, has been that after six months of me standing on the sidelines, just being there, they come across and say, "Can I say hello?" So they've weighed you up – and I'm happy to be weighed up – and thought, "I think I can trust this guy." Then they talk and open up. I don't push people and if they start talking, I tell them to stop when they're uncomfortable.'

As for his early breakthrough with the cyclists, Peters reckons he was 'very fortunate to get a couple of athletes who were just massively underperforming for reasons which I knew I could sort out quite easily. I sorted them out, they both bounced up, and everyone then said to me, "Maybe you can walk on water." Which I can't,' he adds seriously, 'but it gave me credibility.'

Sometimes, Peters admits, he does encounter resistance. 'I've gone to new sports where the immediate perception is, "Who's he seeing? Who's crazy? Who's not coping?"' He won't say which sports. 'I've worked with Premier League footballers who have been brilliant to work with,' he points out. 'It's the public perception that these lads are not intellectual, which is often wrong.'

Peters' work with different athletes in different sports has not convinced him that there are traits, or personality types, common to elite sports people. 'It's a spectrum,' he says 'You'll get highly driven people and you'll get people who lack motivation – that's unusual at this level, but it does happen. You get people who are highly strung and nervous; you get people who are very laid-back.

'I've seen obsessional behaviours, but obsessional behaviours could be for a number of reasons. For one athlete, their obsessional behaviour might *work* for them. Another could be obsessional because of a lack of confidence. What you have to do is tease that out. You wouldn't want to touch the person who's obessional for the right reasons. But the person who's not happy, you would look at it. Sometimes you get common outcomes but totally different underlying causes. Athletes are people – we don't seem to understand that everybody feels the same. We're all vulnerable, we're all anxious, we all get depression, we all get down.'

So how, in a nutshell, might he work with an athlete? 'I have a structured way, a structured process,' he says. 'An eight-stage process of assessment: how you function at the moment and all the influences on you; your biological influences; cognitive factors

– the way you think; behavioural influences – familial influences; schemers – the beliefs you have about yourself and your world; the support networks you've got, the environment you live in … and it goes on.'

Is all this information gleaned through conversation? 'Generally speaking it's just by verbal communication and body language, so you're reading people all the time; you read their body language and signs, then you make an assessment. They're not tricks of the trade, as such, but there are techniques whereby you can take people down certain routes and see what they do, and how they respond … and you can apply what you find to sport, because by and large we tend to respond in our personal lives the way we do under pressure in sport. There isn't a change in personality; that doesn't normally happen.'

Peters, after several years now of working with cyclists and other sports people, still gives the impression of being a little surprised at finding himself in this environment. And I'm not talking about the dingy office in the bowels of the velodrome. 'I didn't plan this,' he laughs. 'I just enjoy working with people.' But he admits there is satisfaction in this field. 'To see somebody who has completely collapsed in on themselves … for you to be able to reconstruct them, and get rid of all the little demons within them, and get them so they're functioning to a level where they feel really happy and content … and their performance as a consequence improves. It's very rewarding. Very rewarding. Dave [Brailsford] said to me, "You're not just getting them to perform, they're different people!" Well, they're not different people, they're just being the people they want to be.'

And then Peters sticks his hand out again, his stopping the traffic motion. 'Can I just pause you for a second?' he asks cautiously. 'I'm aware your book is about Chris Hoy. But all this is about me. Are you sure you're heading in the right direction?' I'm never sure

I'm heading in the right direction, I tell him. 'That wasn't an analysis,' he replies.

Well, I tell Peters, prior to meeting him all I really knew about him and his work was something I'd read in a newspaper interview with Britain's triple world champion Victoria Pendleton, in which she raved about his influence on her. According to Pendleton, Peters likes to compare the cyclists to dogs ... or, rather, likens them to different breeds of dog.

'I made that up!' he smiles. 'Suddenly you think, I can explain this with an example. All I was trying to get across, at the time – and I was speaking to the coaches in fact – was the fact that everybody's different. Some people are like Rottweilers – *excellent* dogs, if you treat them with respect. But you've really got to know what you're doing and handle them carefully. Others are like Labradors. Again, excellent dogs, but family dogs; they love a lot of petting and reassurance, and then you'll get the goods from them. I was really unkind, when I used that analogy, to poodles, but that was just personal bias. I'm sure they're excellent. But I apologize to poodles.'

The point of the dogs analogy was that different athletes need different 'handling'. As Peters says, 'If you want to remove anxiety from a dog, you're not going to reason with it – you use behavioural techniques. And, yes, I can use these techniques with people. So you might have a rider with no insight [into themselves], who says, "I don't want to hear any more of this jargon, I just want to get rid of my anxiety." That's when you'll use behavioural techniques.'

Peters does keep dogs himself. 'Irish wolfhounds,' he smiles. So go on then, I ask, what kind of dog is Chris Hoy? 'Chris?' he smiles again. 'Oh, he's a German Shepherd: an Alsatian. Absolutely certain. Intelligent. Will work for himself and for you; a team player. Perfect, in fact, for an athlete.'

Of course, Hoy described the 2003 season, when he lost his world kilo title in Stuttgart, and failed even to medal in the event, as 'a huge psychological blow'. He added that he was determined to find answers for the mysterious dip in form, and he adopted what might look like a scattergun approach – which is to say that he approached everyone he could think of, seeking help, advice, counsel. 'I realized,' says Hoy, 'I wanted to leave no stone unturned and to try everything – within the rules, obviously.

'After Stuttgart I went back to just being a contender again. I had to fight to get back up there. It changed my outlook. I was far more open to criticism and more open to advice. I said to myself: "I'm going to go to everyone I can think of who has some area of expertise." Even if I thought they would have nothing to offer, I would go to see them. And that was when I went to see Steve Peters. Two thousand and three had been a bad year in all sorts of ways. I'd split up with my girlfriend of six years. I was here, there and everywhere; I had no permanent base; it was all temporary places to live – pretty chaotic.

'I had no problem seeing Steve and talking to him,' continues Hoy. 'There's this myth that sports people are very confident, but I'd say a high percentage are racked with self-doubt. When you see someone perform at the highest level, you think, how can you not be confident? But ten minutes before the start you'd rather be anywhere else. You're like a kitten … trying to act like a lion.' Or an Alsatian with a confidence crisis.

Hoy's state of mind around the end of 2003 sounds as though it might fit a pattern described by Peters. 'There are parts of your brain which are going to send you into chaos,' he says. 'If you invest a lot in something, or you have a belief system around something, and it goes wrong, then you go into chaos. An elite athlete who believes the whole of their value in life depends on them getting a medal … if it doesn't go according to plan then they are likely to cave in, or become aggressive.'

On the other hand, Hoy didn't cave in or become aggressive – on the contrary, he proactively sought help, and answers, in order to make a positive difference. When Hoy went to see Peters that winter, Peters realized he didn't need to open the bonnet and dismantle the machinery of his brain. 'With Chris there was instant engagement,' says Peters enthusiastically. 'He more or less knows what he wants: he made that quite clear. He listens and works with you. He's the ideal athlete to work with. There are others like him; they tell you what they expect, they're very positive in their approach, they let you know if something's working, they let you know if it isn't … For the Olympic games the question Chris had was, "How do I get into the right mindset to be able to focus on what I do and not be distracted? How do I avoid thinking emotionally, and lose the game plan?" This was the biggest disaster which he presented to me – which was nice; he had thought about it, and it was straightforward.'

This, Brailsford had told me, was what he perceived to be one of the major contributions Peters could make to his team. 'Differentiating,' as Brailsford puts it, 'between emotional and logical thinking. Emotional thoughts can hijack you. Look at a footballer taking a penalty. Whether one person or 10 million are watching, it doesn't change how you kick a ball; what does change is the mind. You start thinking about consequences; ego gets in the way.'

The fear for Hoy was a repeat of Stuttgart, when Stefan Nimke, the German, popped up with a sea-level world record and panicked Hoy into abandoning his strategy. It had happened, Peters told him, because he had allowed emotional thinking to interfere with his game plan; emotions had clouded his thinking, overriding or displacing his rational thoughts.

The trick, then, was to switch off those emotional thoughts. Sounds easier said than done. But Peters insists it is easy – that it is all in a day's work for him. 'In a nutshell' says Peters, 'you've got to switch from using one part of your brain to another. You have to learn which part of your brain is operating, and why it's operating, and then when you've learnt that, you switch it off, and switch on the bit you want … and you learn the skill of controlling that. That's what Chris did. And he did it very easily. He could see the reasoning, he understood it, and he learnt to do it. He mastered it.'

Peters describes sessions where they worked through various scenarios, all relating to the high-pressure environment of the Olympic kilo. 'What's your biggest fear?' he would ask him. 'What's unsettling you as you sit there? It could be your own ego; the fear of failure; it could be the size of the crowd; it could be the idea of letting your parents down. You have to define what's going through the mind and then determine where it's coming from.

'How would you react to a fast time by one of your rivals while you're waiting to go? How would you react to a world record? You have to visualize these scenarios. I have to dig into a person's mind to do this. But the part of your brain I want to work is the logical part. The part of your brain I want to turn off, or control, is emotional. Your emotions aren't rational. They create irrational thoughts that can mislead you.'

Fast forward from those winter sessions with Steve Peters to Athens, on the night of 20 August 2004 – the Olympic Games.

It is the kilometre final: arguably the most gladiatorial of all the track cycling events, with the competitors waiting patiently for their turn, watching their rivals, the pressure being ratcheted up as each one goes and their start draws nearer; then stepping up,

Top Chris Hoy and his haul of trophies after his first season racing a BMX, 1984.

Left The podium at the 1986 British championships at the Greyhound Stadium, Derby. Hoy is second, with Matt Boyle first and Nick Gill in third.

Hoy in aerial action during a 1987 National Series round in Sennelly Park, Birmingham.

Chris Boardman speeds to Britain's first Olympic gold cycling medal in 84 years at the 1992 Barcelona Olympics.

Chris Hoy, Craig MacLean and Jason Queally, team sprint silver medallists at the 2000 Sydney Olympics.

Hoy wins gold for Scotland in the kilometre time trial at the 2002 Commonwealth Games in Manchester.

The tried and tested trio: Craig MacLean leads Ross Edgar and Chris Hoy on the opening lap of the team sprint, resplendent in the white outfits of World Cup leaders.

Separated by 0.185 seconds and a step on the Olympic podium: Hoy commiserates with silver-medallist Arnaud Tournant, Athens 2004.

Craig MacLean is the first to congratulate Hoy after his Olympic winning ride, while his coach Iain Dyer reaches to shake his hand

Supercharged: on the way
to winning in Athens.

Top left Keirin world champion, Palma 2007, Theo Bos looks glum.

Top right Hoy steps on the gas, on his way to winning the keirin, with Ross Edgar in his slipstream.

Left 'There have been times I've wanted to throttle the guy' – Shane Sutton.

Dave Brailsford, British Cycling's performance director, outlines his strategy for world domination.

The Man with the Plan, Peter Keen embraces one of his early stars, Yvonne McGregor.

Hoy eyeballs the world's highest track in La Paz
while Scott Gardner fixes his bike to the starting gate.

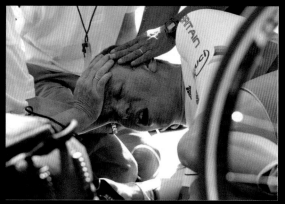

Bolivia lows: the pain of missing the world record by
5,000ths of a second.

Boliva highs: celebrating a new world 500m record
with parents Carol and David.

Hats off for Hoy: the first Brit in 54 years to win the world sprint title, Manchester 2008, with the defeated Kevin Sireau of France in the background.

Left All that glitters: Hoy shows off his three gold medals from Beijing, which establish him as Britain's most successful Olympian in 100 years.

An emotional reunion with his father, David, after victory in the sprint in Beijing. His mother, Carol, looks on, as do girlfriend Sarra and sister Carrie.

Above Philip Hindes, Jason Kenny and Chris Hoy with their gold medals after the team sprint at the London Olympics.

Right Hindes leads Kenny and Hoy in the final, where they beat their old rivals France.

Below Hoy stands on the top step of the Olympic podium for the sixth and final time, having defended his keirin title at the London Games.

going through hell for the pleasure of the spectators, and collapsing in a heap of oxygen-debt.

For the kilo might also be the most painful event: like the 400 metres in athletics, it requires acceleration and speed, so it attracts sprint-type athletes. Yet there is also an endurance element: you cannot sprint flat-out for forty-something seconds. In the closing stages of the 400 m, after the final bend, oxygen runs out, lactic acid takes over – it stings; it hurts. But the kilo is like that and worse. It lasts just over a minute – another twenty seconds of pain. A quote from the Squadra Coppi website, attributed to Sky Christopherson, describes the kilo as 'known to produce the highest lactic acid levels on record. My blood was turned into battery acid. Even my teeth would ache unbearably … I would commonly ride that fine line of losing consciousness.'

Hoy saw his first kilo in 1991, at the East of Scotland championships at Meadowbank. 'I just turned up on a cold, windy night and watched these riders one by one get up there and go through absolute agony. I may have a bizarre sense of fun, but for me it looked like a real challenge, and from the guy who was first, to the guy who was last, they all went through that last lap really giving it everything, the pain etched on their faces. You could actually see the pain. From then on, I was interested in it.'

He offers this description of the experience of riding it: 'The feeling of being one of the last riders to go, you're riding around the little pen in the track centre, it's gladiatorial; when it's down to the last three you're stalking each other. Then you're up; it's cards on the table time. You have one chance. Your body is on the line and it's cruel, because everyone cracks. You start feeling pain within a lap and a half, so the last two-and-a-half laps are pretty grim, but the awful pain comes with a lap and a half to go. It's just a shutdown; you're fighting a losing battle at that point. The body's slowing down, and if you fight it you slow down even more. You have to try and remain smooth. I used to try and fight it, but you become a mess. "Like a monkey on a stick," as Doug Dailey would say.'

In Athens, in the closing stages of the kilo competition, Peters is watching from the stand, observing Hoy in the track centre, pedalling slowly in small circles on the warm-up track, deep in thought, 'locked in', headphones on, oblivious to the fact that, one by one, his sixteen rivals are taking to the start line, blasting out of the gate, being roared on by the crowd, and crossing the line; oblivious, too, to the presence, near him, of the other late starters, his fellow-favourites for gold.

So far so good, thinks Peters, who led him through his final 'mental dress rehearsal' two hours before he was due to compete, 'visualizing everything, stage by stage. What are the demons and gremlins at each stage? How will you confront or deal with each one?' Because the doubts and fears would appear, Peters told him. 'You have to be rational; they're going to appear – we're human … But when they come up, do you know what to do to "box" them?'

Also in the stand are Hoy's parents, David and Carol, his sister, Carrie, and fourteen family members and friends. Carol is so nervous that 'I'm convinced I'm going to be physically sick.' David is calmer. 'We'd seen Chris two days earlier in the athletes' village and he looked like a racehorse. I'd never seen him look so healthy, or relaxed. I thought: "You're flying."'

That was the impression some of his rivals had, too. Martin Barras, now coaching the Australian team, had his spies out to watch the British team. 'In the lead-up to the 2004 games we had reports from people who'd seen him in training,' says Barras, 'and I had people saying it was the most impressive thing they'd ever seen in their sporting careers. He would put in these sessions on the track, come off, puke his guts out, go back and do it again.'

However, two days before the visit from his parents, there was near-disaster: Hoy was knocked off his bike by a bus while negotiating a roundabout in the athletes' village. It could have been catastrophic, but the only legacy is a large, dark red graze on his lower left leg. 'It was embarrassing more than anything,' admitted Hoy, who, earlier in the year, had confirmed that he was on the way back up from the low of Stuttgart by reclaiming his kilo crown at the world championships in Melbourne. That gives him the honour – and added pressure – of being last man to go in the Olympics. It puts him in the hottest of hot seats.

The real test on the night comes in the final twenty minutes before his ride. The warm-up is over. All he can do is wait – and watch his rivals; or, rather, not watch them, nor, if possible, be aware of them. He remembers the drills and mental rehearsals he has gone through with Peters: negative thoughts are natural, don't panic when you have one; displace it with positive thoughts. And always, always turn your focus to the start, and the routine: bang! you're in the start gate, breathing deeply, tightening your toe straps, sitting up, leaning forward, gripping the bars, pulling back, lunging forward.

Finally the Olympic gold medal comes down to five riders: Shane Kelly (Australia); Stefan Nimke (Germany); Theo Bos (Netherlands); Arnaud Tournant (France); Chris Hoy (Great Britain).

Kelly thunders around four laps of the track and through the finish line in 1 minute, 1.224 seconds: a new Olympic record; a sea-level world record. The 6,000 crowd, many of them Aussies, roars the roof off the velodrome. Hoy glances up at the scoreboard and sees the time. Shit, he thinks, and feels a ripple of panic. But then: 'Okay, it's fast in here, it's warm, my training times have been excellent, I know I'm going to do a personal best,' and:

Bang! you're in the start gate, breathing deeply, tightening your toe straps, sitting up, leaning forward, gripping the bars, pulling back, lunging forward.

Nimke goes. The tall, rangy German, who administered such a crushing blow to Hoy twelve months previously, is fast, fluid, a blur of white, black and yellow, and as he crosses the line the clock stops at 1minute, 1.186 seconds – even faster than Kelly. Hoy can't help but look again at the scoreboard, and think: 'I'm going to have to do a personal best just to get a medal here.' But then he checks himself: 'I *expected* that; I knew it was coming.' The start gate, the start gate …

Bang! you're in the start gate, breathing deeply, tightening your toe straps, sitting up, leaning forward, gripping the bars, pulling back, lunging forward.

Bos fluffs his start. He doesn't recover: 1 minute, 1.986 seconds is 'all' the young Dutchman can manage.

Now, with only the penultimate rider to go, Hoy is in the chair. 'It's like the gallows. That's what it feels like – an execution. In those last few minutes it's the last place in the world you ever want to be. You know it's inevitable now and you've got to do it; there's no getting out of it. You've put yourself in this position; you've committed four years to it, it seems ridiculous …'

Now it is Arnaud Tournant: the ultimate world record holder; invincible until Copenhagen in 2002, but who messed up in Sydney four years ago. Possibly the best kilo rider the world has ever seen; certainly the best never to have been crowned Olympic champion – yet.

Tournant flies around the track. He is stocky, he has a punchy style; with his enormous legs he jabs the pedals aggressively around four laps, hunched over his handlebars, sliding forward on the saddle with the effort, mouth open, gobbling up the track. He is up on Nimke after one lap; up after two laps; up after three laps … but as he crosses the line the time that flashes on to the scoreboard doesn't attract a tumultuous cheer; the reaction instead is one of stunned disbelief, followed a nanosecond later by a tumultuous cheer. The time is 1 minute, 00.896 seconds: the first ever sub-sixty-one seconds kilo at sea level. Olympic record. Sea-level world record.

Hoy doesn't see it. He is in start mode. In fact, he isn't. He's had to hit the fast-forward button. An error by an official means that the clock – the countdown to his ride – has started too early. It is supposed to begin the moment the rider mounts the bike. Then he has fifty seconds to settle on the machine … breathing deeply, tightening your toe straps, sitting up, leaning forward, gripping the bars, pulling back, lunging forward.

It's Jason Queally, sitting in the main stand by the start line, who notices what has happened. 'The clock's started!' he shouts at Hoy, and Hoy – somehow – hears him. When he realizes, he doesn't walk towards his bike, he jogs. He doesn't panic. The negative thought – 'Shit! The clock's started!' – is displaced by a rational one: 'In training I can do it in less than fifty seconds.'

Hoy's strength is in the start – it goes back to his BMX days. He 'really attacks' this one, as he says later. But this time, unlike in Stuttgart, he is not attacking Tournant's time; he is not conscious of chasing anyone, only – in his 'locked in' state – of himself, speeding around the track, getting everything out. There is a palpable urgency in his riding; his mouth is open, his face fixed in an angry snarl. 'The only thing that made me aware of how I was doing during the ride was the crowd,' says Hoy later. 'I couldn't believe how much support the British had. It was phenomenal – like a home crowd. I heard the roar, and I knew I was up. You don't ride to a schedule. You don't pace it. Well, you do slightly. You go as hard as you can and just hang on in there.'

The roar comes at the end of lap one: 17.984 seconds reads the scoreboard; Hoy is the first to dip below eighteen seconds. After two laps he is still up; after three laps he is holding on, the pain kicking in, the lactic starting to burn, the snarl more pronounced, and as he crosses the line the crowd turns en masse, like a tennis crowd tracking a tennis ball, towards the scoreboard. It reads: '1min 0.711 seconds OR.' OR means Olympic Record. Hoy has beaten Tournant by 0.185 seconds. But he does not celebrate. He seems oblivious, circling the track in a daze, a look almost of confusion on his face.

'You watch all my other rides at world level and as soon as I cross the line I'm punching the air,' he explains later. 'But this was different. I just couldn't absorb it. I have spent so many hours training and thinking about it, and so much visualization of the ride; then it went so exactly like I'd rehearsed it that I thought it wasn't real. I tried to put my hand up immediately when I saw my dad [David Hoy had rushed to the front of the stand, and was leaning out into the track, a Saltire billowing from his hand] but then I just rode round with my head down for a bit. I burst into tears because there was this massive feeling of relief and disbelief at what I'd done.'

Another factor in his failure to celebrate, reckons Hoy now, is that he had focused so much on the ride itself that he hadn't considered the aftermath. He and Peters hadn't covered that in their sessions; when the end came, it came as a shock.

Peters, meanwhile, remained in the stand. He had been watching Hoy throughout, 'studying his body language'. 'A big cheer went up when the first guy [Kelly] broke the Olympic record, and I saw Chris look up at the board, which I hadn't wanted him to do. But I said, okay, well if you look at the board then what would happen – we'd gone through that scenario. He knew he'd feel some panic. So: there the demon raised its head and he just chopped it off. He had the expectation that was going to happen, that negative thoughts would encroach, and so he wasn't surprised. It gave him control; he had control immediately, as it happened. He put his head down, focused on what he was going to do. Same when the next guy broke the record. By then he'd neutralized it.'

Peters shifts a little in his seat and begins speaking more quickly. 'From my perspective, he was brilliant, superb,' he says. 'And the body language was perfect on the bike, perfect. He was focused, his eyes were in the right place, he wasn't distracted, his emotions didn't come into it, he wasn't looking at the crowd; he was clearly within his own head at that point. In a team game you want them being very visually aware, but this was all internal. He was locked in. When he finished he was still so focused that he'd almost forgotten where he was. For me that was perfection. Perfection.'

When Hoy told Peters about forgetting to celebrate – or not being aware that he should celebrate – Peters chuckled. 'That feedback was brilliant. There's no point in looking at the consequences. You focus on the process.'

The first member of the British team to greet Hoy as he slowed to a halt in Athens was Craig MacLean. He had also ridden the kilo, but after a season blighted by illness, he could only manage seventh. As they both warmed up, he had turned to Hoy and said: 'Twelve years ago we were out at Turnhouse [by Edinburgh Airport], shivering in the snow between sprint efforts. Who'd have thought we'd be here?'

'It meant a lot that Craig was one of the first to congratulate me,' said Hoy at the time. 'Twelve years on, it was nice to share the moment with him. But there was also some disappointment for him. If he'd turned up and done what he's capable of then I think he'd have been on the podium with me.'

The moment was Hoy's, though. He was Britain's first gold medallist of the 2004 Olympics, and a headline-writer's dream: GOLDEN HOY; HOY OH BOY; HOY WONDER; GOLDEN BOY HOY; HE'S THE REAL McHOY; GOLD A-HOY FOR CHRIS.

Hoy's games were not over with the Olympic gold medal, of course. He had another event, the team sprint, which presented a more than decent chance of a medal. Pre-Athens the British team had continued its medal-winning run – every year since 1999 – with bronze at the world championships in Melbourne. In Athens, a medal of some colour seemed close to a certainty.

The only uncertainty concerns who should be in the team. MacLean is renowned as the fastest man in the world over the opening lap. Jamie Staff, the former BMX racer, is a recent addition, and he is fast and in form – a good man to have for the middle lap. Then there's Hoy, who, as Olympic, world and Commonwealth kilo champion, is indisputably the best man for the anchor leg. But there's Jason Queally as well – kilo champion four years earlier in Sydney – who couldn't even claim one of the two spots in the British team for the kilo in Athens, due to the form of Hoy and MacLean.

Three into four won't go, leaving the selectors with a tough decision. Prior to the games, Queally had exposed the rivalry between the sprinters, fuelled, he said, by competition for places in the team. 'It's not the best,' he admitted in one particularly candid interview, 'because we are individuals coming into a team environment. I'd be lying if I said we were the best friends in the world. It's human nature that you are protective of what you can achieve, and what you want to achieve. There's no real cama-raderie in the team. There's no point in dwelling on it because it creates negative feelings and we don't want to jeopardize our chances by falling out with one another.'

All of which seems surprising. And indeed, there was, say those involved, little obvious tension in the team – certainly not around Hoy or Staff. Relations between Queally and MacLean, however, appear to have been a different matter – even if nothing was explicitly said. Queally was, therefore, not best pleased to find that MacLean was favoured over him for the qualifying round of the team sprint.

Nor did his mood improve when, in that qualifying round, MacLean was off the pace. The team could only manage seventh, recording 44.693 seconds for the three laps. It gave them a difficult first-round ride against Germany, for which Queally came in for MacLean. The new British trio went considerably quicker (44.075 seconds), but Germany went even faster, recording 43.955 seconds. In fact, the British team's time in the first round made them the second-fastest of the competition – not that it was any consolation, because they were out, without a medal. Queally was furious. MacLean was inconsolable.

But there is another side to the story. MacLean – alone of all the sprinters – had decided to focus virtually all his energy and efforts on the team sprint. It was, he reckoned, his best chance of an Olympic gold medal. He had therefore devoted his career to team sprint success, pretty much since the Sydney Olympics. The commitment paid off – he became the fastest man in the world over the first lap: the best in the business.

But MacLean's commitment wasn't matched by his teammates, albeit for valid reasons. Both Hoy and Queally preferred to focus on their individual discipline, the kilo. It wasn't incompatible with the team sprint – but inevitably they didn't put as much into the team event as MacLean. And for all that the 2004 Olympics were a huge disappointment for the British team sprinters, there had been numerous occasions in the past when MacLean had been the one left feeling let down. 'I don't recall being aware of any animosity at the time from Jason,' admits MacLean. 'I do recall his lack of desire to train for the team sprint, which probably cost us gold medals – or meant we didn't get as close as we might have done – on other occasions, such as Sydney [Olympics in 2000, when they won silver], and at the world championships in 2001, 2003 and 2004.' In the Stuttgart championships in 2003 – which perhaps saw MacLean at his best – his opening lap gave the British team a lead of nearly half-a-second. But that significant lead evaporated over the next two laps – and the British team could only finish third.

In Athens, as MacLean points out, he didn't expect to be so below par in the qualifying round of the team sprint. 'After the kilo I was still very optimistic and confident. But then, to find out what my time was for my opening lap [in qualifying] – I just felt utter disbelief. I was six-tenths off my best. Sixty or seventy metres into the ride I thought I was going to pass out. There was no subconscious about it – I consciously had to back off at that point. And obviously that was very detrimental [to the team's time].'

The disappointment is still evident when MacLean discusses Athens. He had put four years into the event, it was his best chance of an Olympic gold medal – and in a fraction over eighteen seconds that dream was extinguished. It was a cruel fate for someone acknowledged as something of a pioneer, without whom Hoy says he wouldn't have won his kilo gold medal. But it seems especially cruel that MacLean, arguably the key figure in the six consecutive world championship medals won up to that point, was held up by some as the fall guy, the guilty party, in Britain's failure to win a team sprint medal at the 2004 Olympics.

MacLean, though, had been hampered by illness in the year leading up to the Olympics – within weeks, in fact, of his stunning form in 2003. A chest infection contracted at a six-day race in Australia in November kicked it off. 'When I came back to the

UK in February I had blood tests done, and they showed I'd been exposed to a virus,' he says. Following that, his form was up and down. Crucially, however, there were days when he was at his best – when all seemed well. Then, four weeks before the games began, he was struck down with tonsillitis. He recovered in a week; there were days he felt alright, days he felt not so good. He worked a lot with Steve Peters. 'As long as there's a chance you have to think positively,' says MacLean. 'I was doing a lot of mental rehearsal, putting myself in a positive frame of mind. And you start believing it – that's how it works.'

For MacLean – for whom the disappointment was compounded even more by the fact that at thirty-three Athens might be his last Olympics – the only positive was the success of his protégé, Hoy. 'What I felt then and now is just immensely happy for Chris, and extremely proud of him. I honestly think there's never been a more deserving champion. He trains like an absolute trooper. He's so single-minded. He really did deserve it. He rode like a champion. Getting up there last as reigning world champion, it's the hardest thing to do.'

In the aftermath of Athens MacLean wasn't sure what the future held for him. Even his place on the British squad was, he felt, under threat – his contract was due to expire after the next world championships in Los Angeles, in March 2005. It underlined to him how fickle sport could be – how thin was the line between the kind of success and acclaim Hoy was enjoying, and the disappointment he was having to come to terms with. But his first priority was to regain his health. 'Apparently what I need is aggressive rest,' he said at the time. 'I've no idea what that means – lying in bed shouting at people?

'If I carry on,' he added, 'it'll be to aim for the next Olympics in Beijing.'

CHAPTER 9

Killing the Kilo

UCI headquarters, Aigle, Switzerland, 23 June 2005

Aigle is a small town in the foothills of the Swiss Alps, eighty miles from Geneva, on the outskirts of which is a strange, futuristic looking building, all smooth lines and sunlight-reflecting metal surfaces. It has a curved silver frontage, is fairly vast in size, and is incongruous, to say the least, among the industrial units that surround it. It is, in short, an ostentatious, attention-seeking building – but then again, perhaps it should be. Because it is the self-proclaimed Centre of World Cycling, the headquarters of the Union Cycliste Internationale, representing the interests of '170 national federations and billions of cyclists'.

On 23 June 2005, the Centre of World Cycling received a surprise visit from two people who had, until that morning, never met. Following a blizzard of emails over the course of the previous week they had – 'on a whim' – arranged to meet at Edinburgh Airport, to fly to Geneva and catch a train along the banks of Lake

Geneva to Aigle. With them, they carried a petition that ran to many pages and contained 10,679 names.

They had felt compelled to make this trip, their motivation fuelled by frustration and anger over an announcement made by the UCI a fortnight earlier. Following a review of events on the Olympic programme, the governing body had confirmed that two events were to be axed: the men's kilometre and women's 500-metre time trials.

Less than a year after what many agreed was the most thrilling and spectacular kilo competition of all time – four sea-level world records, a nerve-jangling, spine-tingling finale – the event was to be consigned to the Olympic dustbin. It seemed an irrational, self-defeating, suicidal move by the body that runs the sport.

Chris Hoy, faced with the possibility of being the last ever Olympic kilo champion, described the decision as 'baffling'. When he received the call informing him of the UCI decision, he had to be convinced, over several minutes, that it wasn't a wind-up. 'All the history and heritage of the event will be lost forever,' he said. 'I certainly don't want to be remembered as the last ever Olympic kilo champion. I feel like they've cut my career in half.'

The reason for the decision, said the immediately under-fire UCI, was that they had been asked by the International Olympic Committee (IOC) to drop two events in order to accommodate a new cycling discipline: BMX. 'Kind of ironic,' acknowledged Hoy, 'that I started out in BMX and it could almost end my career.' Not that he harboured any resentment or bitterness towards BMX; his bitterness was directed at the UCI, who claimed that a 'detailed study' had led them to their decision. The precise details of their detailed study remained, for the moment, sketchy to say the least.

So two people, Julie Dominguez and Carlton Reid, decided to travel to the UCI headquarters in Aigle. They went in search of answers. Through his cycling website – Bikebiz.com – Reid had organized a 'Save the Kilo' petition. Dominguez, a track cyclist from Edinburgh, was one of the first to sign up. Though they didn't know each other, they united to lead the campaign to get to the bottom of what they regarded as an outrageous decision, which could have serious repercussions for track cycling at the Olympics. The beauty of the kilo, after all, lies in its simplicity. For the viewing public, it has the advantage of being straightforward and easy to follow, unlike some other track events. It is also exciting to watch, unlike – many would argue – the road time trial, which was added to the Olympic programme in 1996. If any event was to go, many would have fancied the road time trial.

There was huge disappointment in Britain, obviously, with Hoy's success still so fresh in the mind – not to mention Jason Queally's in the same event in Sydney in 2000 – but there was also indignation in Australia, China and elsewhere. Doing away with the kilo wasn't just unfair to Hoy and the other athletes whose careers were devoted to specializing in it, it seemed perverse. Some wondered: was this an act of wilful perversion by the UCI, or a statement every bit as attention-seeking as the governing body's headquarters? And if so, why?

When Reid and Dominguez arrived at the UCI they walked straight into Pat McQuaid, the Irishman who was then UCI president-elect; he was due to succeed Hein Verbruggen three months later. McQuaid was coming out of a pre-lunch meeting when he was handed the petition. Reid asked him if it would have any impact. 'No,' replied McQuaid. 'No.'

To his credit, McQuaid invited Dominguez and Reid to sit down and discuss the issue. And at 1.55 p.m., within minutes of their meeting with McQuaid, Reid filed a report on Bikebiz.com. In it he said that McQuaid, upon being handed the petition, 'flicked through the names and comments, some of them highly critical of the UCI [and] said any anger should be directed at the IOC, not the UCI. "The petition is a very powerful statement," said McQuaid. "I'll make sure Verbruggen sees it. He'll make sure the IOC sees it. It's up to the IOC to change this decision. It can't be changed by the UCI."'

Throughout their meeting with McQuaid, neither Reid nor Dominguez took any notes. Reid explains: 'I committed everything to memory. When I came out of the meeting I didn't even say anything so I wouldn't forget exactly what he'd said. Then I sat down and wrote it verbatim; Julie did the same and we compared what we'd written. As he was speaking I concentrated very hard on remembering exactly what he said, but even as he was talking the juicy bits stood out a mile.'

According to Dominguez and Reid, McQuaid said that the IOC had approached the UCI eighteen months earlier, requesting the inclusion of BMX on the Olympic cycling programme. 'We agreed to that,' McQuaid told them, 'and knew we'd have to drop two medals to accommodate BMX. We didn't make any decision at the time. We tried to brazen it out with the IOC, hoping they'd forget about events having to be excluded. It was the IOC who told us to exclude track events, not road, because the women's 500 m, for instance, was only introduced [to the Olympics] at Sydney [in 2000]. We got a letter in March [2005], I think it was, reminding us about the exclusions.'

Reid's antennae twitched in response to McQuaid's claim that an IOC reminder had arrived in March, effectively catching the UCI unawares. Before meeting McQuaid he had in fact visited the UCI library and read the minutes of a UCI management committee meeting, held at St Wendel, Austria, on 28 January 2005 – two months before the alleged IOC reminder. The significant line noted by Reid in the minutes said: the 'mgt [management] committee will take a decision in June regarding the withdrawal of two specialities at the 2008 Olympic Games ...'.

As for the 'detailed study' that led to the decision to drop the kilo, McQuaid told Reid and Dominguez that this had involved sending a survey to the twenty-four national federations which had sent track squads to the Athens games. 'If we surveyed all 170 federations we'd not get many replies,' reasoned the UCI's president-elect. 'As it was we had to keep reminding the twenty-four to send us their replies. Only nineteen replied. You've got to realize that each federation votes in its own interests. Those countries that don't have any specialists in the kilo voted against the kilo.'

But the question that troubled Reid and Dominguez – and others – was why a track event was targeted in the first place? Why not just put it to a straight vote? Was it really true, as McQuaid claimed, that the decision to drop a track event had been at the request of the IOC?

In fact, Reid believes the decision to axe a track event must have been taken before the UCI management committee meeting on 28 January 2005. Because as well as noting that the management committee would make their decision in June, he spotted something else – that the discussion on the exclusion of events came under the heading 'UCI Track Commission'.

Reid believes that the 'exclusion survey' dispatched to the twenty-four national federations in March 2005 was flawed from the outset. According to a 'highly placed source', Reid was told that, although 'road events were listed [on the survey] as possible options for exclusion, and many federations picked out the road time trial for deletion', their votes were discounted. According to Reid, these federations voted for the road time trial 'not knowing that their votes would not be counted because the UCI would only be deleting track events ... National federations were not told any vote for a road event would not be counted.'

Towards the end of their meeting, McQuaid suggested another context in which to consider the decision: the UCI's fear that cycling might be excluded from the Olympics altogether. 'At the Singapore vote in early July [2005] the IOC is voting on which country gets the 2012 Olympics,' McQuaid told them, 'but a couple of days later there's a vote on which sports stay in the Olympics, and which have to come out ... We're worried about the vote. Well, not worried so much; we know cycling will be voted in again, but if cycling is the fourteenth or fifteenth most popular sport, it weakens our position for the future.' McQuaid finished the meeting by telling Reid and Dominguez that he was having lunch with Hein Verbruggen and Jacques Rogge, the IOC president, the following month. 'We'll discuss this petition with Jacques then,' he promised.

Reid and Dominguez left Aigle, catching the train back to Geneva but stopping off in Lausanne en route. They had a copy of the petition for the IOC, too. At IOC HQ they were met by a 'helpful and sweet' PR man.

Dominguez explains: 'He said, "We've been expecting you ..." I think he'd already seen the report [of their meeting with McQuaid] that Carlton put on his website before we went to the IOC. He was really nice, very open, and he told us straight off that the IOC had *not* told the UCI to bin two track events.'

The IOC weren't the only ones to see Reid's report of the earlier meeting with McQuaid. It was picked up by a sports news website, sportcal.com, who had already contacted the IOC for a reaction to what McQuaid had allegedly said. The IOC spokesman told sportcal.com: 'Requests for changes to the Olympic programme come from the federations, in this case the UCI. They came to us wanting to put BMX on the schedule.' The IOC spokesman flatly denied that the IOC had told the UCI to axe track, rather than road, disciplines.

The IOC man who met Dominguez and Reid told them the same. Dominguez now believes that, among the 'many conspiracy theories', the UCI might have been 'playing Russian Roulette with the IOC', given that the Olympic body's limit on the number of disciplines is understood to be motivated by a desire to limit the overall number of participants. As she points out, dropping the kilo and women's 500 m time trials will make no difference to the number of participants; all these riders compete in the other sprint events in any case. Dropping the kilo and 500 m could therefore be interpreted as a two-fingered 'up yours' gesture aimed by the UCI at the IOC. 'I think the UCI thought that if they dropped these events there'd be an outcry against the IOC,' suggests Dominguez. 'It was a way of bullying the IOC I think, forcing them to allow the reinstatement of the dropped events, because they wouldn't want to lose the kilo from the Olympics. But the backlash wasn't against the IOC, it was against the UCI.'

'In my opinion the whole thing was a set-up,' says Reid. 'For the UCI it was all about protecting what they really love, and which brings in all the money, and that's road cycling.' As Reid's dispatches from Switzerland were picked up and reported more widely he found himself at the centre of what in Scotland is known as a 'stushie' – a controversy. McQuaid was unhappy. 'He rang me up straight after the story appeared in *Cycling* magazine,' says Reid. 'He was extremely angry and denied everything. His main beef was that I didn't tell him I was a journalist. But at the same time, I didn't hide it.'

In the end, and other than to cause some embarrassment to the UCI president-elect, Reid and Dominguez's trip to Aigle made little difference. Neither, it seems, did the petition, which has never been heard of again. 'It was really sad,' says Dominguez, who had ambitions to specialize in the women's 500 m time trial. Its axing was, in fact, even more unfair on the female sprinters than the disappearance of the kilo was to the men. It left only one event for female sprinters. At least the men still had three other medal chances – sprint, team sprint and keirin. 'Nothing really happened after our trip,' says Dominguez. 'Lots of riders and fans supported the cause, but no federations really got behind it. I thought China would do something, because they had high hopes in the women's 500 m, and with the next Olympics in Beijing … McQuaid actually told us it was a "catastrophe" for Chinese cycling and that he'd had some grief over that. But nothing happened. It died a death. I wonder if it was ever even discussed by the UCI.'

After speaking to Dominguez and Reid, I thought I should travel to Aigle myself, to meet McQuaid and ask him about the process that led to the UCI decision to drop the kilo. Having submitted my questions, I was granted a meeting in November 2007. And although McQuaid admitted with a sigh that he had thought the episode was 'done and dusted' he agreed to reopen the can of worms, and examine the contents. How thoroughly – or not – I would find out when I arrived at that strange, futuristic building, which stands against the backdrop of the Alps, but whose incongruity is emphasized by the fact that Aigle itself seems a small and sleepy town.

I got there early, intending to visit the library, to read the minutes of the UCI management committee meetings. Reid had read these in the library. He told me they were there, and available for public inspection. But when I looked I couldn't find them. I asked the receptionist. She shrugged her shoulders and said she couldn't help. I looked again. There were shelves of glossy books and biographies; countless annual reports from national federations; cycling magazines from around the world – but no minutes.

When I meet McQuaid, I ask him. 'I must admit I don't know,' he says. 'I'll take you to our head of information, he should be able to help.' Which, later, he does, but it seems that the management committee minutes are no longer available for open public inspection. I wonder if they were removed after Reid's visit.

McQuaid is not a man to be envied. He comes across as decent – arguably it was his decency that got him into trouble when he met Reid, a stranger to whom he opened up easily, not realizing he was a journalist. But, that aside, he is permanently embattled, with 'beleaguered' the adjective attached so often to the organization he leads that non-English speakers might believe its name really is 'Beleaguered UCI'.

It is ironic that he and the UCI stand accused of being biased in favour or road racing, because the source of most of their problems is road racing – from a succession of catastrophic doping scandals to a hugely damaging rift with the organizers of the major road events, including the Tour de France. But the road remains, despite all that, the most lucrative area of cycle sport; it acts as a magnet to millions in sponsorship and TV money. And this, you imagine, means the UCI needs it, not least for the upkeep of its swish headquarters.

Does this apparent road bias, I ask McQuaid, explain why the UCI appeared determined to sacrifice two popular track events, while leaving the road events alone? 'Well,' he says, 'the question that went out [in the survey] included road events as well.' But what was the point in that, if votes for road events were discounted? 'We had twenty-four federations involved in the track events in Athens, so we sent the survey to them,' replies McQuaid. 'We consulted with them. That was the decision we took.' Why? 'It was sort of inferred by the IOC that it should be track,' he says, unconvincingly. 'Bear in mind that in Sydney we added new track events; so it was obvious they should go – in the Olympics it tends to be last in, first out. We didn't have much choice in mountain biking [where only one event, cross-country, features on the Olympic programme] or in road [where there are two: road race and time trial].'

You say the IOC 'inferred' that track events should go – but the IOC say it was nothing to do with them. 'Yes, that's right,' says McQuaid, 'it was a UCI decision.' So was he aware of any IOC opinion on which events should go? 'No. No, none at all.' So they didn't 'infer' that track events should go. That is balderdash. Given which, does he understand, from a track cycling point of view, why there is frustration that the road time trial wasn't considered for the chop? 'I can understand the view, but we had to take the overall position for cycling. [Road] time trialling itself is a discipline which is under certain pressure … big time trial events like the GP des Nations are off the calendar, so we felt we needed to support that. The road time trial is equally a test of man and machine, and man against man in the pure sense …

'We felt that if we were to drop the road time trial,' continues McQuaid, 'we'd be left with only one road event: the road race. And there are a lot more nations involved in road than track – a lot more take part in the time trial than the track. The track could afford to lose two disciplines, road and mountain biking couldn't; that was the bottom line. I can understand Hoy and Queally feeling personally affronted, and British cycling feeling affronted, but we have to take decisions for the overall good of cycling. And it was the federations that decided.'

Well, twenty-four of them. Though, in the end, it was nineteen – nineteen from the 170 federations, and billions of cyclists, who all shelter under the UCI umbrella. It doesn't seem very democratic that such a huge decision came down to just nineteen federations: in effect, a handful of people. McQuaid cannot say how many of these nineteen federations voted for the kilo to go – or how many voted for the road time trial to go, whose votes were apparently discounted. 'The events that won the ballot – or in effect lost the ballot – were the women's 500 and the men's kilo,' says McQuaid. 'The 500 was fairly widespread; the kilo was by a small margin.'

It seems grossly unfair on female sprint specialists that they have only one crack at an Olympic medal. 'I understand the women feeling strongly about that,' says McQuaid. 'It is an issue. It's something that's been generated over several Olympics. It's something we need to talk to the IOC about.'

What if the IOC come to the UCI and tell them they can add two events to the Olympic programme? Would the UCI reinstate the kilo and 500? 'Yes,' says McQuaid. 'We are continually lobbying the IOC. If we were asked to add any discipline the first thing we'd bring back would be the kilometre.' In time for the London Olympics in 2012? 'It's not been discussed.'

Like Queally four years earlier, Hoy suffered 'a wobble' following his success at the Athens Olympics – and it was only partially linked to the sudden loss of his event from the Olympic programme. Initially it had more to do with the fact that he'd reached the top of the mountain. As Peter Keen might have put it, the mist had cleared, he'd pushed on for the summit, and planted his flag there. What now?

As there had been for Queally, there was also a big increase in 'extra-curricular' activities – or 'opportunities that you have to weigh up', says Hoy. 'If you can do things that ensure you have financial security then you owe it to yourself to take some of them. I had a few weeks after the games when I didn't touch my bike because there was so much going on. But then I cut back on that

stuff when I started training again. There is no danger of complacency on my part. There never has been.'

Yet when it came to racing, Hoy discovered a new and unexpected challenge. The Olympic final had been such a highly pres-
surized occasion, and that pressure had, of course, brought the
best out of him. There was, he realized, something quite intoxi-
cating about it. When it came to other races, with less at stake, he
missed it. The sense of anticlimax was striking. 'No race was the
same,' he says, 'and I found that really hard to get my head around.
I did the World Cup meeting in Manchester and did a 1.01.6, the
fastest I'd gone there, but it felt very underwhelming. Then I went
to the world championships in Los Angeles [in March 2005] and I
was only third in the kilo [more than a second down on Theo
Bos, with Queally second, though Hoy joined Queally and Staff
to win gold in the team sprint]. The kilo was a really bad ride. I
just didn't have the fire in my legs. Two months later, I discovered they were dropping the kilo from the Olympics. I felt a bit
directionless.'

Steve Peters, who had helped Queally cope with the pressures
of being Olympic champion, clearly had an important role to play
in helping Hoy in this period. 'His career was more or less perfect
up to the Olympics,' says Peters. 'He had setbacks, but he always
had focus. But after the Olympics it … wasn't perfect. There's a
difficulty in dealing with reaching something that is apparently the
pinnacle of your career, of focusing on one single thing, and
getting it. I think for Chris this is when things started to get a bit
more difficult,' continues Peters. 'This is where he's an Alsatian –
he needed to focus on a new goal. And I don't think he did
initially.'

Hoy says that someone else who helped enormously in this
difficult period was someone who had by now been assigned to
manage the sprint group. It was a surprising appointment, because

the individual in question, one of the best known in British cycling circles, had no background in track sprinting. He is an Australian who had been a road rider, one of the best British-based professionals of the 1980s and early 1990s – he even won the country's premier stage race, the Milk Race, in 1990.

But Shane Sutton – for it was he – is a character with a capital C, larger than life itself. Sutton didn't replace Martin Barras, because his job wasn't to coach. His job is to manage; when necessary, to bang heads together – to confront people, challenge them. It's something he's good at. Still, his appointment raised eyebrows, as Dave Brailsford admits. 'I remember everyone really drew in their breath,' smiles Brailsford. 'I can remember Doug Dailey saying, "Bloody hell Dave, I hope you know what you're taking on here!" Shane's a bit of a wild man,' continues Brailsford, 'but what I saw in Shane more than anything was an empathy for the riders – a natural feel, an instinct, for how people are feeling.'

'There were big problems at that point in the sprint group,' says Sutton, alluding to the tension that Queally had mentioned in the run-up to Athens. 'The boys weren't getting on, so the management asked, "Will you help with the sprinters?" Wasn't really my area, I told 'em, but we had a meeting, and I decided I'd take over.'

Sutton is a wiry, ageless character, a bundle of nervous energy, a fast-talking, fast-living, fast-thinking, ducking-and-diving dyed-in-the-wool Aussie. Having lived in Britain almost a quarter of a century he appears to have inherited not a hint of British reserve; he remains, resolutely, a larger-than-life Aussie. He is edgy, always fidgeting, apparently always – always – with his mobile phone either in his hand or attached to his ear. He is not someone who appears to switch off. Frankly, it is impossible to imagine him dressed in anything other than Team GB gear, hurrying somewhere, or fidgeting nervously. He tells me he has an addictive personality. Not for Sutton, though, your common-or-garden addictions. 'Jeez, at one stage, mate, I found myself addicted to buying houses,' he says, dead seriously.

Alongside Steve Peters and Chris Boardman, Sutton is one of Dave Brailsford's key lieutenants – he sits on the four-person management committee. If nothing else, that must liven up their meetings. In these meetings, he tells me, he considers himself to be the riders' representative; prides himself on it. If their interests look like being compromised then he threatens to quit. 'If they don't get what they want, and what they need, I'll walk,' he claims to say to Brailsford on a fairly regular basis. 'I say to him, "I'm walkin' – get me bloody redundancy package ready!"'

His title is performance manager; his role, effectively, is people person. You imagine that on occasion he could raise a smile merely with the sheer force of his personality, with a nugget of wisdom, or with his refreshingly direct style. He sees his role as being to get to the root of problems, then dig them up. 'I think that's me job, basically,' he admits. 'Chris might have problems that are not cycling-related. I can tell if he has problems. I'm quite good at managing that day-to-day lifestyle thing, if they need it, if they need a bit of guidance, need a bit of help. Chris and I have been through thick and thin. Through the Stuttgart thing [at the world championships in 2003], he had problems then and I gave him personal advice. I had him sat on my bed pre-Stuttgart bloody virtually breaking down with the pressure. My job is to make sure the guys are getting everything they need; they know my door is open and they can walk in and talk to me about anything.

'After Athens we said to Chris, "Go away and do what you want to do, but you've still got your grant; everything is still in place for you." Jason [Queally] didn't have that [post-Sydney]. But it was a tough time for Chris. And I could understand that. I was with him in track centre in Athens, as those times came in, and I saw the strength. When he looked in me eyes, and I looked in his eyes, he saw the strength in me, and I certainly saw it in him: I didn't have to put it in, it was there. Don't get me wrong, what Tournant did was special, but if Chris wobbled, I didn't see it. I just saw sheer bloody strength; sheer bloody character, mate. But it was a big, big high.

'Here's the thing about Chris,' says Sutton, continuing his torrent of words, barely pausing for breath, 'three days before the kilo, I went up to his room, and I said, "What can I do to make a difference to your performance?" Because that's me job, see. And he said: "I want you to get me one of those disability skinsuits." The paralympic team, you see, were wearing different skinsuits, and Chris felt it was a better fit. That said it all to me. I spoke to all the riders, asked them all, "What can I do to make a difference to your performance?" Some guys said, I want apple juice, or other kinds of food, or superstitious things, quirky things, but the thing that struck me was this – Chris wanted something to do with performance, nothing else. Performance. He was the only one.'

It was Sutton who called Hoy to tell him the kilo had been axed. Which probably explains why it took Hoy so long to accept that it wasn't a wind-up. There is more to Sutton, though, than his role as joker or Mr Motivator. Hoy admits that Sutton was the one that finally made him, and the sprinters, feel like an integral part of the British team, purely by connecting with them at a human level. 'There was a real change for me when Shane came on board,' says Hoy. 'He was the first person who really understood us as riders. He didn't have the background in sports science or physiology, but he knew us as riders. He understood our personalities. Plus, all he's done is race bikes all his life. He knows bike racing inside out; it doesn't matter what discipline.

'The funny thing with Shane is that he has a very, very small ego,' Hoy continues. 'He's not the sort of coach who'll be standing next to you when you're having your picture taken with your gold medal.

He steps back. He doesn't seem to need credit or adulation, or even want to be seen to be part of it all. He's low-key when it comes to that. But his personality is not low-key. He is unique. That's what most people say about him. You will never meet anyone like Shane. He's a person who you never have a mediocre time with. It's either great or horrendous, but it's always intense. I mean, the number of times I've wanted to throttle the guy …'

Laughing, he explains: 'In the moments I've wanted to throttle him part of me thinks we should have a fight, because that would settle it. But another part of me thinks he'd probably kick the hell out of me, even though he's half my size. It's a no-win situation. Either I beat him up and that looks bad, because I'm half his age, twice his weight … or he kicks the shit out of me and I look like an idiot!

'You get annoyed,' Hoy continues, 'but Shane lives for the job, and you have to remind yourself of that. He puts in as much if not more than we do – and that's very rare. I think, to be honest, there are riders who put in less than Shane.'

If 2005 saw Hoy wobble, he came back in 2006 determined to bow out as a kilo rider 'with a flourish'. With the kilo gone, his first instinct was to focus on the team sprint, as Craig MacLean had done, while also trying his hand at the other two sprinters' events, the keirin and individual sprint.

First, though, there was unfinished business as a kilo rider. He would have to bounce back again from his disappointing third at the 2005 world championships in Los Angeles to try and retain his Commonwealth crown at the games in Melbourne, then regain his world title in Bordeaux. Then, he said, he would retire from the kilo. The only thing that might tempt him to extend his kilo career a little longer was the outside chance of an assault on Arnaud Tournant's ultimate world record, set at the highest track in the world, in Bolivia, in 2001. It would be a huge logistical feat;

it would be expensive; it would also be a supremely difficult record to beat, with Tournant's mark of 58.875 seconds recognized as one of the best in cycling. But Hoy was keen to have a go. And his father, David, was on the case.

The 2006 Commonwealth Games came early, in March. Hoy had a title to defend. His form was decent. But, on the night, there was an upset. One of the early riders to go, the Australian Ben Kersten, recorded 1.01.815, setting the mark for the later starters, including Jason Queally and last man Hoy, to try and beat. A curious thing happened, though. There seemed to be unusually long gaps between the starters. And, in those gaps, there was a noticeable dip in the temperature.

It has been noted before that the air temperature makes a big difference in the kilo. A sports scientist with the British team, Scott Gardner, has calculated that a degree is worth as much as a tenth of a second: a significant margin. How much the temperature dropped in the Melbourne arena is unclear – but most were agreed that it did get decidedly chilly. How did this happen? It has been suggested that external doors or vents were opened, though there is no evidence that it was part of an Australian conspiracy. Hoy insists that he wouldn't have won anyway. Ahead of him, Queally, another late starter, was back on top form, and, with his 1.01.849, he claimed silver behind Kersten – he perhaps had greater cause to be upset by the chill in the air. Hoy clocked 1.02.071 and had to settle for bronze.

When the open door 'conspiracy' was put to him at the time, Hoy rejected it: 'I got beaten fair and square; I have no complaints at all.' And Shane Sutton, a proud Aussie, has no time for any such conspiracy theories. 'You can quote me on this: "Bullshit!" The door might have opened, but that's not the point. Bottom line is he got beat. And he got beat because he hadn't done the yards. He was three weeks behind.'

Hoy admits the defeat to Kersten was 'a little depressing'. (Characteristically, Sutton puts it more dramatically: 'He's a classic mega-depressant, doesn't take defeat well at all. Doesn't show it in public though.') MacLean, who was fourth in the kilo (with 1.02.983), was also disappointed. 'We were both down after it,' says Hoy, 'but a day later Shane, Dave [Brailsford], Craig and I had a chat in one of the cabins in the athletes' village. Shane is brilliant at that – he helped turn round my attitude after Stuttgart [in 2003], but it was something that Dave said that resonated: "True champions aren't just people who get up and win all the time; the champion is someone who can deal with setbacks, turn it round, not be defeated by that ..." I remember thinking, yes, we've still got a chance to win a gold medal, in the team sprint. Scotland were not favourites by a long shot, but [with MacLean and Ross Edgar] we got up and put in a world-class time, 44.2 – it would have won the Sydney Olympics. And we beat England in the final. It was a great night.'

Better was to come a few weeks later in Bordeaux at the world championships: a rematch in the kilo with Kersten, which motivated Hoy no end. As Sutton puts it: 'The only way for Chris to turn it around is to go back and win the worlds. He has to remind people he's the man, he is number one.' It would also ensure there was no lasting hangover from his defeat at the Commonwealth Games. And, in the event, Hoy delivered, inflicting a crushing defeat on Kersten, his 1.01.361 over half a second better than his Australian rival (1.02.085). It re-established Hoy not only as the best in the world but as one of the best kilo riders of all time. His three world titles (2002, 2004, 2006) now left him just one behind the two riders who led the all-time list with four titles apiece – Lothar Thoms and Arnaud Tournant. Brailsford led the tributes. 'He's a phenomenal athlete and a joy to work with,' said the British performance director.

Another British success story in Bordeaux was a resurgent MacLean. The thirty-four year old was angry at being overlooked for the team sprint – Staff, Queally and Hoy were preferred for the qualifying round, though, in the reverse of what had happened at the Athens Olympics, MacLean came in for Queally in the final, with the British trio losing out again to the French. Then, just when he most needed to prove himself, MacLean did something in the individual sprint that no British sprinter had done since Reg Harris. He marched to the final, beating Mickael Bourgain in the semi-final, to meet the dominant Theo Bos, the reigning world champion, in the final. Bos won in two straight rides, but MacLean's silver gave Britain its first medal in the discipline since 1960, when Dave Handley claimed bronze, and the best since 1956, when Harris took silver in Copenhagen.

Hoy, who in the aftermath of his Bordeaux success spoke again of having suffered self-doubt ('It meant so much to me; I had a lot of doubt after the Commonwealth Games, and as you get older you start to question whether you are past your best'), maintains that his setbacks have acted as 'springboards to my real success. They give you a kick up the backside and force you to say, okay, you maybe need to change things, tweak things. If you keep winning all the time – and maybe this is what happened to Tournant, I'm not sure – then you're frightened to change things. That's only natural, because you think you've found a winning formula. But you have to change – if you don't, you stand still, and you don't progress. But in 2003, and to a lesser extent 2006, when you win after a setback, it's an amazing feeling. It's all the sweeter.'

If 2006 was a partial disappointment then 2007 was anything but. 'Almost a perfect year,' says Hoy, referring most obviously to the world championships in Palma de Mallorca, arguably the British track team's finest hour. It was here that Hoy won two world titles, the keirin and that fourth kilo, to leave him top of the all-time list, alongside Thoms and Tournant.

As with Frank Sinatra, Hoy's retirement seemed to be a long-drawn-out affair. In Palma, MacLean asked, jokingly, 'Is this your last kilo again Chris?' It was as if he was reluctant to take a final bow – and who could blame him? But, with the event absent from the Beijing Olympics the following year, it was definitely, finally, time to move on, and to focus on a discipline that could enable him to try and become the first British cyclist ever to win two Olympic gold medals.

There was only one thing left for Hoy as a kilo rider, one piece of unfinished business: the ultimate world record, set at the altitude of La Paz, Bolivia, by Tournant.

PART 3

Bolivia to Beijing

CHAPTER 10

What Are We Here For?

La Paz, Bolivia, May 2007

It is six weeks after the world championships in Palma de Mallorca, and we find ourselves in a sun-bleached sand-coloured concrete bowl, high in the Andes, perched on the only bit of flat ground for miles, and surrounded by jagged peaks. It is just after 9 a.m. on Saturday, 12 May 2007, and a crowd has gathered. From where, who knows, but the grandstand is half-full, mainly with dark-skinned locals from the city of La Paz, the Indian women in their flowing dresses and bowler hats, and, seated in the centre of the stand, some white faces – expats – including the British ambassador and his wife.

In the back row, the Bolivian Army brass band sits in a line, erupting into song every few minutes. But their cheerful tunes, belonging firmly to the oompah-oompah oeuvre, are incongruous: to a man, they wear surly expressions and dull army fatigues; as do the Bolivian police, who mill around in the centre of the track, keeping a wary eye on proceedings.

Just before 11 a.m., a hush falls. It is part nervous, part excited. Chris Hoy's track bike is being fixed to the start gate, right in front of the stand. And a few moments later, from a bright yellow tent in one end of the track centre, Hoy emerges. Lumbering and a little ungainly, he walks to another bike, mounts it, and pedals slowly around the track, reaching the home straight and silently dismounting. Then he walks onto the track and sits down before the bike.

Everyone is staring at him, even the army band, who performed a drum roll a couple of minutes earlier, when it was confirmed that the ride would go ahead. It is an intense kind of quiet, like a minute's silence. Hoy's face is set in a look of grim determination; we can stare all we like, he can't see us, can't see anything other than the bit of the track where his gaze is fixed. Hearts beat faster, throats constrict.

Hoy's mother, Carol, standing beside me in the track centre, with her knuckles fixed around a flag that, in a few moments will unfurl above her head, manages to lighten the mood. 'I must warn you that I'm *very* embarrassing to stand beside,' she confides, in hushed tones.

The bike stands in the start gate, as ominous as a scaffold. In front of it, Hoy sits on the slope of the track, arms hooked around his knees, head bowed, with the expression and demeanour of a condemned man. The sun threatens to break through the thin layer of white, hazy clouds; the high altitude air is cool but slowly beginning to warm; it is so thin, and so dry, that it feels as though a deep breath would scorch your lungs.

Eventually Hoy rises from his seated position on the track, walking awkwardly, in his cleated shoes, the couple of paces to his bike. He climbs aboard, sits up, breathes in deeply, and adjusts – with an aggressive slap – his helmet. Its mirrored visors conceal his eyes, making him look a little robotic or otherworldly, even sinister, like Darth Vader. The clock reads 30, then it starts counting down the seconds. Time begins to speed up; and the words from an old Guinness advert, featuring a curious and strangely terrifying melange of surfers and horses, come suddenly into my head. 'He waits; that's what he does.' Then: 'Tick followed tock followed tick followed tock followed tick.'

We are in the Alto Irpavi velodrome, which at 3,408 metres is the highest velodrome in the world – the highest sports arena in the world, say some. It is truly surreal. It is on the outskirts of the highest city in the world, La Paz in Bolivia, and Hoy is here, in the aftermath of his triumphant world championships in Palma, to try and break one of cycling's toughest records: the 1 km.

The existing record, 58.875 seconds – to date, the only sub-minute kilo ever ridden – was set on the same track in 2001 by Hoy's great rival, Arnaud Tournant. As we know, three years after establishing that apparently unbreakable record, Tournant travelled to Athens to try and add the Olympic crown, though he could only go agonizingly close, losing out to Hoy.

Hoy says this will be his final kilo. And he means it this time. It is his swansong. What a place for it.

With him here in La Paz is a ten-strong support team. It has been a long journey to get here. Most of the party travelled from Edinburgh – between thirty and thirty-six hours door-to-door. As I had observed to a friend before leaving, it was a hell of a long way to travel to see something that could last only fifty-eight seconds. 'Fifty-seven,' he replied.

For those who have organized the trip the journey has been longer – more than a year. By 'those' I really mean one person: Chris's father, David.

'Do you know what it feels like?' says David on the eve of our departure. 'It's like Chris is a teenager again and we're loading up the car and setting off on an adventure, not really knowing how it'll all turn out.' It was an adventure that had actually started twelve months earlier, and it was as meticulously planned as it could be. It had been Chris's idea. 'The catalyst was dropping the kilo from the Olympics,' David explains. 'He was looking at a way of signing off, and maybe he wanted to thumb his nose at the UCI; tell them, "This is what you're losing." There were a lot of ideas floating around but the world record was the one that got everyone excited. And Bolivia, of course, was the only place to do it.'

So David Hoy went to work trying to arrange sponsorship. He reckoned they would need £100,000. Chris was Olympic and world champion, as well as the sea level world record holder; raising £100,000 for an attempt that was sure to generate publicity couldn't be that difficult. Could it?

Yes, in fact it could. It proved impossible to raise that amount, and difficult to enthuse people in an event that might be witnessed by a couple of hundred locals, and perhaps some mules and llamas. Nobody seemed to understand that it was precisely this quirkiness that lent the project its appeal; that the surreal nature of the event made it more, not less interesting; that this was a record attempt that followed in the established, if eccentric, tradition of famous record attempts, especially by crazy Brits.

David Hoy's initial thinking was to sign up ten sponsors, paying £10,000 each. 'I wrote to some of the biggest companies in the country. I was thinking, let's get £100,000 and anything left over is a bonus for breaking the record. But there was nothing – a standard rejection letter in most cases.' It was only when the BBC came on board, to make a TV documentary about the attempt, that commercial backing was secured – though in the end the total raised was less than half the targeted £100,000. For Chris, it meant no bonus for breaking the record. He was doing it, in effect, for nothing; nothing except the glory of the world record. It added to the sheer quirkiness and eccentricity of it all.

Ultimately the money raised was enough: enough to transport nine large wooden crates, containing everything from Hoy's state-of-the-art carbon bike and wheels to the electronic start gate required for the kilo, and timing equipment; enough also to pay the travel and accommodation costs of the UCI officials and dope testers.

I arrive in La Paz on Wednesday, three days before the record attempt. Chris's parents had been there since Monday. But preparations at the rarely used Alto Irpavi velodrome had been going on for at least a fortnight, overseen mainly by 'Mr Bolivian cycling', Ruben Martinez, president of the Federacion Boliviana de Ciclismo.

Martinez is seventy-three but looks more like a forty-something. He holds every Bolivian age-standard record from forty upwards. From out of the blue, and with no prior introduction, David Hoy sent him an email to run past him the idea of his son's record attempt. Martinez responded by immediately travelling from his home in La Paz to the Alto Irpavi velodrome, armed with a video camera. Then he walked around the track, his camera honed on the line Hoy would take for his kilo attempt, his narrative describing every hole, blemish and crack in the concrete, his hand – hovering over the surface – indicating the bits that Hoy should pay particular attention to. 'Bumpy surface here,' said Martinez on the grainy video that he then emailed back to David Hoy.

The Alto Irpavi track is seldom used for international competition – some claimed that Tournant's world record in 2001 was the last event of note – and so a lick of paint and tidy-up were well overdue. In fact, more than that was needed: work was also needed to fill in some of the cracks and gaps, and to smooth the bumps, on the track itself. David Hoy's reaction upon seeing it for the first time was damning: 'It's worse than Meadowbank!' But it is thanks to Martinez, and a few other Bolivian cyclists, that it remains in use at all.

On Thursday, two days before the record attempt, I pay a visit to the velodrome, a journey that involves a taxi ride out of town, down a hill, through the suburbs, and then up a winding, dusty track, with one recurring question occupying my brain: there can't possibly be a velodrome at the end of this, can there?

Astonishingly there is, and the scene, just forty-eight hours before the world record attempt, is extraordinary. There is bustling activity, with around thirty locals, including women in traditional Indian dress, all supremely focused on their tasks. In their flowing polleras and bowler hats – sitting square on their heads if they are married, tilted at an angle if they are single – the women sweep the steps of the stand with their traditional brooms. On the back wall an old man skilfully applies the last drops of paint to a message extolling the virtues of sport at altitude. Meanwhile, painted depictions of racing cyclists are being added at the entrance to the sand-coloured structure, much of it a spider's web of cracks and crumbling concrete. It is strange and a little poignant to see such intricate artwork being applied to such a building – almost as if it is being glued together by the paint.

In the track centre, Carol Hoy describes all this activity as 'moving'. She says the locals' efforts to transform the velodrome 'is like something you see on a TV makeover show – it's like Changing Velodromes'. A few days earlier, she tells me, the women had spent the day in the track centre with scythes, hacking back the grass. At that stage it had looked like a field; you could barely see the back straight from the main stand. Now, from the distance of the stand at least, it resembled a bowling green, albeit one scorched brown.

What makes this all the more humbling, or moving, is that Bolivia is a country blighted by serious poverty. Of the country's 8.8 million population, almost 15 per cent live on less than a dollar a day. Of all the South American countries, it has the highest proportion of native Indians.

La Paz itself is an incredible, otherworldly place. Driving into the city from the airport, you travel initially through areas of shanty town, with fragile looking shacks by the sides of broken, crumbling roads, which in places are little more than dirt tracks. But eventually the track turns to a road that crests the lip of a hill, and presents the most amazing scene: the city itself, crammed into a giant crater, sparkling and shimmering at night like a billion diamonds thrown into a well.

During the day the scene is far more revealing of the poverty. Daylight reveals not diamonds but a mass of tightly packed, uniformly pale buildings, nestled in the crater and clustered around a small business district, a tiny dot of high-rise towers and glistening black glass, hemmed in on all sides by extreme poverty.

It is sights such as these – the crumbling buildings, the stoicism and resilience of the people who live there, and the regular-as-clockwork early morning protests on the streets of La Paz – that prompt Carol Hoy to describe the scene inside the velodrome as 'moving'.

The daily demonstrations provide a diversion. The most serious of them, in the week we were there, was on the Tuesday, when the security police protested about poor pay in comparison with the normal police. The normal police fired tear gas and for a moment it threatened to spiral into a violent confrontation. But the other protests passed without incident, including Friday's. 'On Fridays it's the teachers,' I was told. So there appears to be a rota.

As well as the efforts being made to make the velodrome fit for a world record attempt, it is apparent that Chris Hoy has been

adopted as something of a hero by people starved of major sporting events. But on the Thursday we realize that there is a problem. The posters produced to advertise the world record attempt
describe the Scottish cyclist, in large lettering, as 'Ciclesta Inglés
Chris Hoy' – 'English cyclist Chris Hoy'. Oh dear. Still, it was nothing that couldn't be sorted out with some black masking tape.
Many of the posters were thus altered to read: 'Ciclista [blank] Chris
Hoy.'

I explore the bowels of the Alto Irpavi velodrome and come
across yet another surreal scene: a clubhouse bedecked with
cycling posters and a counter serving as a café. Behind the counter
is a picture of Jesus Christ, yet it isn't this portrait that forms the
centrepiece to the small gallery: that instead is another icon, Fausto
Coppi, the Italian cyclist of the post-war years. Coppi won the Tour
de France and Giro d'Italia – the picture is a familiar one, showing him climbing a pass during the Tour – but it isn't clear, other
than in deference to his status as a cycling god, why he is afforded
pride of place in the Alto Irpavi clubhouse. Perhaps because he
was one of the first European stars to race on South American
roads, in the Tour of Colombia.

Beyond Christ and Coppi the walls of the clubhouse comprise
an eclectic gallery. There is a picture of Chris Boardman, en route
to gold at the Barcelona Olympics. Then there are old posters
advertising events at the velodrome, and a list of the fifteen world
records established here: no other velodrome in the world can
boast so many. There is no question, however, of the Alto Irpavi
velodrome's proudest hour – or minute. Or, to be absolutely
precise, 58.875 seconds.

There is a collage of pictures from Tournant's kilo record
in 2001, dominated by a spectacular image of the Frenchman
circling the track at its highest point, the jagged peaks of the
Andes rising up behind him. It is as if the velodrome is perched

at the summit of a mountain, with a sheer drop all around. There are also faded cuttings from *L'Equipe* and other newspapers, proclaiming Tournant's feat as one of the greatest in the history of cycling. The other world record set that day, by Tournant's countryman Arnaud Dublé, for 500 m, is almost a footnote; and poor Laurent Gané, who was here to tackle the 200 m mark, is shown in a bloody, painful state. He crashed heavily during his ride, apparently, in part at least, because of the dizzy state he found himself in, a result of the lack of oxygen.

Or so the rumour goes. And this is one of the intriguing aspects of Hoy's record attempt: that Tournant's is shrouded in so much mystery. 'There's no real information out there of Tournant's ride,' explained Scott Gardner, the sports scientist who accompanied Hoy to his pre-record training camp in Florida and then on to La Paz. 'There's no footage of it, no real data at all.'

Yet some of the stories – true or false – about Tournant's attempt have passed into folklore, and now contribute heavily to the mythology surrounding the kilo record. What is known is that his approach was very different to Hoy's. Whereas Hoy is flying in at the last minute, and is due to arrive in La Paz just twenty-four hours before his record attempt, Tournant was apparently in La Paz for longer, allowing his body to acclimatize and adjust to the oxygen-starved air. The story goes, however, that he remained in his room for the first three days – why, nobody in the Hoy party seemed to know. Perhaps he, like most of us, had been struck down by altitude sickness – a condition that, as I can attest, renders you barely able to move.

But another Tournant story had caused more alarm. Following his ride, we were told the Frenchman collapsed and passed out. He was, we were told, unconscious for almost half an hour. This is an aspect of this adventure that Carol Hoy is understandably concerned about. A sleep nurse in Edinburgh, she knows all about the dangers, for those with sleeping disorders, of being starved of oxygen. It was also felt that the dangers of competing at altitude would be heightened in Hoy's case by the approach he was choosing to take.

Like many, I had been under the impression that if an athlete competed at high altitude then he must first acclimatize: I thought that was the whole point, that the body adapted to the thinner air by producing more oxygen-carrying red blood cells, thus gaining a physiological advantage. But Hoy's record attempt in La Paz has nothing to do with physiology. As he explained: 'Because the kilo is essentially an anaerobic event, there is no real advantage in being acclimatized. From a performance point of view, any adverse reaction from making a maximum effort at altitude is going to come after the effort. It's going to be grim, I know that, but if you've got a world record … you can handle a bit of pain then.'

In other words, there was a refreshingly unscientific – for a non-scientist like me, at least – explanation for going to La Paz to try and break the world record. The air was thinner – literally less dense – and it therefore offered less resistance: you travelled faster through it, or slowed down at a slower rate. This was illustrated when my plane landed: it took an alarming length of time to slow down. Apparently the runway at La Paz airport is one of the longest in the world for this very reason. Similarly, when football matches are played in La Paz a disproportionate number of goals tend to be scored from speculative long-range shots – and by long-range I mean forty or fifty yards – whereby the ball thunders, as if jet-propelled, into the net. It is one reason why international football matches have been banned in La Paz, which is something the Bolivians aren't very happy about. Never has the term 'home advantage' carried so much weight.

For Hoy, it had been a question of weighing up the different risks in the two possible approaches – arriving early and acclimatizing, but risking picking up an infection or being unsettled by an unfamiliar environment; or remaining in a comfortable sea-level environment until the eleventh hour, then flying in and attempting the record before the body has had the chance to realize that it is at altitude.

But this approach carried risks too, as Hoy himself had hinted at with his casual 'you can handle a bit of pain then' remark. The problem would be that when his body really needed oxygen – in the closing stages of the ride, or just after – it would be shocked to find that the air contained – to be strictly accurate – 33 per cent less of the stuff than at sea level. It might react badly to that.

That is putting it mildly. And so it is no wonder that Carol Hoy is concerned. Back in Edinburgh, she approached a specialist in human physiology at altitude, Dr Kenneth Baillie, a young Scot with the quiet self-assurance and cool detachment that is reassuring to discover in a doctor. Baillie runs an organization called APEX (Altitude Physiology Expeditions), and he has been on several field trips to Bolivia with subjects, mainly students, to observe the effects of altitude on their bodies. He is, he says, 'fascinated by the effects on human physiology of altitude'.

What he reveals is just as fascinating, in a ghoulish sort of way. He states, for example, that if you were to be instantly transported from sea level to 6,000 metres – the height of the mountain looming up behind the velodrome – then you would die. 'Within twenty minutes,' he says earnestly. 'The risks are very real and I have explained them to Chris,' Baillie continues, as he demonstrates the oxygen-filled 'body bag' that would be trackside, awaiting Hoy, should he slip out of consciousness.

'The procedure he's following, flying in at the last minute, is designed to give him the best possible chance of breaking the record,' explains Baillie in a mildly disapproving tone. 'Well, his sole aim is to get the record. But my aim is different – I want him to be healthy. When he finishes the kilo he will be enormously short on oxygen and he'll have acidic blood. He's prepared for the fact that he's going to feel extremely unwell. But he seems quite up for that. He's a very determined man.'

Can it really be that dangerous? 'Yes. It can be that dangerous,' replies Baillie. 'There are very real risks. My fear is that he suffers high altitude pulmonary edema [HAPE], where fluid builds up on the lungs. For someone already in oxygen debt that can be fatal. But he is an elite athlete. If anyone can take the strain on their body, he can.'

Forty-eight hours out from the record attempt, Baillie was going through several possible scenarios. The oxygen canisters and inflatable body bag were in place. An ambulance would be on standby, and Baillie has calculated that he could be in a first-class medical facility within minutes.

Or so he thought. He has neglected, however, to take into account the strict anti-doping rules that exist in international sport; and he is duly informed, by the UCI official who has travelled to La Paz to monitor the attempt, that Hoy would not be permitted to go anywhere until he had submitted a sample to the anti-doping officer.

A compromise was reached: if necessary, Mr Dope Control would travel with him in the ambulance.

'Have you heard?' asks David Hoy. It is early – very early – on the morning before the record attempt.

'No, what?'

'Chris's plane has gone missing.'

This has the effect of waking me up – conjuring up images of another plane to go missing over the Andes, an event that led to the book and film *Alive*, chronicling cannibalism in the mountains. But the report proves to be a slight exaggeration.

En route to La Paz, from Miami, Hoy's plane developed problems with its hydraulics. 'I knew we were in trouble,' said one of those on the flight, 'when the pilot came on and introduced himself as Captain John Thomas.' Given the added complications of landing at high altitude – specifically the difficulties of stopping – Captain John Thomas opted to divert to another – sea level – Bolivian city, Santa Cruz.

'It shouldn't be too much of a problem,' says David Hoy, after clearing up the initial confusion, and admitting that his son was unlikely to be devoured by cannibalistic fellow passengers. 'He should be in by ten. Eleven at the latest.' It is 7 a.m. The overnight flight had been due to land at 5.45 a.m.

By 10 a.m., the expected arrival time has been adjusted to midday. By midday, the expected arrival time has been revised to 2.30 p.m. By 2.30 p.m., there is even more uncertainty. Hoy, Gardner and the official photographer are still at a small airport in Santa Cruz. Waiting.

At 7 p.m., roughly twenty-two hours after leaving Miami, after approximately ten hours of hanging around airports, and after a two-hour transfer between airports in Santa Cruz, Hoy finally arrives in La Paz.

There is a small party to meet him. Ruben Martinez, all seventy-three years of him, appears as excited as a child as he chats to reporters. 'There were not very many people for Tournant, but Tournant didn't have the results that Chris has – Chris is a superstar!' he says. Martinez smiles broadly, his lean frame exuding enthusiasm and his pencil moustache bobbing up and down as he speaks. 'There hasn't been this much excitement before and everyone is waiting for Saturday. The stand will be full; it's been on Bolivian television and they have been writing a lot about Chris in the papers. Nobody expected Tournant to go under a minute – it was incredible – but I'm very confident Chris will go faster. Oh yes, definitely! Chris is going to fly!' Martinez was also making a world record attempt – the 2,000 m mark for over-seventies. 'After Chris it will be my turn,' he beams. 'I think I'll be inspired by him.'

From the airport, Hoy travels directly to the track. First he walks slowly around it, studying the surface, visualizing the ride. In his grey hooded top, with his head down, he looks like a boxer. Then he completes a full race warm-up – a forty-minute routine. It is a stunning evening, the sun bathing the track in a pleasant, glowing heat. There is not a breath of wind; it is almost eerily still. Tiny tubes carry oxygen into Hoy's nostrils whenever he is off his bike; but on it, without the oxygen, he says he hardly notices that he is at altitude. Everything is perfect. He is ready to go; has never been readier. He confirms: he will go for the record in the morning.

But in the morning the conditions have changed. It is cool, chilly even. Hoy rides around the track in long sleeves and leggings. His support team, especially Gardner, appear anxious and nervous.

Warm-up completed, Hoy disappears into the tent, where he continues his warm-up on static rollers, an oxygen mask clasped to his face. A decision has to be taken. It is cool, but relatively still. As the morning wears on, and the sun rises, the wind would pick up – this has been the pattern all week. It had been twelve degrees at 8 a.m., rising to fourteen degrees at 8.45: sixteen was the minimum at which he would attempt the record. 'The effect of temperature on time is substantial,' explains Gardner. 'It's almost a tenth of a second per degree.'

Behind the blanket of clouds the sun is rising, slowly warming the air. But the wind, blowing in brief gusts through the velodrome, and lifting the three flags from their poles – Bolivian, Union Jack and Saltire – appears to be picking up.

Gardner, who had been checking the data with the time-keepers, and discussing the conditions with Hoy's parents, eventually disappears into the tent. It is rumoured that Hoy might go for the 200 m or 500 m record instead, saving the kilo for tomorrow, when there might be more favourable conditions. But the idea of not going for the kilo is anathema to him. 'Realistically, Chris has three days to get this record,' Gardner explains. 'That's the window. He might not get to try it tomorrow. We don't know what the weather's going to do. He could be floored by altitude sickness, because it usually takes twenty-four hours to hit you. I feel that it could be now or never.' Gardner goes to see Hoy, still warming up on the rollers inside the tent, and asks him a question that requires no answer: 'What are we here for?'

Tick followed tock followed tick …

The silence is broken by a bang: Hoy explodes from the start gate, his mouth open in silent roar, the crowd providing the soundtrack, shouting and cheering, his mother fulfilling her earlier promise, screaming 'Come on Chris!' and waving her Saltire – 'The Real McHoy' written across it – above her head.

Because the Alto Irpavi velodrome is long – 333 m as opposed to the 250 m of the indoor wooden tracks where Hoy normally races – there is a curious, deathly silence as Hoy completes the first corner of his kilo world record attempt and enters the back straight. The noise dies away completely, and we watch him race up that straight for what seems like an eternity: it looks as if he is pedalling in slow motion, as if he is in a silent movie.

Then he appears in the home straight, appearing to speed up as the noise erupts again. He flashes across the finish line, mouth still open in silent roar. The timekeepers pore over their computer screens and then convey the information to Gardner: he is almost a second up on Tournant's record. A second. A second!

Now he is on the back straight again, pedalling silently, looking as if he is far more in the distance than he actually is; taking an age to reach the bend. Then, again, around the corner, the volume increasing, the sense now that it must all come out – the noise from the crowd as much as the strength in Hoy's legs – for the final lap, the final push. And again the study of the computer screens, and the information passed to Gardner. The lead has fallen slightly, but he is still 0.873 seconds up on Tournant.

The back straight, the silence, the slow motion; then around the arc of the final corner, and the first sign that the effort is beginning to tell, a noticeable wobble as he enters the back straight, shoulders swaying; and now a roar as loud as the one that greeted his starting effort as he races down the home straight, across the line, and into silence. It is a horrible silence that can only mean one thing: failure. The clock has stopped at 59.103 seconds. We have just witnessed the second fastest kilo in history: twenty-three hundredths of a second slower than Tournant.

Hoy knows. He knows as soon as he hears nothing. His momentum carries him around the bend and into the back straight, where he slows rapidly, and stops by Kenneth Baillie. He collapses to the ground as the doctor attaches an oxygen mask to his face.

A small crowd gathers around him, including his mother, who, still clutching her flag, has sprinted across the grass. But after seven minutes he removes the mask, and gets back on his bike, cycling around to the home straight. He stops to clap the crowd as they in turn shower him with warm applause. Then he turns towards his father and embraces him. But already he is preoccupied by two thoughts. The first is that the effort hadn't taken as much out of him as he feared. The other is that he hadn't come 6,000 miles, at a cost of £40,000, to become the second fastest man in history.

He describes the ride. 'My head exploded on lap three. It was all I could do to keep pedalling. It's really frustrating and disappointing, but I rode the best race I could in the conditions. I deliberately went out quick – that was the decision we made in training, and I was nearly a second up when my head blew off. I've never experienced anything like it; there was no oxygen coming in. It was like being underwater. Last night when I was training here it was fifteen degrees warmer – so if a degree is worth a tenth of a second, as we've calculated, then do your own maths. But I'm not downhearted. We're here for three days and I haven't come all this way not to break the record. We'll monitor the weather carefully and if there's any possibility of another attempt we'll take it.' Baillie, meanwhile, declares himself 'blown away' by Hoy's recovery. 'I'm delighted, and as far as I'm concerned he can go for it again – but it's up to Chris.'

Nobody disappears from the track yet, though. First there is the small matter of Martinez and his record attempt. The atmosphere is initially muted, but as the seventy-three-year-old retired mining engineer enters the closing stages there's clapping and cheering, reaching a crescendo as he crosses the line, 0.2 seconds inside the old record. He raises a hand and wobbles, almost falling. When he stops on the home straight Hoy goes to meet him and lifts Martinez's arm, then steps back to lead the applause and to allow Martinez to enjoy his moment.

On the journey back to the hotel Hoy speaks to his father, and what follows is exactly the same kind of conversation that father and son used to have after BMX races: a rational discussion of what went wrong; logical rather than emotional – Steve Peters would be impressed. 'If that's as bad as it gets at altitude then I can go tomorrow and hit it,' Hoy tells his father. His father asks him if all the talk of the potential danger had bothered him – more to the point, had the prospect of imminent death put him off his ride? 'I think so, yes, with people telling me I could die doing it. You're never going to give 100 per cent with that thought in your head. You're going into the unknown and you might subconsciously hold something back if you're a little bit scared.'

Speaking later to the media – both of us – Hoy says, 'I will invoke the spirit of Obree,' recalling the exploits of another Scottish cyclist, Graeme Obree, who failed in 1993 to break the world hour record, but, remarkably, got up the next morning and smashed it. A second kilo in twenty-four hours was more doable than a full hour, reasoned Hoy. Plus, he wouldn't be scared. And he wouldn't hold anything back – not even subconsciously.

It is Sunday morning, 9 a.m. The sun is climbing, the sky is blue; it is warm, breathless. The crowd that had half-filled the velodrome the previous day has gone; the place is virtually empty, filled only with echoing voices. In this rarefied atmosphere, there is a distinct lack of atmosphere.

Of the few 'supporters' in the velodrome, some of us position ourselves on the inside of the second bend. It was here, the previous day, where Hoy seemed to wobble – a wobble that was probably enough to cost him the record. A little bit of encouragement here on the third lap, on the final bend, could make a difference – could make *the* difference. So we stand and wait, and Hoy goes through the same routine: sitting on the track, staring down, then rising and climbing aboard the bike, sitting upright, aggressively slapping the helmet into position, and then leaning forward and gripping the handlebars. Then, bang!

After a lap he's up, less than yesterday but perhaps he's holding something back for that final lap ... after two laps, he's still up: and now there is nobody in the velodrome who doesn't think he'll claim the record; that we are on the brink of witnessing something special; and so we steal ourselves to erupt into wild celebrations as he crosses the line.

But first, on that final bend, we clench our fists and pump our arms and yell at Hoy as he whizzes past. There is no wobble this time – or none that we can see. He flashes across the line. I am running to the finish area. 'Awesome ride, Chris,' screams Gardner after Hoy, but it echoes around the stadium. The wild celebrations have not erupted; it is ghostly silence again. And it says it all. His mother looks crestfallen. Hoy manages half a lap and then slows to a halt and all but falls off his bike. He slumps to the grass, head bowed between his legs, as Baillie goes through the routine of attaching an oxygen mask to his face, and his mother tries to hold him upright.

Although there are virtually no spectators today there are several photographers. They cluster on the track in front of him, snapping away. After several minutes he pulls the oxygen mask to the side and asks his mother for a towel, which he drapes over his head. His mother politely waves away the photographers, who oblige. When Hoy removes the towel his eyes appear puffy.

The clock said 58.880 seconds. That was his time this time: 58.880 seconds, compared to Tournant's 58.875 – five thousandths of a second is the difference. An analysis of his split times showed that his strategy had been subtly different to the previous day: he started slightly slower (22.553 seconds for the first lap; 22.35 the previous day), and was still marginally down after two laps (40.174 compared to 39.997), but on this occasion he managed a steadier ride – a final lap of 18.706 (19.106 the previous day) that saw him flash across the line in 58.880. Five thousandths of a second, or 2.3 cm – that was all that he missed the record by; 2.3 cm, the difference between success and failure, though 'failure' seems an inappropriate description. But that was it, says Hoy. 'It's not a possibility to go for it again,' he says. 'In an ideal world I could stay, recover and go a bit quicker, but not tomorrow, not after doing two rides like that in tweny-four hours. I've always said when I've been beaten by a small margin that you can't be disappointed if you feel that you've got it all out – and I feel that I did get it all out. I gave it absolutely everything I could and really put my heart and soul into that ride. But when I crossed the line and there wasn't a cheer I knew I hadn't done it.'

Later, he reflects some more on the closeness of it all: 'I didn't realize how close it was. The margin was a little waver off my line, that's all. You can speculate – if I hadn't gone yesterday I might have gone better today; if I hadn't had the problems on Friday with the flight … you know, there are 101 excuses I could make, but I don't want to make excuses, because that's what life's about. It doesn't always go your way.

'It's an amazing record. I've always respected Tournant but I've got a huge amount of respect for what he achieved here. I laid everything on the line here and it wasn't enough. Today was the best chance I had. Yesterday I was fully committed but today was perfect, though the effort hurt more. The defeat makes it worse. When you win you don't feel a thing; when you lose you really feel it. You feel that all that pain and suffering has been in vain. I'm so deflated. But I gave it my best shot and it wasn't enough.

'But hey,' he smiles, 'nobody died.'

He sends a text message to Arnaud Tournant. 'Your record's safe,' it says.

'Hi Chris,' comes Tournant's reply, 'Thanks for your message. That remains a big performance. Do not forget we are the only two to pass under the mythical time of one minute. Congratulations on your time and see you soon to share your experience.'

Hoy writes back, saying that Tournant should feel proud to have kept the record. 'Yes, it's true, I'm satisfied to keep my record, but you deserved to beat it,' responds Tournant. 'You remain all the same a major figure in the kilo and a big champion. Do you take a new attempt?' Hoy doesn't reply.

CHAPTER 11

Finally, a World Record

Still in La Paz, Bolivia, May 2007

There is a postscript to the Bolivia adventure. And it is a happy one. There was a sense, after the second kilo, the one that was 0.005 seconds slower than Tournant's record (had they been racing side-by-side then it would have taken a photograph to separate them), that Hoy had got everything out. That it had taken him so near to – and yet so far from – the record was agony, of course. But, having made two attempts, he had nothing left, physically, psychologically, emotionally. He needed, for peace of mind if nothing else, to forget about it. To put it behind him. To move on.

But, equally, he couldn't quite bring himself to leave Bolivia without a world record. And so he decided, as the blazing sun heated up the Alto Irpavi velodrome in the late afternoon, just hours after his second kilo attempt, to have a crack at the flying world 500-metre record. That was the other record broken on the day that Tournant set his magical kilo, by another Frenchman,

Arnaud Dublé. Hoy thought initially about a crack at Dutchman Theo Bos's flying 200 m record. But ultimately he decided not to, reasoning that it could be construed as unsporting behaviour to attempt to snatch a world record at altitude that had been set at sea level. Bos's super fast time, of 9.772 seconds, was achieved in Moscow.

Since Dublé's 500 m mark of 25.850 seconds was established in La Paz, it was an entirely different matter – fair game. And so, in the late afternoon of a perfectly still Bolivian day, Hoy went through his warm-up all over again, all forty minutes of it – slow laps of the track, punctuated by brief sprints, laps where he wound up the pace and then slowed; then on to the rollers, legs spinning on autopilot. And then, finally, he was ready to go.

Unlike the kilo, the 500 m involved a flying start. He circled the track slowly at first, winding it up. Lap by lap his pace increased, and so did his position on the track: from the inside he gradually moved up until he was hugging the top of the track, at the highest point of the banking, that astonishing and vast backdrop of mountains just over his shoulder. And then, following Scott Gardner's instruction, he swooped down, diving from the top of the banking to gain maximum speed as the clock started at the line halfway along the back straight – 500 to go.

A lap-and-a-half. He thundered through the finish line directly in front of the main stand – not across it, but through it. The sheer speed was remarkable – Hoy admitted later that it felt as though he had never ridden a bike so fast before. He rode as if liberated – from the pressure of going for the kilo, and from the fear of collapse as the longer effort told. With the 500, the gloves were off: he attacked it with everything he had – everything he had left. And that initial, blistering speed was maintained – possibly increased – around that final lap, the clock stopping at 24.758 seconds as he hit the line.

It was tempting to wonder, later, what he might have done for the kilo had he just kept going, but there was no time for that now – this time there was, finally, the much-anticipated outburst of applause and cheering. There might not have been many people in the velodrome, but they generated the noise that had been building, without release, since that first kilo attempt, thirty-two hours earlier.

A time of 24.758 seconds – more than a second quicker than Dublé. The record hadn't been broken – it had been obliterated. Hoy had put it on the shelf; a very high shelf at that. Because the shorter distance is rarely raced, it perhaps didn't get the headlines it merited – and of course it didn't give Hoy the satisfaction that the kilo record would have given him. But here's the thing: it is difficult to imagine it ever being beaten.

This time there was no collapse. As Hoy had said, there is no tiredness when you win. He rode around the track, into the home straight, waved at the small crowd in the stand, and then stopped to embrace his father, then his mother, as they draped him in the Saltire and posed for pictures, all three of them. 'I put all my frustrations from the kilo into that,' said Hoy. 'I've never gone so fast in my life. I've got a record. It's not the one I wanted, but I'm happy that I can go home with that.' He still had one more day in La Paz. He definitely couldn't be tempted to go for the kilo again? 'No, definitely not. Right now I'm just looking forward to a night without oxygen tubes stuffed up my nose.'

That night, back in the Ritz Plaza Hotel in central La Paz, the Hoys threw a party in their top floor suite. It seemed that everyone who had been in the velodrome over the course of the weekend was there. It was a celebration, though an understandably muted one. People were willing a party to happen, which wasn't easy. Nobody, of course, wanted to acknowledge the elephant in the corner – the kilo record, still in Tournant's hands. In fact, the

Frenchman's grip on it had never looked tighter. Much of the conversation concerned Tournant, in fact. The sense of wonder at his record had increased, the questions had become more pressing, the mystery heightened. Fertile ground for rumours to flourish.

'He locked himself in his room for three days and no one saw him.'

'I heard it was a week.'

'They had a budget of £500,000.'

'I heard he went in the late afternoon.'

'He must have done – in the pictures the sun is in the west.'

'The technique he used was to ride a measured first couple of laps and sprint the final one – he did it totally differently to Chris.'

Hoy allowed himself a couple of beers and then made a speech. He thanked Ruben Martinez and presented him with a gift. He thanked all the Bolivians who had helped with the record attempt.

'I'm not just saying this,' Hoy told the small gathering, 'but although I've been around the world and competed in so many incredible places, I've genuinely never had an experience like I've had here. It's been an amazing trip, an amazing experience. The people have been so warm, friendly and helpful, and the place itself is like nowhere else on earth. I'll never forget it.'

The next day we all became tourists: a day trip was organised to Lake Titicaca. In a convoy of two cars we travelled through the streets of La Paz, climbing out of the city, glancing back down at the incredible sight of it crammed into the crater, and up through the shanty towns, to a road block. A queue of traffic, alongside an enormous protest march, filtered slowly through a wall of policemen, but the car containing the Hoy family had a problem.

'Licence!' barked the policeman.

'No licence,' said David Hoy.

'Passport!' said the policeman.

'Hotel,' replied Mr Hoy, shrugging and holding up his hands. 'Chris Hoy, campeón del mundo,' he added, handing over a signed postcard of his son, sitting cringing in the passenger seat (and still, surreally and a little comically, with an oxygen mask attached to his face).

'Ah!' said the policeman. 'Gracias.'

The road to Lake Titicaca took us across a desolate, lunar land-scape. It felt very close to the sky. We arrived, via primitive ferries, punted by ferrymen across a short stretch of water, in a small village, and entered a restaurant. It was, all agreed, 'a nice day out', but Chris seemed a little distant. As soon as he finished lunch – an unidentified fried fish, washed down with some local beer – he got up and left. 'He doesn't do small talk,' joked his mum.

From Bolivia Hoy had a few days in Miami with his parents before travelling on to Mauritius for a holiday with his girlfriend – finally, the end-of-season holiday that most of his rivals and team-mates had enjoyed six weeks earlier, after the world cham-pionships in Palma. Would Bolivia play on his mind? Could he switch off? He wouldn't have his bike, but he had made sure to book a hotel with a gym – of course he had. How long would he stay out of it?

'I didn't feel too down at the end of it all,' he said when he came back. 'It was more a feeling of closure, knowing that was the last kilo. It was almost relief. I could move on and focus on Beijing. And I did stay out of the weights room … for a few days.'

No, he insisted, he didn't go over and over that second attempt in his head, agonizing over the five-thousandths of a second that separated him from the record. 'If you overanalyse stuff it can rip you apart,' he explained. 'There were small things,' he added. 'Like the front wheel …' The front wheel? 'Er … well, yeah, the front wheel. I went online when I was in Miami. And I was on a website

– a forum where they were discussing the record attempt. And someone, an American, said something: "I noticed Chris Hoy's wheel was in backwards – I guess the British team must have done some tests in the wind tunnel and found that those wheels are more aerodynamic when reversed ..."' If only. 'It was a mistake, my fault,' said Hoy. 'I've no idea what it cost us in terms of time. You think about it, but I don't blame anyone. I should have noticed ...'

There was still something from Bolivia that I wanted to clear up. It was the mystery surrounding Tournant's record-breaking ride in 2001. We heard so many stories and rumours, many of them contradictory, that the task of separating fact from fiction was impossible. And as Scott Gardner noted, there was little published information on his attempt – either the preparation or the record-breaking ride itself.

Could Hoy not just have asked Tournant? Well, no – not really. While on the one hand the two have become good friends, on the other, they are also rivals. It is true that Tournant could have volunteered information that would have been useful to Hoy. But Hoy would not have asked. And, tellingly, Tournant, though he encouraged Hoy, and supported his effort, did not rush forward with advice. Yet who could blame Tournant for keeping his cards close to his chest? He had been there, done it, and learnt the hard way – why should the man trying now to break his record benefit from that?

After we returned from Bolivia, though, it seemed reasonable to put some questions to Tournant, in the hope of gleaning some more information – and dispelling some of the myths. When I next saw him I asked him; and with a smile, Tournant willingly agreed to help. 'Yes, of course,' he said in his near-perfect English. 'You send me email Reechard, and I will answer questions.'

'Are you sure?' I said, 'we could just talk like this, face-to-face, if you prefer.'

'No-no-no, I prefer email.'

Five months, several emails, numerous texts, and a few phone calls later, Tournant emailed back (my questions are in italics).

When did you arrive in La Paz – how close was it to your world record attempt?

'We arrived one week before the attempt. We actually planned to make the attempt three or four days after our arrival, but the [electronic] start gate was kept at customs in America, and we had to delay our attempt for a few days until it arrived.'

What did you think of the city, and how did you adapt to the altitude? Did you do any specific preparation, in advance, for the altitude?

'La Paz is a stunning city and a little surreal. When I arrived there, I asked myself, can there really be a velodrome here? And when I discovered it, it was really incredible to see the velodrome lost in the mountains. It took me a few days to get used to the altitude, and I confess that the hardest thing for me wasn't the effort of riding the kilo in itself, but rather these peculiar conditions. But I managed to get used to them, under very tight medical surveillance. [Tournant was accompanied by a sizeable entourage, with, as well as Dublé and Gané, members of the Cofidis professional cycling team's staff.] In terms of preparation I didn't do anything special except one very specific test at altitude, before my record attempt, to make sure I wasn't in danger.'

Your kilo world record is incredible, incroyable! Is that the best you have ever felt on a bike? If so, how do you think you were able to find such form?

'It is true that this record is incredible; even today I can hardly believe that I have managed to go so fast! It is true, as we saw with Chris, but also with previous records, that the altitude contributes to excellent times. In my case I think that what was very important – crucial – was the organization of my sponsor Cofidis, who supported my record and allowed me to concentrate on it without having to worry about anything else at all.'

How would you compare your performance in Bolivia with your performance at the Olympics in Athens in 2004 [where Tournant was second to Hoy]?

'These two kilos for me are the most beautiful kilos, but it is true that the conditions at altitude are very particular. I think that the main difference is what is at stake; at the Olympic Games we find ourselves in the very biggest competition, with all of our adversaries, whereas for the world record you are alone against yourself. It is the difference: in one you are competing against others, in the other with yourself.'

You must have been surprised when you saw the time you recorded. Can you remember what your reaction was on seeing that you'd done 58.875 seconds? Did you think such a time was possible?

'I remember very well this moment, but when I finished my kilo, I thought more about the physical pain of the effort and the lack of oxygen than the time. However, when I saw the smile on the face of my trainer, I understood that I had broken the minute barrier – I realized then that I had passed under the minute! But 58.875 remains a time that I couldn't believe; that I couldn't think I could do.'

We were told that you collapsed after your world record, and that you were unconscious for 20 minutes ... is that true? Do you remember how you felt? And were you aware of the dangers of competing at altitude in advance of your ride? Did it scare you at all?

'No, I was not unconscious, but I had to wait thirty minutes before I could talk ... and it took me about an hour before I could

walk again! I remember that my team had to cut open my suit –
my top and shorts – because I had the feeling that my legs doubled
in size! I was conscious before my ride of the dangers of altitude,
but I wasn't expecting such pain.'

*The difference between your ride and Chris's seems to be that
you went faster at the end. Chris went fast at the start but slowed
down, while you maintained incredible speed. Was that the strategy you planned in advance – to hold a little back at the start in
order to maintain speed, or even try and accelerate, in the final
lap?*

'I think that the difference between my last race, which was
the world championships in Antwerp, and La Paz was the gear I
used on my bike … in Bolivia I used a bigger gear because the
altitude allows it, and I think that this bigger gear allowed me to
better manage my kilometre. We did a few trials before leaving,
but we took the decision to use the [larger] gear only when we
were there. It was last minute, on the spot. But I believe that helped
me.'

Do you think anyone will ever beat your world record?

'I think that the record is an incredible time but records are
meant to be beaten, and so I think that one day it will be … maybe
by Chris if he takes up the kilometre again, but even if the record
was beaten I would still be proud to be the first man to go
under a minute … this is something nobody can ever take away
from me!'

And still there is one final postscript to Bolivia, from Scott Gardner,
the sports scientist who accompanied Hoy to Florida for his training camp and then on to La Paz for the record attempt. An
Australian, from Melbourne, who worked for his own national
team before jumping ship to the British camp, Gardner smiles as

he tells the story, as if pleased with the sheer mischievousness and audacity of joining the enemy. 'The team I was with in Australia won a ton of medals at the [Athens] Olympics,' says Gardner when I meet up with him for my own Bolivia debrief.

Gardner says he's happier working with the British team because, as he says, 'it's recognized as the best in the world'. You'd think his Aussieness might be a problem, but no. More important than nationality, he wanted to work with people on the same wavelength as him – just as ambitious, and just as prepared to make the same sacrifices. 'Achieving in sport is about people self-sacrificing, putting their lives on hold to achieve a goal. Working with the Brits has taken over my life, but it's given me an opportunity. The opportunity to work with Chris, for one thing, because I was in Athens, in the opposition camp, and I saw his Olympic kilo, and it was just spectacular; one of the greatest things I've ever seen. The guy is a physiological phenomenon, he has got class, he's intelligent. It's a privilege to work with him.'

We talk about Bolivia; the maybes and what-ifs of the record attempt; the little things that went wrong. 'I know we could have done it better,' says Gardner. 'It was a shame that for his big moment, the 500, nobody was there. That was the moment he let it all out. Everything was relaxed and calm and he could let it out. The pressure that was on him for the kilo … it did come out, but it wasn't that relaxed, awesome performance that we see from Chris. The kilo was still a major ride, but the 500 was a beautiful, perfect ride. He was right on the line, he sailed over the bumps, he held the track nice and tight; he was going so fast. It was perfect.'

Gardner exudes the same passion, and the same quiet intensity, as Hoy, which is probably why they work well together. But, having talked to both of them, I was struck by a difference: Gardner seemed more troubled by Hoy's failure to beat the kilo record than Hoy appeared to be. It was – in his mind at least – his failure as much as Hoy's failure – even if 'failure' seems an inappropriate word in the circumstances – but he seemed to be finding it more difficult to come to terms with that failure than Hoy.

Five months on, Gardner seems to be still hurting. 'I have 260 emails in my inbox on this project,' he explains. 'It was a learning experience, and there were lots of little things … lots that we could have done better, and it reinforced and drove the point home that you need everything, everything, to be perfect. I mean, I don't think the delay was too much of a factor, but Chris was pulling luggage off carts. You tell him not to, but he'll still be saying, "I'll get it" – that's just Chris.

'It felt rushed … everything had been spot on until the last twenty-four hours … it wasn't panic stations, but it almost was. Also, the health aspect … ethically, Chris had to be told the worst case scenario in terms of the risks, and maybe it played on his mind … but after that first kilo he knew he couldn't hurt more than he does sometimes in training; he does sessions where the body basically goes into shock. You can't hurt yourself any more than he does in training on a regular basis.

'At the end of the day I look back on the most amazing, unique experience of my career, but …

'I'd love to go back,' he adds with feeling, 'and Chris is the man to go back with. There's no question in my mind he can get that record. I'd love another crack at it.'

There seems to be nothing to add to that, so we stand to leave. But as we do so, Gardner begins talking again: 'When I saw Chris next, after Bolivia, I felt there was something still there between us, you know? We had our debrief and went through everything, from start to finish: what did work, what didn't work, what can we learn from it – we just got it all out. We sat down and talked about it; about everything. It was about two hours and we pretty much got everything out. Next time I saw him I felt normal again. But I realized that he'd switched quicker than I had. I was still thinking about it, turning it over in my mind, thinking about some of the decisions I'd made. Chris had let go. He was thinking about Beijing. That reassured me.'

CHAPTER 12

Looking After Number One

Cottbus, east Germany, October 2007

I am sitting with Shane Sutton in the stand of the Cottbus Velodrome, a municipal-style facility on the campus of this German town's sports school. It isn't the fanciest cycle track, but seen in this context – as part of a school, with nearby athletics track and stand and a range of other facilities on a sprawling campus – it is hugely impressive. The velodrome comprises concrete track surrounded by rows of seats – there is capacity for a few thousand; it is partially roofed – the track and seats are covered, the track centre is in the open; and it forms part of the enviable infrastructure built up by the East Germans when they ruled the sporting world.

Sutton, Hoy and the rest of the British sprint squad – minus Craig MacLean, who has just returned from Japan – are in east Germany for a training camp, but tonight, as a diversion from the grind of endless training, there is an opportunity to race at the Cottbus GP. The programme says 'Grobier Preis von Deutschland im Sprint'.

It is October, five months after Bolivia, ten months before Beijing, and Hoy is easing himself back into training. Ten months to the Olympics. A little early for the riders to be racing at full pelt, but this doesn't dampen the enthusiasm of the crowd, who attend the Friday night meeting in large numbers. On buying their tickets at the entrance they are offered a choice of rattle, whistle or horn. These will become very irritating, very quickly – especially the rattles.

As the evening progresses, burger and sausage vans open and do brisk business at the main entrance, alongside a beer tent. The crowd is highly educated in the nuances of track cycling. And also in other important matters – they all bring square pieces of foam to place on the rigid plastic seats.

As well as coming to witness some of the best sprinters of the current generation, tonight also offers spectators a trip down memory lane. There is a golden oldies' event, featuring the past masters of East German – and therefore, by definition, world – sprinting, including Michael Huebner and 1980 and 1988 Olympic champion Lutz Hesslich. Old habits, however, die hard. In the build-up to the meeting one of the golden oldies – or Masters of Sprinting, as they are known – had been in the press talking up his chances but with the caveat, 'I hope there's no dope test! My piss would melt the bottle!'

The Masters receive a rapturous response, though one or two are beginning to look slightly ludicrous in their Lycra. They're still as muscle-bound and bulky as in their pomp, though in some cases some of that bulk has gravitated south. Their world champions' jerseys (because most of the Masters are resplendent in these) bulge around the stomach, though they try, manfully, to puff out their chests. Their legs, however, remain extraordinary: like gnarly, knotted trunks of oak trees. And here they are, raging against the dying of the light. It is quite a spectacle – and possibly a little sobering for Hoy and the other younger sprinters. Is this what they'll be doing in twenty years?

Watching the main competition unfold alongside Sutton provides me with an education in the black art of sprinting. 'He lives and breathes cycling,' Hoy had said of Sutton, but it is revealing to witness this in the flesh. It is instructive, too, to observe his uncanny ability to 'call' a race – he predicts the outcome of each race accurately and unfailingly, in the process offering a forensic analysis of the tactics.

We watch Hoy, Ross Edgar, the young British sprinter Jason Kenny, and Britain's world champion Victoria Pendleton, in their one-on-one bouts, during which Sutton tells an endless succession of stories and anecdotes, interjecting his narrative with yelled instructions to his charges. He is like the football coach who mimes kicking and heading the ball from the touchline, his movements mirroring those of his protégés. He lunges, kicks for home and body-swerves; he is with them every pedal revolution.

Yet, 'There comes a time when I can't do anything for these guys,' Sutton admits. 'What can a coach do for a rider forty-five minutes before the race? He can only fuck it up. Nah, the job's more than that, mate. I make sure they're okay – that's me job. Even when they're being right awkward bastards.' He shrugs. 'That's the nature of the beast.

'We're going to Australia a couple of years ago, right? And Jason [Queally] phones. "I want to fly to Australia from Manchester." Rest of the team is flying from London. So I go, "Aw Jeez Jason, you want to fly on your own and not be with the team?" "Yeah," he says. "There's two-and-a-half inches more leg room on the flight from Manchester – I've measured it." "Jeez, alright," I say to him. "Fair enough. You've got to look after number one. That's fair enough, I respect that."

'Thing was,' adds Sutton, with visible glee, 'he was delayed eight hours in Singapore! I picked him up from the airport. You should 'ave seen him. "Alright Jason mate, how'd you like that two-and-a-half inches extra leg room?"'

Sutton has been involved with cycling, as Hoy said, all his life. He has seen it all. He has certainly seen how badly teams can be run – he was part of a British team that started the 1987 Tour de France, whose owner vanished halfway through, and was never heard of again (with the riders going unpaid for their three weeks of toil around France).

He is therefore in a good position to analyse what makes the British team successful, to define what it is that has led to such a spectacular transformation from laughing stock to superpower. Does it come down solely to the investment of millions of Lottery funding? 'Nah, the thing that makes us successful is good leadership,' says Sutton, not pausing even to consider the question. 'But it doesn't just come from the PD [performance director]. Leadership happens throughout the programme and it's the key to everything. Now we've got underpinning groups – young riders who are following the lead of the Chris Hoys, the Jason Queallys. These senior athletes are responsible for their own success but also for the success of the programme downstairs. So these athletes provide leadership in that way. If you're a young junior and you're training with Chris Hoy, he's an icon for them, and you need icons. These guys have been instrumental in the way this programme has moved forward.

'Chris and Jason are special,' he continues. 'They're great bike riders, and that's a big word. I don't use it lightly. Queally's a great athlete – he won his Olympic kilo through brute strength. Chris is great in a different way ...'

Mid-stream, Sutton's attention switches to the track – a sprint match featuring Hoy and a German opponent. The bell sounds for the final lap, Hoy feints an attack, fooling his rival into making the first move. Sutton is animated: 'That's a good move, GOOD MOVE CHRIS … not too early … not too early …' – while his opponent is sprinting flat out, Hoy positions himself on his rear wheel – 'Gotta go, gotta go, HIT HIM NOW …' – and Hoy accelerates, moving alongside his opponent – 'He'll get him, he'll get him … yeah!' Hoy pips him on the line. 'That's the best ride I've seen Chris do in ages. Tied him up well.'

Turning away from the track, Sutton continues, seamlessly: 'Chris and Jason are … okay, I'll say it, they're nice guys, but they both have that C-U-N-T element. You gotta have it. Need it. A prime example. Stuttgart, 2003 worlds, Chris is in a bad way. He isn't in the team for the team sprint. Chris is the guy who'd stay back at the track and have a quiet word, convince you why *he* is the man who can do the ride. I shouldn't say this, but he'd come up here [into the stand] and sit here and convince me he was the man to do the job. He believes in himself 100 per cent. Bottom line, he's selfish. He'll admit that. It's all about Chris. But he needs to be like that, and when you take him away from the performance, from this arena here, you wouldn't get a nicer guy. He's not a show-off. He's not an extrovert. He's a gentle giant with the big Mike Tyson neck who gets on with his business. Outside here, I don't associate with people from work at all, but Chris and Queally are people I'd maintain a real close association with. They're great guys, nice guys.'

Meanwhile, Hoy returns to action, and Sutton's attention switches back to the track. 'Height! Height!' he yells, urging him not to panic, to move up the banking, even if it means his opponent opens a gap, so Hoy can use the banking to his advantage, swooping down the track when he begins sprinting. 'He needs to feel it, needs to learn what the gap can do. HIGHER CHRIS!'

Is it not unusual, I ask Sutton when the race finishes, with Hoy registering another comfortable victory, for nice guys to win? 'Yeah, but remember that element, the C-word – it's there when he needs it. And when it comes to training this guy is the epitome of what elitism is all about. I've seen a lot of world-class athletes, but he and Vicky [Pendleton], I've never seen two people so devoted to training. They thrive on it. Chris loves training. Loves it. Very few are like that. Normally you're pushing athletes, saying, "Come on, you gotta get your arse in gear." But with Chris you're pulling him back, pulling him back, pulling him back. He's a trainaholic: he just loves getting up, going to work and leavin' everything on the track. That's it.'

Much of what Sutton says chimes with what Peter Keen tells me. 'The thing that stands out among hugely successful athletes and coaches is a fascination with the process,' says Keen. 'They are genuinely fascinated by the process, not just the end result. It's something Chris Hoy and Chris Boardman have in common. In fact, they have quite a lot in common: a total unwillingness to accept mediocrity around them; a willingness to challenge for better in quite a constructive way. Chris Hoy doesn't complain – he is relentlessly positive; he does raise his head above the parapet, but subtly. He invites you to align with him and help him; he positions himself as somebody people want to work with and see succeed.'

Keen laughs. 'With both Chris B and Chris Hoy, there've been moments when … well, in a sense it's that selfish gene, isn't it? But they can make you feel special, because, effectively, they say: "I need *you* to be a special person, and I'll be really positive and support you, because I need you to do this for me. It's all about *me* really, but I can make you think you're special …" That is a great gift!'

When I ask Hoy about this there's a knowing smile. 'You mean I'm manipulative?' Well, I recall the ingenuity of his fund-raising efforts for that first BMX, where he invited his parents' friends to 'align with him' and help him with a fiver in the pot towards the bike …

According to Sutton, it is Hoy's trainaholism that should see him continue to perform at a high level for several more years. 'I was thirty-nine when I retired,' says Sutton. 'Queally wanted to pack it in a while back, but I told him, "Keep going as long as you can. Stop if you start going backwards and looking stupid. But enjoy it, because before you know it, it's over." I wish I could go back and do it again, mate. Take it a bit more seriously.'

Meanwhile, Hoy is back on the track. 'Aw, that's a bad move Chris,' says Sutton. 'GO UP THE BANKING, GO UP, GO UP … I think Chris has got him, Chris has got him, Chris has got him … beautiful.

'Chris will know when it's time to stop,' Sutton continues, performing another perfect segue. 'He's got too much pride in himself – look at the way he dresses. But I think he enjoys himself in this group. We have been to hell and back but it's okay in the sprinters' group now. The environment is high-intensity. It's thousands of a second we're talkin' about, and there are a lot of big egos. When I came in here it was me-me-me. But then Vicky [Pendleton] came in, the first woman, and when she won her first world title [in LA in 2005] she proved she deserved to be recognized alongside these guys. That helped the dynamics. I've never seen them take so much time out for Vicky as they do now. She's part of the group. Their attitude is: she's one of us; don't mess with her.'

Sutton seems to enjoy his role as confidant. Relationship counselling forms part of his work, he says. 'I tell 'em, "Whatever you do, make the decision quick. Short-term pain, long-term relief guys. Be honest with yourselves, make the decision quick, in whatever walk of life."

'Chris is the character we're unveiling here, right? He's a decent looking bloke, he's got everything going for him: well organized, financially settled, an elite sportsman … you think he'd be settled now, right, married and all the rest of it? Nah, he's not willing to share the moment. It's all about him, and I think that is one *really* good trait to have if you want to reach the top. Some people do it in different ways; they have the family – they need that stability. But you get ones like Chris who won't let anyone in. He doesn't need it. It reflects in his training. Nothing comes before training. That's why he's so good.' An Alsatian, as Steve Peters said.

'And you get guys who need to be reassured,' says Sutton, 'guys who need an arm around 'em, tellin' 'em how special they are.' Ah ha, the Labradors? 'Yeah,' says Sutton, 'we've got guys who are scared to pick up the phone for a week because they're frightened to tell you they can't do this or can't do that. They're frightened to upset people. Chris, on the other hand, will tell you it as it is. He'll come in, say what he has to say, and know you're going to be pissed off, but he accepts that. He's got that self-belief, but he's not a big-headed bastard. When he comes off the track, whether it's a win or defeat, he's the first guy to shake the other rider's hand. Then he thanks the coaches and the staff.'

The previous day, I'd attended a training session at the track involving Hoy, Pendleton, the coach Iain Dyer, the sprint coach Jan van Eijden, the now-retired 2000 world sprint champion from Germany, sports scientist Scott Gardner and mechanic Ernie Feargrive. There were other riders there, members of the Australian and New Zealand squads. Dyer appeared on a motorbike, riding it onto the track, and Hoy fell in behind while Dyer ramped the speed up.

He follows the motorbike, just a centimetre or so from its rear wheel, for lap after lap, eyes trained on that back wheel. They reach 74.9 kph – 47 mph – with Hoy pedalling in a blur, up to, at the end, 192 revs per minute – all of which requires a massive amount of skill, on the part of both Dyer and Hoy. And it is, when you think about it, enormously dangerous – all it would take for a calamitous crash would be the slightest contact between the two wheels. It is also all in a day's work. ('You don't think about it,' said Hoy later, 'because you can't. If you thought about the consequences of touching the bike, at 80 kph, wearing thin lycra … but I think I'd come off worst.')

Backing up one of Sutton's observations, as he leaves the track Hoy pats Dyer on the back. 'Thanks Iain,' he says, 'you're pretty good on that bike.' 'You're not so bad yourself,' replies Dyer.

There is something else going on at the track during this training session, though. The British team has set up its own timing equipment, but there are Australian and New Zealand riders here. Gardner watches one of the Australian women launch a flat-out effort – though he isn't just watching; he is also timing her, and others, scribbling the relevant information. 'I got her on 13.6,' he says quietly to Dyer. 'Yeah, she backed off a bit,' replies Dyer.

Later, I ask Gardner about this form of espionage, which carries echoes of the Formula One spying scandal that erupted in 2007, but with one difference – in cycling spying on other teams might be underhand but it is not illegal. 'One thing I do is that I make sure people from other teams know we're doing stuff,' says Gardner, smiling. 'It's part of the game. You walk around the centre of the velodrome, check what other people are doing. I make sure I'm seen on a laptop every now and again. Then they think: "What's he doing? Oh shit!" In terms of gathering information from other teams, yes, we do it. You can only learn that way.' It occurs to me later that Gardner – an Aussie who worked with the Australian team at the 2004 Olympics – might have been the 'spy' who fed reports on Hoy's training back to the Australian coach,

Martin Barras. 'Spy on Chris?' he says, outraged, when I ask him. 'Nah, no way mate!'

However, the man who oversees the British spying operation, and also the secret development of equipment, is the director of coaching, Chris Boardman. A couple of weeks after Cottbus I meet Boardman at the British national track championships. He looks pleased with himself; it wouldn't be an exaggeration to say that he is almost rubbing his hands with glee. 'Hundreds of thousands of pounds is the bill I've just agreed downstairs with the accountant,' he says in his flat Merseyside tones, which don't even hint at the excitement he is obviously feeling. 'The accountant knew it was coming, he'd budgeted for it, but everything will be new for Beijing, pretty much everything. And most of it will be so subtle you won't be able to see it, apart from the suits.

'They're shiny,' adds Boardman, a twinkle in his eye.

He is talking, of course, about the equipment, the Secret Squirrel Club, the armoury for the Beijing Olympics, which loom ever larger on the horizon. Later, when I meet Peter Keen and tell him about Boardman's glee at the prospect of all this top secret weaponry, he looks momentarily serious. 'You're not supposed to know about that. I'm going to have to kill you.'

But it is clear that Boardman takes great enjoyment and pride in his work on the equipment front – that the challenge of trying to stay ahead of the opposition, of innovating, appears to engage him in the same way as the process of training, of trying new things and finding solutions to make him a better cyclist, did during his career. Keen has mentioned the similarities between Boardman and Hoy and these are quite striking in the way they talk. In fact, one of the people Hoy visited after his Stuttgart nightmare in 2003, when he was determined to leave no stone unturned in his build-up to the Athens Olympics, was Boardman. And Boardman offered a tip that proved priceless, telling Hoy: 'Your training plan has to excite you.'

Hoy explains: 'He said that, because planning is such a big thing for him, that if you write your year's training plan and don't get excited by it, if you don't think, in my hand I have a piece of paper which is like a recipe, or blueprint, for a gold medal … then scrap it and start again.' This appealed to Hoy; and he has followed the advice ever since, even ripping up his first training plan for Beijing, written in August 2007, and redrafting it until he had a document in his hand that excited him. It took several weeks.

It is interesting, in this respect, also to contrast Hoy with Craig MacLean. While Hoy and Boardman are process-driven, my impression is that if Hoy lives to train, then MacLean lives to race. He admits as much when acknowledging, during a run of indifferent form, that 'It'll be different when I have a number on my back.'

Perhaps their different personalities are also reflected in their homes. Hoy's flat, neat and tidy, features mementos of his cycling career: a rainbow world champion's jersey in a glass case; a large print of his world record attempt in Bolivia; numerous other pictures and medals. But in MacLean's house there is nothing – not a single reminder of his medal-laden cycling career, not a scrap of evidence to indicate he's a cyclist.

The only clue seems to be a wall planner on the kitchen door, with 'OLYMPICS' scrawled in big letters over a fortnight in August 2008. It even seems out of character for him to have a wall planner. 'I know,' he replies, 'I hate that, having it in my face every day reminding me what I have to do.' So why does he have it? 'Steve Peters suggested it. But it's coming down …'

There might have been a nice painting of MacLean on his living room wall. In 2007 he returned to his hometown of Grantown-on-Spey to be the VIP at a special ceremony. To honour his status as a local legend the town decided to name their smart new sports centre the Craig MacLean Leisure Centre. MacLean was flattered. And after he'd cut the ribbon, he was presented with a large painting, commissioned to mark the occasion, done by a local artist, who'd worked from a picture of MacLean in action. Or it was supposed to be MacLean. But as MacLean studied the painting he realized it wasn't. It was Chris Hoy. 'Typical,' says MacLean with a wry smile.

Possibly the best observation ever made of Hoy and MacLean, which sums up their different temperaments and approaches, comes from the former Scottish national coach, Graeme Herd. 'Chris is a scientist,' says Herd, 'Craig's an artist.'

And Chris Boardman is most certainly a scientist as well, of course. But although he has sometimes been depicted as a cold, calculating, numbers-obsessed athlete – his nickname, according to Wikipedia, is 'The Professor' – there is more to him than that. There is certainly passion – and that is not a word often associated with Boardman. When he retired he needed to find something else to fascinate him, to fire his passion. (Boardman says he remembers 'the day, the hour, when my career effectively finished, at the end of the 1997 season, when I realized, during our debrief of the season, that what I was planning the following season was to stay the same – I'd tried all I could to get better, and as soon as I realized that, I lost interest'.)

'Nothing will fill that void,' he says of retiring from cycling. 'When I got rid of all that pressure, life became … pretty bland. So I had to introduce things, go looking for challenges. My primary passion now is scuba diving. I do quite enjoy looking at the pretty fish, but it's the challenge I like. I do a lot of quite extreme diving, cave diving.

'I don't like risk,' he stresses, 'I like challenge. I don't do things that are dangerous, but I like things that are really hard to do. But

I also know, from my experience in sport, that you do need some risk, that there is no elation without risk. Two weeks ago I dived on a new wreck that was found in Egypt: it was ninety metres down, we had sixteen minutes of gas … it was a really carefully executed plan, with six bottles of gas to make it work. I really enjoyed that. Chris Hoy will probably have to go and look for something like that.'

Boardman's involvement with 'the programme' – as he refers to it – 'gives me satisfaction because you're surrounded by problems all the time'. Also, 'you have to take risks to stay ahead.' Boardman therefore likes to think 'outside the box', or outside the sport of cycling. 'On the equipment research and development front,' he reveals, 'there is no one with anything to do with cycling involved in that. There are fifteen people who we work with on everything from clothing to handlebars. They come from Formula One and further afield – we'll be taking another new step soon.' (A few months later I find out what he means, when a tie-up between BAE Systems, the global defence and aerospace company, and UK Sport is confirmed, to 'deliver expertise in structural and mechanical engineering, aerodynamics, hydrodynamics, mathematical modelling and simulation, human factors and materials science' to the sports of cycling, sailing, canoeing, rowing and bob skeleton.)

It is one thing to look beyond his own sport, but Boardman's approach – to look *exclusively* beyond the cycling industry – seems an extreme one. 'It's because as soon as you have a handle on something, if you have a preconceived idea of what a bike looks like, or what it can do, then you can't think in an original way,' he says. 'Preconceived ideas kill genuine innovation. So we go to people who have no idea about bikes, who don't even really know what a bike looks like. It takes a bit of self-discipline on my part to work out whether you've reached a dead end with some

guys, or whether I've just stopped them with my own preconceived ideas ...'

But how much of this, I wonder, is merely a game with the
other teams, designed to make them paranoid that they will be at
a disadvantage. 'There is a psychological warfare element to it,
yes,' admits Boardman, 'but we've never had anything like what
we've got for Beijing. That's the truth. The only thing limiting us
is that we have to work within the rules. And the rules are shit,
because they're not hard and fast. Virtually every bike in Beijing
will be illegal ... but ours will be the most legal.'

So much for the equipment; how about the athletes? How are
they prepared? How do they compete – within the rules? Like
Sutton, Boardman has pretty much seen it all. He has been part
of pre-Lottery British teams. He has been part of continental
professional teams. He says there is no comparison between either
of these entities and the current British set-up. He says he could
never have envisaged what exists today. Even by continental
professional team standards, it is a world apart.

'When I joined a pro' team in 1994 we were just a group of
guys in the same coloured jersey,' Boardman shrugs. 'I won the
[Tour de France] yellow jersey in the [1994] prologue and there
was no strategy at all, no plan. There was a team time trial, which
was crucial to defend the jersey. Before the Tour I'd given my
bike to the mechanics telling them "That's how I want it set up."
But on the morning of the race some of my team-mates
were adjusting their positions, going "Yeah, that feels okay." No
preparation, no thought had been given to it at all. And it was a
disaster.'

And it mattered: the team time trial was on the eve of a rare
visit by the Tour de France to Britain. Had Boardman been in
yellow he – and his team – would have received acres of publicity. Instead, he raced on British roads not resplendent in the yellow

jersey, but merely as one of the pack, a virtually anonymous member of the peloton.

The picture Boardman paints is of an ad hoc, chaotic world. But underpinning the continental road scene, as a never-ending stream of revelations over the past few years have informed us, was a deeply ingrained drugs culture. It seems paradoxical: while some of the teams, with their multimillion pound budgets, had sophisticated and expensive doping programmes (administering potentially life-threatening drugs), they ignored other, far more basic, aspects of performance.

Dave Brailsford has an interesting theory on this, which goes to the heart of his approach, and reinforces his belief that his – clean – team can win at the highest level. 'My personal take on it is that a lot of the guys who dope actually use it as such a crutch that they stop doing other things.

'We've got this saying, "performance by the aggregation of marginal gains"', says the fast-talking Brailsford, repeating the phrase more slowly for emphasis: 'performance … by … the … aggregation … of … marginal … gains. It means taking the 1 per cent from everything you do; finding a 1 per cent margin for improvement in everything you do. That's what we try to do from the mechanics upwards; if a mechanic sticks a tyre on, and someone comes along and says it could be done better, it's not an insult – it's because we are always striving for improvement, for those 1 per cent gains, in absolutely every single thing we do. Now, it's my belief that some guys don't do that; that they rely on doping instead. And they neglect all the little bits. I suspect some look on doping as a substitute for training properly.'

There is no question, though, that outside observers will look at recent performances by the British team and conclude that drugs must play a part. Brailsford knows this. 'The Italian [cycling federation] president said something about our track programme being doped. People do say things like that and it really doesn't bother me. I haven't got a problem. I can sleep with a clear conscience.

'When I first got involved with the programme,' he continues, 'I thought, sod it, why is this such a taboo subject? Some people are very quiet on doping, but I've always been open about it. I introduced blood testing a long time ago, and I said to the riders, "We're going to take your blood, and if there's anything suspicious I'm not going to send you to the police, or the anti-doping guys. We're going to do it in-house, and if I see anything dodgy, I'm just going to phone you up and say, 'Look, we know what you're doing. You can tell me about it if you want. But you ain't riding, that's for sure.'" And there have been three or four riders, Great Britain riders, who didn't get selected, where I've had to say: "No, you're not riding, because we know what you're doing." And they just said: "Oh, alright then."' The 'three or four' riders Brailsford is referring to here, I subsequently find out, were road riders, with continental professional teams. Their names, however, have never been disclosed.

Brailsford continues: 'If you're open and frank about it, and you're not pussyfooting around, then what's the big deal? Look, life's pretty straightforward in my view. You can tell from the way people talk if they're hiding something. They come up with far-fetched, bollocks excuses, but look in their eyes. People don't want to talk about it because they're frightened they'll get caught. If you're hiding a secret, you want to avoid the topic. If you're not frightened, and have nothing to hide, then you'll talk openly. It's like the guy who's cheating on his wife.'

Brailsford has witnessed the effects of doping at first hand – not in a performance sense, but he has seen what might be called the collateral damage. In June 2004 he was with David Millar, the Scottish road cyclist who would later confess to using EPO, when the French police arrived at a restaurant in Biarritz to take him away for questioning. 'People say, doping is this big door – you come to it and then decide whether you want to walk through it or not,' says Brailsford. 'But it's not like that. What often happens with doping is that you get yourself in a *right* mess; you get yourself in a real situation and it doesn't seem like there's any other way out. I had quite a bad – but very interesting – experience with Dave Millar. I'm pretty close to him – he's been very open with me – and I chose to stand by him and try and support him, because I realized that he'd found himself in what he felt was a pretty desperate situation. It gave me an insight, an invaluable insight. It made me even more convinced that doping is a crutch – nothing more. And it made me even more convinced that we can win without doping.'

The big question, of course, is whether an athlete who has trained to his absolute potential, who has taken care of every tiny detail – who has aggregated all the marginal gains – can beat an athlete on drugs? Can this be as effective at 'enhancing performance' as doping? 'I don't know,' says Boardman. 'I don't think we'll be able to tell for another couple of years. But I do think, like Dave [Brailsford], that doping can be a shortcut for some athletes.'

But currently there exists, in sports such as cycling and athletics, something close to an assumption of guilt, certainly in events like the Tour de France and the men's and women's 100 m. It has reached the stage that if an athlete speaks openly and articulately on the subject, he is praised – which is as sad an indictment of sport as the football crowd which is praised for observing a minute's silence. Cycling has its drugs; football has its yob culture.

Just as football fans can all be tarred with this brush, so all athletes bear the weight of the crimes of the dopers. So do their parents. 'It's hellish,' says David Hoy, shaking his head slowly. His mother, Carol, says: 'I tell you something that, as the mother of an athlete, I find really upsetting. It's that I know when Chris is standing on the podium getting a medal there are people look-ing at him thinking, "I wonder if he's taken something." That suspi-cion is horrible. I'm proud of how vocal he's been about it, and I don't have any doubts about him because he's always known the difference between right and wrong – he knew as a child that if he stole the last biscuit then Jiminy Cricket would get him …'

Hoy says the first time he became aware of what some people might be thinking was at the world championships in Copenhagen in 2002, when he stood on the top step of the podium having won the kilo. It should have been the proudest moment of his career to date, and it was, but there was the hint of a sour taste, the whiff of suspicion. 'I don't actually blame people for being suspicious, because it's what they're told in the media – that top athletes take drugs,' says Hoy. 'There are guys I know who are still racing who would probably bet their entire life's earnings on the fact that I take drugs, because they will not accept that I could be beating them without taking drugs. It would shatter their ego, all their beliefs; it would destroy them. I'm sure there are even some guys who wouldn't feel resentment towards you if you told them, "Oh, I'm taking this or that …" The reaction from them wouldn't be, "You cheating bastard!" It would be: "Right, okay, thanks for the advice."

'I'm less and less aware of that doping culture though,' adds Hoy. 'There are about two or three left in the world of sprinting. Ten years ago I would have said there were maybe a dozen or so. But I would agree with Dave [Brailsford]: I think some guys maybe do see drugs as the biggest part of their preparation, with the result that they don't pay as much attention to every other detail, trying to squeeze everything out of every other area. But that's what motivates me to put in 100 per cent everyday. I try to go into the major competitions knowing that I've done absolutely everything I possibly could.'

When he addressed an anti-doping conference in London in 2007, David Millar – who, since serving a two-year ban, has become a fervent anti-doping campaigner – raised an interesting question. 'I think we have to learn a lot more on a human level, a psychological level, about why athletes dope,' said Millar. 'When I was preparing my presentation [for the conference] and thinking of that key question – why did I dope? – I got to thinking, why did I *not* dope for so long? I think it's useful to look at what factors might prevent an individual doping. It comes down to their core values, ideals, ethics, but also their peer group, and their belief in the system. If you don't believe in that system, if you think you're being let down by it, if you know that other people around you are doping, and you know they're getting away with it, then you start to lose faith in the system ...'

It is a good point; and given the apparent prevalence of drugs in the highest echelons of sport, and the fact that so many – evidently – *have* got away with it, there are numerous reasons not to have faith in 'the system'. So why, in that case, and to pose Millar's question, does Hoy *not* use drugs?

'It would require so much deception, and living a lie,' he says without a moment's pause. 'People who do it find their own morals, or code of conduct, or some way to justify it or rationalize it, by saying that everyone else is at it, and it's the only way to reach the top, or whatever ... but I don't know how you could stand on the podium, with everyone applauding you ... I think you'd need to be psychopathic to deal with all that and not let it affect you.'

Peter Keen thinks along similar lines, and takes Brailsford's argument a stage further, suggesting that doping could actually be detrimental in some circumstances. When asked if he thinks Hoy has beaten athletes on drugs, he says, without hesitation, 'Oh yeah definitely, without a doubt.' His belief is that the robust anti-doping procedures now being applied will 'subtly level the playing field'. Keen's theory is that, with methods of detection improving, and sanctions increasingly severe, the stakes are being raised – and in some cases the fear of being caught could nullify the advantage of taking drugs in the first place.

'What Chris doesn't have to do is worry when he goes to sleep at night whether the phone is going to go, or the door is going to be kicked down,' says Keen. 'He doesn't have to worry whether he is trusting the right supplier; he doesn't have to worry whether the people he has confided in can be trusted. He can sleep at night.

'Yeah, okay, all the science says that there's a 10 per cent improvement in performance through EPO-like interventions … but is that a guaranteed 10 per cent? And unless you're a psychopath, how do you sleep at night? Where is your focus or attention? Can you afford to relax sufficiently to do the kind of constant re-evaluations that Chris is doing everyday, or are you worried instead about your supply; are you worried about the efficacy of what you're doing? Are you happy living a lie? I have to keep putting that to athletes who are making the choice, and saying: "Is that a better place to be?"

'If you genuinely don't care and you hate the world, then you're not going to lose any sleep, but I think the majority of athletes are actually human. They do care, they do have a conscience, and it eats them up. And when you look at the behaviours that many of them develop around [doping], I don't think those are optimal in terms of training. So I don't think it's as simple as saying that Chris has to overcome the 10 per cent he's not getting from using drugs … because the person who's using them is probably not getting the 10 per cent advantage, due to all those other factors. It's a subtle argument that gets lost in all the hyperbole around the rights and wrongs of doping,' says Keen. 'But it's a good argument for pushing on with anti-doping controls.'

Talking to Hoy, it is abundantly clear that he doesn't lose sleep about drugs; he is just mildly irritated that the subject is always there, like white noise. Looking ahead to the Beijing Olympics, he did have one overriding concern, and it had nothing to do with drugs.

The axing of the kilo left him with a dilemma: where should his focus now be? He had maintained, since the kilo decision, that it would be the team sprint. But his gold medal in the keirin, at the 2007 world championships, seemed to give him another realistic shot at an Olympic title – not that he necessarily saw it that way. 'It's a lottery,' he kept saying of the keirin, recognizing the apparent fact that, with six sprinters racing head-to-head, there was an inherent unpredictability about it. 'So many variables,' he insisted. And Hoy – like Boardman – isn't a huge fan of lots of variables, or, more accurately, lots of variables beyond his control. It was what he liked about the kilo: he only had to rely upon, and worry about, himself, not others. The keirin is different. It's a race against other people, with tactics and countless different connotations.

But in the early part of the 2007/08 track season, Hoy turned the received wisdom of keirin racing on its head. On the eve of the Sydney World Cup he totted up his keirin wins: he reckoned he had won twelve international keirins in a row. This record surprised him; it also seemed to rubbish the notion that the event was a lottery. With Hoy riding, these theoretically crazy, chaotic races didn't appear unpredictable at all – on the contrary, they seemed, on this evidence, to be quite predictable.

In Sydney, the serious track season – and the countdown to the Beijing Olympics – got underway with the first of four World

Cup meetings. Having won a tough qualifying heat from the Frenchman Grégory Baugé – taking his tally to thirteen consecutive keirin victories – Hoy lined up for the semi-final, and deployed his favourite tactic: going from the front – and winning. Fourteen …

The final featured most of the big hitters, including Theo 'the Boss' Bos of the Netherlands. A different approach this time: Roberto Chiappa of Italy led it out, with Hoy tucked in behind, and with a lap to go he 'nailed it', launching a full-on attack, opening a big gap that nobody came anywhere near to closing. To make the victory even sweeter, it was a British one-two: Ross Edgar came through for second, with Bos third. Fifteen …

The following weekend, in the early part of December 2007, the show moved on to Beijing, and the new Olympic velodrome, for World Cup number two. 'I expect to lose my unbeaten record before the Olympics,' insisted Hoy. 'I've found a formula that works for me – riding from the front. But I want to try different tactics, different ways of riding the keirin, between now and the Olympics, so I'd be surprised to remain unbeaten. The others know how I ride, and although knowing what I'm going to do and being able to do something about it are two different things, I know that I need to add new strings to my bow.' In heat one, though, it was the tried-and-tested tactic, Hoy leading out and qualifying, 'nice and safe'. Sixteen …

Heat two was a potential banana skin, featuring two of Hoy's oldest rivals, Arnaud Tournant and Stefan Nimke. He decided to take no chances, leading it out again, winding up the pace and, once again, proving too powerful – Tournant qualified in second; Nimke was eliminated. Seventeen …

The final was a fraught affair. It also offered some evidence that Hoy's dominance was starting to influence the tactics of some of his rivals, dictating how they rode. As the derny passed the start line – the cue for the riders to be released, and fall into line behind the motorized bike – Hoy did what he invariably does: he accelerated sharply to be first behind the derny. Behind him, at least two riders, Ryan Bayley of Australia and Morne Blignaut of South Africa, reckoned there was only one place to be: both fancied being directly behind Hoy, where they could effectively be towed to the finish – though this, as Hoy acknowledged, might be easier said than done … and of course there wasn't space for two. The South African shoulder-barged Bayley out the way, which, in the old days, would have been dismissed as the argy-bargy typical of the event. But the rules have been tightened and, like the two-footed tackle in football, shoulder-barging has been deemed illegal.

Blignaut was disqualified. The race restarted with five. Hoy again led out, but with two laps to go, Arnaud Tournant took a flyer. He opened a lead of several lengths but Hoy didn't panic, riding his own race, gradually applying more pressure, slowly catching Tournant. Finally, having sat a couple of lengths off his back wheel, leaving Tournant hanging on for dear life, he launched a counter-attack, going over the top of a tiring Tournant, with the Frenchman holding on for second. Eighteen …

CHAPTER 13

Big in Japan

Kokusai Keirin Gakko, Izu-shi, Shizuoka, 2005; and Rotterdam Six-Day, January 2008

The keirin is one event in the track cycling repertoire – and there are several – that can provoke bafflement in the uninitiated, their confusion owing to one aspect: the presence of a motorbike. It is not what people expect in a bicycle race. As with the pole vault, or Australian Rules football, it's reasonable to ask: who on earth started that? And why did anyone take them seriously?

Keirin racing began in Japan in 1948, and Japan – not a country renowned for any other form of cycle racing – remains the hotbed. International keirin racing is a relatively new discipline: it was introduced to the world championships in 1980, to the Olympics as recently as 2000.

But Japanese keirin racing remains quite distinct from the international version – fields are made up of nine riders rather than six; and instead of a motorized 'derny', the pacer is a nominated cyclist, who sets off just ahead of the pack of nine, and whose job it is to build up the speed to around 50 kph (31 mph) before peeling off with two laps to go, setting up the mad dash for the line.

This, admittedly, makes the Japanese keirin less bizarre to the outsider than international keirin racing, where the appearance of an invariably potbellied derny pilot, riding his moped at the head of a string of six honed sprinters, makes it one of the most surreal events. Equally, however, there are oddities unique to Japanese keirin racing: the padded suits, the full motorcycle-style helmets, a preponderance of primary colours.

To dispel one myth, though: 'keirin' is not Japanese for 'fight,' as some – prominent commentators among them – insist on claiming. It is an amalgamation of two Japanese words: 'bet' and 'wheel'. And this offers a clue as to what Japanese keirin racing is really all about: money, or betting.

The figures are staggering. The Japanese Keirin circuit, which features 5,000 professional riders and 1,200 events, spread around Japan's fifty velodromes, attracts 20 million spectators – or more accurately punters, who generate a whopping £3.7 billion per year in betting income. The top (Japanese) riders are wealthy, with some worth £4 million to £5 million, and earnings of up to £1 million possible in a single season. It is no wonder, then, that non-Japanese riders want a slice of the pie, but their slice is limited. Only nine 'internationals' per year are admitted, and they earn a fraction of what the Japanese riders earn. And it is, in any case, extremely difficult for an international rider to win in Japan.

Craig MacLean has had four stints in the crazy world of the Japanese keirin circuit, including the summer of 2007. 'The top Japanese riders drive Ferraris and Lamborghinis and they're shocked at how poor we are,' he says. 'To them we're penniless. They have a totally different lifestyle. You see them drinking and smoking between races. It's a different culture. They baffle us and we baffle them.'

One of the curiosities in all of this is that the Japanese riders have made very little impact on the international scene – at the Olympics or world championships. The only exceptions are the silver medal-winning team sprint trio at the Athens Olympics, and the remarkable Koichi Nakano, the most prolific winner on the Japanese keirin circuit, who also managed to notch up ten consecutive world professional sprint titles between 1977 and 1986. It is worth pointing out, however, that, to win these titles, Nakano did not have to overcome any East Germans – or other Eastern Bloc sprinters – all of whom were restricted to the world amateur title. (The irony being that, throughout the 1970s and 1980s, the world amateur champion would have – probably – wiped the floor with the world professional champion.)

These days, the lack of impact made by Japanese riders on the international stage is not necessarily through a lack of talent. 'They just don't put a lot of effort into international racing, because it'll compromise their efforts – and their earnings – in Japanese keirin racing,' as MacLean says. 'Financially it doesn't make sense to target the Olympics. Although the guys who won silver in Athens were all given a suitcase of cash when they arrived back in Japan … But there are good riders: when the talent pool is 5,000 professional riders, there have to be some good ones …'

When Jason Queally went to Japan to ride the keirin circuit after his Olympic success in 2000 he finished last in his first race. A restless crowd responded by shouting 'Go home Queally!' 'It's not like you're treated as royalty,' says MacLean. 'Some have that perception – that because we're international riders, who have won Olympic and world medals, we'll get special treatment, and given pots of money. That is definitely not the case. Most of the Japanese riders don't want us there, because we're a threat to them. And the punters don't seem to want us there – there is generally less money bet on races with foreigners, because the outcomes are less predictable. It's all pretty bizarre. It's a strange experience.'

The strangeness starts the minute the internationals arrive. Because before they are allowed to race – and regardless of how many world and Olympic titles to their name – they must go back to school. All the budding Japanese Keirin riders – the annual intake of nine international riders and around 200 Japanese, which represents only 10 per cent of applicants – have to enrol at the Kokusai Keirin Gakko (International Keirin School). The school campus comprises an austere collection of buildings perched high on a hill in Izu-shi, Shizuoka. These contain dorms, classrooms – and four high-quality cycling tracks. (It is interesting to note that, while this school on a hill can boast four velodromes, Hoy and MacLean's native Scotland has none – or one if you count the soon-to-be demolished Meadowbank.)

Chris Hoy, who raced the Japanese keirin circuit in 2005, describes the school accommodation as 'quite sparse, a bit like university halls of residence. Every morning we were woken at 7.30 a.m. by a voice blasting out of a loudspeaker above our door. It scared the life out of me. I thought it was a fire alarm the first morning.

'You get up, put on your robes, and the day is completely regi-mented,' continues Hoy. 'We would go to the classroom to learn the rules of keirin racing. The lecturer would speak and then four different interpreters would translate everything he said. Just like the film *Lost in Translation*.'

'Halls of residence?' says MacLean. 'I don't know what kind of halls Chris stayed in. It's like the worst halls of residence you'll ever stay in, and, although we only do two weeks in keirin school, it's our base the whole time we're out there – nine, ten weeks. We have a room to ourselves; it's paid for the first two weeks, then we have to pay for it out of our winnings for the remainder of the time. I'm reluctant to call it a hotel, though I suppose it's in the style of a hotel – with several thousand cockroaches as its main residents. If you go to the canteen at night and switch on the light, all these cockroaches scatter everywhere. It's pretty gross.

'There are usually around 100 Japanese students there with you at any one time,' continues MacLean. 'They have to spend ten months going through the schooling process. There's an entry exam, which isn't cycling related – they have to do vertical jumps, that kind of thing. A lot of them don't have any background in cycling – it's a career choice, a job. There are some from other sports, like ice skating, who've done the Olympics and now want to make money. The international riders are fast-tracked. The Japanese spend hours riding the bike; they do a ridiculous volume of work.' Indeed they do, reputedly spending fifteen hours a day training and studying for the official Japan Keirin Association qualification that will permit them to race.

'For the internationals, it doesn't matter if you've been before: you have to enrol in the school,' explains MacLean. 'There's a lot of classroom stuff, learning the rules and regulations of keirin racing – because they're specific to Japan, and pretty complicated.'

In 2007 one of MacLean's fellow 'internationals' was the Australian Ben Kersten, who posted a thoroughly entertaining blog. Reporting that all communication devices are banned in keirin school – and at races, to keep the betting clean – Kersten notes the irony of 'being in the country that has made a name for itself by mastering such devices to then be reverting to letter-writing and carrier pigeons'.

Here in the 'land that time forgot,' Kersten adds that 'bicycle evolution has bypassed the Japanese keirin'. Again this is ironic, given the Japanese contribution to advancements in cycling components and other bike-related technology, yet there are sound reasons for the bikes being at least twenty years out of date.

As Kersten writes: 'because of the gambling involved, there must be total equality and consistency for each keirin racer. There is no flexibility on these rules ... hence prehistoric bicycles for everyone.' In fact, riders like Kersten find it very difficult to get their hands on such old-fashioned machines. With his sponsor, the French firm Look, having ceased to make steel bikes – and with carbon fibre banned – they were obliged, at great expense, to produce one-off frames for Kersten and another of their sponsored riders, Mickael Bourgain.

At keirin school, the physical tests – on, writes Kersten, 'a stationary bike with more wires and sensors than Apollo 13 ... all very unpleasant to say the least and [to] serve no purpose other than data collection for the school' – are followed by practical classes on 'bicycle maintenance and safety'.

This is when it gets even more bizarre. In what other sports would Olympic and world champions be expected – or indeed willing – not only to go back to school but to be proficient with a set of tools? Imagine Lewis Hamilton or Fernando Alonso going along with all this, lying underneath a car, spanner in hand. Wouldn't happen. But such is the lot of the international track cycling superstar rider in Japan. Although, as Kersten acknowledges, the bike maintenance classes are rooted in common sense, given that riders are responsible for their own machines, and also that safety is paramount – not so much out of concern for the riders but because a crash would upset the punters, ruining their carefully and expensively placed bets. On the maintenance classes, Kersten writes: 'We had to completely disassemble a bicycle under careful observation from an instructor. It must be done piece by piece and in perfect order, as we'd been taught. No sound must be made by the tools touching the bicycle, and no part or tool can be dropped. When finished you yell "Owarimasu!" ... then proceed to do it all backwards ... oh yeah, did I mention the twenty-minute time limit? In practice I was pushing it and rolled in under ten minutes. [In the test itself] I wanted to be safe and do it perfectly (Virgo), and did it in around fourteen minutes.'

The point of all this, explains Kersten, is so that 'no one dies the next time they go to ride their bike'. Crashes are a common feature of Japanese keirin racing – and they can be nasty, given that the tracks are coated with a sandpaper-like material. In 2005 Hoy suffered one of the heaviest crashes of his career, when, in a test race, a rider in front of him fell. Hoy hit him, and then the deck, at 64 kmh, landing heavily on his hip. MacLean has suffered several bad crashes, breaking his collarbone on one occasion. So the crashes are painful, which is unfortunate. They can also upset the betting – which is even more unfortunate.

After bicycle maintenance, there's a written examination. 'Comprising about fifty totally obvious and unfailable questions,' writes Kersten. 'We didn't need ten days to answer: "Is Keirin a Gamble sport? Y or N." [But] the fact there is a test at the end of the course is the most productive learning instrument … you always pay attention, thinking, do I need to know this?'

Towards the end of their ten days in school, the international riders are subject to tests on the track, with some fairly modest targets for a flying 200 m and kilometre time trial (twelve seconds and one minute, twenty seconds respectively). For the international riders, these targets are not a problem – although, just as in the tests on the stationary bike, 'pride is always a factor', as Kersten says.

One of the most important lessons taught at keirin school concerns the types of punishment applied for any transgression of the rules. There are three levels of offence, which, in order of seriousness, are Shikaku, Juchu and Sochu. 'You don't want one of these,' writes Kersten of the Shikaku. 'Say goodbye to all your prize money.' A Juchu is 'a serious warning', carrying a fine and percentage loss of prize money – 'However, it may be worth the risk [of receiving a Juchu] in trying to win.' It is a gamble, in other words, that could pay off – or not. MacLean admits he has incurred one or two Juchus in pursuit of victory. Finally there is a Sochu, for minor infringements. 'From what I can figure out, this one is given out for breathing,' writes Kersten.

A few other curiosities about Japanese keirin racing: one is the outfits. No skimpy lycra, but full motorcycle helmets and padding, with protective plates for the spine, arms and shoulders, and carbon knuckled gloves. Each rider wears a distinct colour – like a jockey's silks – and number. Another oddity is the spectators. 'They aren't really sports fans,' says MacLean. 'Most of them aren't into cycling. They're into betting.'

But one of the most curious aspects of Japanese keirin racing is the tactics, which must be declared in advance, allowing punters to bet accordingly. Spontaneity is banned – a rider must reveal at least twenty-four hours before the race exactly how he intends to ride, adopting one of the following strategies: Senko (lead-out man), Makuri (second or third in line), or Oikomi (third or fourth). The Senko must attack 800–400 m from the finish; the Makuri must not attack any earlier than 300 m out; and the Oikomi must leave his attack until the final 150 m. This information then appears in the newspapers' betting guides. 'NOTHING can be done to change it,' notes Kersten.

This doesn't, however, make the outcomes of the races predictable. Results are ultimately still dependent on the strength and ability of the rider, not least the ability of the rider to carry out instructions if, for example, he is assigned a particular role. If there is one predictable aspect it is this: that international riders rarely win.

'The Japanese riders gang up against you,' explains MacLean, who won the top international rider award in 2006. 'It's bad for them if a foreigner wins, so they make sure you don't.' They can do this, he says, simply by exploiting their numerical advantage – often there will be only one international rider in a keirin, against eight Japanese. 'It's very lonely,' claims Kersten.

'Your first race is pretty nerve racking,' says MacLean. 'I'm still nervous every time I go out there, just because, even having been there four times now, there are so many unknown elements. There's so much money on the line as well, not just for you but for the others. If you're there to do a job for some guy, who is sat on your wheel, you have to do it right.' Or you might get a Shikaku? 'Well, I've had other warnings,' says MacLean. 'Sometimes you risk breaking the rules to try to win. But I've managed to avoid a Shikaku.

'I wouldn't say the racing's rough,' he continues, 'but the Japanese are far more familiar with the rules and how much you can bend them … and the judges are far more lenient with the Japanese guys, so they tend to get away with murder, whereas the slightest infringement and we can be penalized quite heavily.'

As Kersten found out. Opening a diary entry with, 'SHIKAKU … I can't believe I got one of these,' he explains: 'In my last entry [headed: "Welcome to Alcatraz"] I touched on the similarities between a keirin tournament and prison. Well, I wasn't actually complaining. I much preferred being locked in the keirin than locked out …' Kersten was racing in Kumamoto, on day two of the three-day event (they're all three days), and riding at the front of a string of riders, waiting – as per the plan – for a line of two riders to come over the top. The plan had been for them to sit in front, with Kersten gaining some shelter, but, as they passed him, they 'broke rapidly and pushed me down inside the track'. Kersten began to drop back, in order to go around them again – the long way, around the outside. Then he remembered something from keirin school: that you are allowed to overtake on the inside, though only when 'a rider is forced from the sprinters' line to the inside of the track with physical force'.

Kersten, feeling he had been 'forced inside with physical force', thus accelerated up the inside, hit the front, and won the race. 'A submarine dive,' he called the tactic, and promptly fulfilled a winner's tradition – buying each of his beaten opponents a drink.

But, unbeknownst to him, the judges were studying his 'victory.' And then came their verdict: 'Shikaku!' 'I met with the judges and they were extremely apologetic and totally understood my manoeuvre,' writes Kersten. 'It is a legal move, but I waited a split second too long to decide to take the lead back, and break-ing that rule is punishable by a Shikaku.'

The punishment was even more severe than he had been led to believe. He thought he would simply be required to sit out the rest of the evening's racing, and be able to return the next day. But no. 'Pack your things,' he was told.

'Eh?' replied Kersten.

'Pack your things please.'

'Eh?!?'

'You're not allowed in the velodrome or dormitory after a Shikaku.'

'Eh??!!??'

'Taxi is waiting.'

'EH!!!???'

'Sorry.'

'Where do I sleep?'

'We booked you hotel. You pay for it. Sorry.'

'Ah Shi … kaku.'

'Sorry,' said the sympathetic – to a point – official.

In his hotel room, Kersten decided to make the best of a bad situation, heading out (alone) for a night on the town, drinking cocktails, and ending up in a karaoke bar with some locals. This, he discovered, helped him get over his Shikaku. 'Fortunately I now have a few fond memories of Japan,' he writes, 'and I can sing a little better.'

As with any industry so reliant on gambling, illicit betting is the big fear of those who run the Japanese keirin circuit. It is why mobile phones, computers and any other communication devices are confiscated; the riders are not allowed any contact with the outside world for the three days of a keirin meeting. As Kersten writes: 'Keirin riders are a lot like horses when it comes to gambling, only horses can't talk …' Even when the riders are racing, any gesture – such as a raised arm on winning a race – could result in a heavy fine. 'You are not searched [for communication devices],' says Kersten, 'but if you are found to have one of these you will be suspended for two years. The maximum penalty for illicit racing or accepting a bribe in Japan carries a three-year prison sentence …'

MacLean is aware of rumours of at least one betting scandal involving international riders in the past. 'It's been suggested that one foreign rider did try to fix it,' he says cagily. 'They changed the system after that – now there's only one international rider per race. They split us up more than they used to.

'We were all interrogated a few years ago,' he continues. 'At one race, a couple of minutes before the deadline for bets, there was a massive bet put on the one-two-three – and that was how it finished. It was completely against the odds. And it was three foreign riders. I wasn't in the race in question. But there was a big investigation; we all got interrogated by people from the keirin association, and independent people … it was quite daunting.'

As for how much the international riders make, MacLean says it isn't as much as some believe. His local newspaper published his (alleged) earnings in 2007, claiming he made around £25,000 in his two months in Japan. MacLean won't confirm if that's an accurate figure. But he hints that it isn't. The actual figures remain shrouded in almost as much a mystery as Japanese keirin racing itself.

Hoy, in any case, and regardless of the financial rewards accrued in his (so far) only season on the keirin circuit, has reason to be grateful for Japan's gift to the world of cycling. The keirin has provided an unexpected lifeline, and a possible source of a priceless second Olympic gold medal. Far from his depressing prediction on the day that the UCI announced the end of the kilo as an Olympic discipline – 'I feel like they've cut my career in half,' was his initial response – it seemed, as the 2007/08 season progressed, as though the keirin could be his best chance of gold in Beijing. Apart from his world-title-winning ride in Palma in 2007, his victories in the Sydney and Beijing World Cups – taking his tally to eighteen consecutive keirin wins – established him as the dominant force in the discipline, as impervious as he was in the kilo.

It prompted him to reassess his career, even to consider the axing of the kilo as a possible blessing. Every cloud, and all that … 'It might turn out to be a good thing for my career,' admitted Hoy, speaking just after the Beijing World Cup in mid-December 2007. 'I would never have wanted the kilo to go, but I would probably have ridden it [at the Olympics] in Beijing then had a couple of years out from it, because it's such a brutal event to train for. It drains you mentally and physically.'

Training for new events, says Hoy, has freshened him up; kept things interesting. And besides, after years of specializing on the kilo and team sprint, he maintains that he still has much to learn about the 'black arts' of match sprinting and keirin racing. More than that, however, what the change in focus, the switch of direction, has done has been to keep training enjoyable. 'What I'm starting to realize,' reflects Hoy, 'is that it's a massive privilege to do this. Before Athens I was really intense about it, but I'm starting to appreciate it more, get more perspective on it. I'm intense when I need to be. People might think, "Is he losing focus, losing the sharp edge?" ... but the world championships this year [in Palma] was the best I've ever been. It's about understanding yourself.'

Even Shane Sutton acknowledges that the 'trainaholic' Hoy is not as tightly tethered to training as he once was. 'He still needs to kill himself on the track to be able to relax at night,' smiles Sutton. 'But he knows when to back off now. He is getting to know his body better, to know what it can do and – just as importantly – what it can't do. There are even days now when Chris doesn't train! That's unheard of! But no question, he's a better athlete as a result of that.'

Some things don't change, though. On Christmas Day 2007, despite lashing rain and freezing temperatures, Hoy headed out for a two-hour ride on the road. 'Always train on Christmas day,' he says, 'because others might not.' But his mother has an alternative explanation. 'It's to avoid doing the sprouts!' suggests Carol.

It's early January, 2008, and I'm with Hoy, Craig MacLean, Ross Edgar, and the British sprint coach Jan van Eijden, at the Rotterdam Six-Day. Most six-day events are for specialist six-day riders – endurance riders who, in teams of two, contest a range of distance races on the track, in front of large, baying and beery crowds. In places like Ghent, Munich, Bremen and countless other European cities throughout the winter months, six-day racing is huge. What they have in common is an atmosphere unique to six-day events. They are part sporting event, part festival. The beer flows, the arena fills with the smells of barbecued meat and cigarette smoke

– in countries where this is still allowed. And every ten seconds or so there is a refreshing blast of cool air as the peloton, which usually includes one or two star names from the Tour de France, sweeps around the velodrome.

Rotterdam is unusual in also featuring a sprinters' grand prix, with the programme including sprint events – sprint, keirin, flying laps, team sprint – on each of the six evenings. The reason for this is, simply, Theo Bos – the Dutchman is a massive star in his native country, a hero. At the entrance to the track there is a 'Theo Bos Fan Club' stand. It sells posters, T-shirts, even a Theo Bos magazine, all celebrating a rider known, inevitably, as 'The Boss'.

He isn't the only one with a nickname in Rotterdam. Since six-day races have such an emphasis on showbiz, all the riders are assigned nicknames. Hoy is 'The General'. Edgar is 'Braveheart'. MacLean is, oddly, 'Sir MacLean'. 'I think it's because I'm from the Highlands of Scotland, and they think I live in a castle,' he suggests. Arnaud Tournant is 'The Gladiator'. Most curiously of all, the Dutch sprinter Yondi Schmidt is 'The Bastard'. MacLean enlightens me: 'It's something to do with Yondi having ginger – or red – hair. In Holland, buoys are all red. And apparently they are known as bastards.' Poor Schmidt. He manages a wry smile every time his name is mentioned by the excitable commentator, who urges the crowd, 'Let's hear it for the Bastard!'

The assigning of nicknames is only one of many theatrical aspects to the Rotterdam Six. It is a colourful, magical event. Picture the scene: it's a Thursday evening in early January, the weather is cold, the wind is biting, the rain is coming at you at a sharp angle, assaulting your cheeks, as, head down, you trudge across the vast and desolate car park that surrounds the Ahoy Arena on the edge of town. The vast, dark building at the other end promises little.

But you enter the arena, filter through the labyrinthine tunnels, climb up the stairs, up more stairs, and eventually reach a tunnel-like opening. Through this and there it is: a scene that floods the senses. There are two tiers of seating, filled with thousands of people – 8,000 to be precise, which is the number that attends the Ahoy Arena every night of the Rotterdam Six, drifting in and out of sessions that start around 7 p.m. and finish as late as 2 a.m. Even the track centre – which at normal track meetings is segregated into teams' pens – is filled with people: 1,000 of them, all enjoying hospitality and sideshows on mini stages erected around the centre. When the riders are not racing, they disappear as if by magic – though there is little that is magic about the basic cabins that provide their accommodation. Traditionally, in fact, and when six-day races carried on virtually twenty-four hours a day, they did provide a place for the riders to live and sleep for the few hours they weren't racing. And while the riders these days stay in hotels, for some of the *soigneurs* and mechanics on the six-day circuit, the cabins still are their 'digs'.

Quite apart from the spectacle of a six-day race, your ears are also assaulted mercilessly, through a combination of excitable Dutch commentators and Euro pop – endless Euro pop, mixed with old staples – 'We Will Rock You', 'The Eye of the Tiger' and so on.

And amidst the madness, encircling the partying crowds in the middle, there is, of course, an oval cycle track, covered in the names of sponsors and illuminated by lights. Entering the arena is like entering a football stadium at night, and seeing the luminescent green rectangle. Actually, it's not really like that at all. It's like a nightclub. As well as the music, there are flashing lights, strobe lights – the arena is regularly plunged into darkness, with the riders picked out by spotlights – and an enormous mirror ball. A mirror ball! How many sporting events have mirror balls? Not enough. But that's six-day racing for you – it is like no other sporting event. Yet, despite all the razzmatazz, there is the overriding and almost paradoxical impression that this is sport in the raw: the cycling equivalent of bare-knuckle boxing. You can smell the sweat, somehow – over the Euro pop – hear the whir of tyres on wood, and see the pain etched on the cyclists' faces as they lap the bowl. The contrast between beer-guzzling spectators and hard-grafting athletes has never seemed so striking.

Yet, in the Ahoy Arena and at most six-day races in Europe, it is a knowledgeable crowd, which mills around the beer and burger stands in the lulls, and switches its full attention back to the racing when it matters. Bos is a big draw, naturally, but in the first couple of days of the meeting Hoy seems to have the measure of him – he subdues the crowd by setting a new track record for the flying 200 m. Then he and MacLean stitch up The Boss in a keirin, rendering the 8,000-crowd momentarily dumb. Just as well that Bos manages to redeem himself with a few victories of his own, living up to one banner in the Ahoy Arena, which declares him 'The Master of the Universe'. 'The Fastest Man in the World' is another popular slogan – but that has some basis in reality, given that he is the world record holder over 200 m.

The real showman, however, is the Gladiator, Arnaud Tournant. The Frenchman laps it up. If Bos, with his serious demeanour, looks like a man not having enough fun, then Tournant looks like he's having too much. It is, he claims, his retirement year. He is still just twenty-nine – two years younger than Hoy – but he reveals that he intends to retire after the Beijing Olympics. It seems premature, but he has been around forever – he was a child prodigy and has been at the top for longer than Hoy. Perhaps because of his early brilliance, he has struggled to maintain the form that propelled him to four world kilo crowns, and, of course, that ultimate world record in Bolivia. Now, with the end in sight, he seems determined to enjoy himself. He engages easily with the crowd. They respond with requests for his autograph. He signs 'Arnaud Tournant58.875', the time of his kilo record cleverly entwined with the letters of his name.

For the sprinters, the main event is on the Saturday. They take centre stage for the Shimano Masters of Sprint competition, which sees them enter the arena like boxers, appearing at the top of a set of illuminated stairs, though these are not so easily negotiated in cleated cycling shoes, with the added distraction of eight cheerleaders in black bikini tops, brandishing pom-poms. Accompanying each of the riders is another glamorous female, in hot pants and knee-length boots, continuing the boxing theme by holding up the rider's nickname on a large board.

It is gloriously unreconstructed. The crowd love it. So do the riders – or some of them do. Tournant's entry into the arena, through the corridor of cheerleaders, takes an age, as, smiling broadly and charmingly, he pauses at each of the girls, embracing them and delivering a continental peck on each cheek. In contrast, Edgar, possibly the most laid-back man in cycling, seems underwhelmed. 'Are you excited Braveheart?' asks the MC. 'Oh yes,' replies Edgar, unconvincingly.

When Tournant reaches the track centre and the MC, he is interviewed. 'You are a real lover of the ladies, yah?'

'Oh yeah, for sure,' replies Tournant.

'But you are here to ride the bike, yah?'

'For sure, I am here to ride the bike this afternoon, but later, perhaps …'

Finally The Boss enters, taking the boxing theme to its obvious conclusion – he is wearing a silk gown, which he removes at the top of the stairs to reveal his predominantly white – with its distinctive rainbow coloured bands – world champion's outfit.

When, eventually, the show – sorry, racing – begins, Hoy deviates from the script once again by breaking the stadium record for the flying 200 m, his 10.438 seconds a full tenth of a second quicker than Bos. It seemed scripted, though, that he would reach the Masters of Sprint final – and face Bos. They certainly make a race of it. It is a full-blooded affair that has the crowd transfixed. With the bell ringing for a lap to go, and Hoy leading, Bos launches his effort, drawing level, at which point Hoy deviates slightly from his line, and the two clash. They don't so much collide as bounce off each other – not once but twice. It all looks pretty hairy. Neither backs off, and they race, shoulder-to-shoulder, for the line, Bos earning the verdict by an inch, and enjoying several laps of honour to a soundtrack of the most exuberant Euro pop.

It has always been rumoured that much of the racing in a six-day meeting is fixed. But that final between Bos and Hoy didn't look fixed. Hoy says no, it wasn't, though there is a glint in his eye as he reflects on the day's work. 'I'm pleased with my form,' he says. 'This is Theo's event, so it's good for the crowd that he wins, but I couldn't be happier with how I'm going.'

Hoy's Rotterdam Six is curtailed, unfortunately, by sudden illness. It strikes him on the Sunday – coincidentally, the day after a rare evening off (as mentioned in Chapter Seven), when Tournant, demonstrating again just how relaxed he was, insisted on buying large rounds of drinks. The next day, Hoy is unwell. But before the sceptics accuse him of a lack of professionalism, let it be said that this was not a hangover – this was full-blown flu. He struggles to the velodrome and takes part in the first race, only to collapse afterwards. The doctor tells him to return to his hotel and not to return. He isn't the only one who succumbs. A six-day race in a smokey, beery velodrome, with 8,000 people crammed in, is not the healthiest of environments – and the flu bug is rampant. MacLean is having none of it, though. 'It's a flangover,' he says of Hoy's illness. A flangover? 'A cross between flu and a hangover.'

Joking apart, it is flu. Of this there is no doubt. And a virus is potentially serious – as MacLean knows only too well, having struggled to shake off the effects of glandular fever over several months leading up to the 2004 Olympics. Hoy says he hasn't had an illness like it for years. Colds and sniffles, yes. Full-blown flu, no. For four days he is, he reports, 'completely flattened'.

Gradually, though, he returns to full training, and the big test comes a little over a month later, in the final World Cup of the season – the final one before the world championships; the final one, for that matter, before the Beijing Olympics. Having missed World Cup number three in Los Angeles in January, Hoy is placed second to Tournant in the overall standings for the keirin. An over-all victory would guarantee him a seat on the plane to Beijing – something which, perhaps surprisingly, he is refusing to take for granted.

The first night of the Copenhagen World Cup is inauspicious. The team sprint trio – Hoy, MacLean and Jamie Staff – could only manage fourth: a rare medalless outing. Indeed, it is clear from the ride that Staff – the first man – is the only one firing on all cylinders. Both Hoy and MacLean appear below-par, Hoy complaining of 'lethargy'.

But a day later, the keirin gives Hoy his chance to extend that extraordinary sequence of wins in international competition. Having not raced since Rotterdam, he is less than optimistic, repeating again the line that he 'expects to be beaten before Beijing'. But it doesn't happen in the first round, which he wins. Nineteen. And it doesn't happen in the second round. Twenty.

Now, he says, he is back. The bad legs and disappointing result from the team sprint are fading from the memory. He has reached the final of the keirin: in front of him is a chance to earn his third

World Cup victory, maintain his 100 per cent record, and get the automatic place in the Beijing Olympics that goes to world champions and overall World Cup winners. It could prove crucial, since it would guarantee Britain at least two riders in the keirin – potentially a significant advantage in an event in which team tactics can come into play, as they appeared to do – by accident or design – in the 2007 world championship final, when Hoy and Edgar combined to such good effect, placing first and third.

To illustrate this point, it is the presence of more than one Frenchman that poses the greatest threat to Hoy in the final in Copenhagen. As well as Tournant there is Grégory Baugé. There are also two Germans. Hoy is isolated. Before the final he speaks to Jan van Eijden.

'How do I ride it to beat Arnaud?' he asks him.

'You gotta ride the way you always ride and not think about Arnaud,' Van Eijden tells him. 'Race to win. Don't think about Arnaud. Don't think about the Olympics. Race the way you race best.'

Which means, of course, going from the front. It isn't the time to be experimenting with different strategies or tactics. What follows is a blood-and-thunder final. Hoy takes up his position behind the derny, focused on its back wheel, just millimetres away from it. Behind him his five rivals jockey for position then fall into line, and, with two laps to go, the derny peels off. The attacks come thick and fast: one, two, three, four. It is chaos. But the big one, the really big one, with a lap to go, comes from Baugé – it could be a French tactic to get Hoy to lead the chase, allowing Tournant to shelter in his slipstream, and come round him on the line. 'But I could see Baugé coming,' Hoy says later. 'So I was prepared for it.'

What Hoy does is subtly alter his line, drifting up the track a little – not enough to infringe Baugé, or incur the wrath of the judges, but just enough to force him to alter his line, to take a slightly longer way around. Then, as Baugé draws level, Hoy unleashes everything he has – 'Absolutely everything,' he says later. And the others, lining up behind him for a late charge, wilt. Tournant emerges from the melee to take second, but Hoy is the winner. Twenty-one.

A Dutch journalist calls Hoy in the aftermath to tell him that it is his twenty-sixth World Cup win. 'I didn't know that,' replies Hoy. But the main thing is Beijing. He's going. Relief. 'I'm delighted. That was a hell of a final – an epic. I've got a feeling tomorrow will be the end of my run. [Copenhagen hosted a one-off, non-World Cup Japanese Keirin, with a £10,000 first prize, during the World Cup weekend.] But that's me on the plane to Beijing – that's the main thing. It's a relief. And regardless of whether I get beaten tomorrow, the confidence from winning the World Cup keirin is … well, after the team sprint I had doubts, all kinds of questions, over whether I'd got over the illness … now I know the answer. I'm back to my old self.'

A silver medal in the sprint on the final day of the Copenhagen World Cup, losing to another Frenchman, Kevin Sireau, suggests that in the sprint, as well as the keirin, Hoy can be a force in Beijing. In the afternoon, on his knees through tiredness, he starts the Japanese keirin. He surprises himself in heat one, somehow, despite the aching legs, managing to win. Twenty-two.

But it can't last. The run shudders to a halt in round two. He can only manage fifth, but it has been, he reckons, the busiest weekend of his career. Including all the sprint matches on the way to the final, he has raced eighteen times. Tournant, incidentally, wins the final of the Japanese keirin – and takes home the cheque for £10,000. The drinks – again – are on him. 'But I'd rather be on the plane to Beijing,' says Hoy. Next stop, the world championships.

CHAPTER 14

The House Is on Fire;
We're Trying to Save the Furniture

Manchester Velodrome, March 2008

It is eight days until the world championships get underway in Manchester, where the British team and Hoy will attempt the seemingly impossible: to match the performance in Palma twelve months earlier, where they bagged a record-breaking seven gold medals. A tall order, certainly, but these championships are on home soil; the World Cups have shown the British team to be in medal-winning form; all is going smoothly, until ...

BANG!

During training, there's an explosion on one of the steeply banked corners of the velodrome.

CLATTER!

A rider hits the deck at speed, slides along the boards, and slithers to a halt.

PANIC!

It's Hoy.

He had been following the motorbike, piloted by Iain Dyer – the kind of session he does almost daily, and which I had witnessed at the training camp in Cottbus. Things had been going well. Actually, they had been going better than well: during an earlier motor-paced session, Hoy reached 82 kph (a fraction under 51 mph) – to his knowledge, the fastest he has ever gone on the track.

On this occasion, he followed the motorbike, eyes trained on its rear wheel, his front wheel just behind it, increasing the speed to 80 kph, legs spinning at 200 revs per minute, putting the finishing touches to his preparation, adding what they call 'top end' speed. After several laps he eased up and dropped back. It was as he was slowing down, and on the steepest part of the banking, that the calm of the Manchester Velodrome was shattered by that BANG!

The rear tyre exploded. Hoy went down – it is impossible to do otherwise. When those in the track centre arrived at the crumpled heap they found him bruised, battered, bleeding – but, crucially, not broken. Later, licking his wounds, he managed to dispatch a text message: 'Crashed in training today. Got blow out straight after an 80 kph motor chase! Luckily I'd slowed down to about 40 so I just lost some skin. Could've been disastrous tho.'

Then again, was it an omen? He had crashed days before the 2002 Commonwealth Games in Manchester, then again on the eve of the 2004 Olympics, and on both occasions, the latter with the livid red scars from his altercation with a bus in the games village still visible, he triumphed. The latest crash leaves Hoy with the kind of wounds that don't prevent training but do interrupt sleep and rest – big burns that take several days to scab, and weep constantly, uncomfortably, painfully; the kind that stick to bed sheets and clothes, which then, in an eye-wateringly painful ritual, have to be peeled off. In Hoy's case the wounds are concentrated in a particularly problematic area: his rear. It is, literally, a pain in the arse. Sitting is painful – except, luckily, on a saddle.

The Manchester Track Cycling World Championships carry special significance this year, of course. It is Olympic year. The British team, with expectations building, want to prove that Palma wasn't a one-off; they need to score the psychological advantage before Beijing. They also want to show off to an expectant home crowd – impressively, most of the five evening sessions are sold out several weeks before the championships begin. The others sell out as the event gets underway.

But these championships are significant in other ways, too. Could they mark the end of an era? Craig MacLean is missing – for the first time, incredibly, since 1995. It is staggering to realize that the last time MacLean didn't compete in a world championship John Major was still prime minister, Wayne Rooney was nine, and British cycling was in the dark ages.

MacLean, unhappy with his form, asked not to be considered for selection for Manchester. Like Hoy, his problems also amounted to a pain in the arse. A torn gluteus medius, suffered back in October, left him 'playing catch up' all season. 'It was like the other guys had a head start,' he explained, 'and I could never get them back. I'm still optimistic I can go to Beijing. But I've not been at my best and as soon as I made the decision not to go to the worlds I felt much happier. It's taken a weight off my shoulders.'

Still, it was difficult not to wonder whether perhaps MacLean, at thirty-six, had ridden his final world championship. Similarly, thirty-eight-year-old Jason Queally, who didn't make the team for Manchester, was speaking optimistically of going to Beijing – but you had to wonder how realistic that was. Regardless of the Olympics, the absence from the home world championships of two stalwarts of the British team sounded a poignant note and served as a reminder that sport can be the cruellest business. 'Compassionate ruthlessness' is Dave Brailsford's creed, remember, when it comes to telling people their time is up. Sentiment is noticeably absent.

Not that this is unique to the British team. Another of the legends of the previous decade, Arnaud Tournant, was feeling similarly marginalized in the build-up to the Manchester world championships – though he at least would be there. Much to his chagrin, Tournant had been overlooked for the team sprint. 'Sacre bleu!' was his response, or words to that effect. He would still ride the keirin, but, with the French the outstanding favourites, the team sprint was – as he saw it – his best shot at a gold medal in Manchester, and Beijing. In the run-up to his final world championships he was not happy and speculated openly, with much extravagant shrugging of the shoulders, about the sanity of the French selectors.

The build-up to the 2008 Manchester World Track Cycling Championships was characterized, then, by the usual bruised egos and bodies, but nothing, absolutely nothing, could have prepared Dave Brailsford for the bombshell that detonated on the opening morning. It was the start, he would later claim, of 'the worst day I've had in this job'. It was pretty bad, then.

It all started at 7 a.m. The British team, ensconced for the duration of the championships in a hotel close to the Manchester Velodrome, received a visit from the UCI blood testers. This is a regular procedure that started in 1997, when it was feared that the use of the then-undetectable EPO was rampant in professional road racing circles – a justifiable fear, as later events seemed to suggest. Back then, there was no test for EPO, a synthetic hormone that boosts the body's production of red blood cells – the cells that transport oxygen – and raises the athlete's haematocrit level. For endurance athletes, in particular, a high haematocrit can confer a significant advantage, having an effect similar to spending many weeks at altitude.

The blood tests carried out by the UCI can indicate the possible use of EPO, though they do not offer actual proof – they are called 'health checks' rather than dope tests. But if a rider's haematocrit is in excess of 50 per cent – unless the competitor has a certificate to prove that his natural level is that high – then he is deemed to have 'failed' the test and is prevented from racing. But such a 'failure' is not regarded as a positive drugs test, and there is no doping sanction – the competitor is simply withdrawn from competition for two weeks and allowed to resume racing if his blood values return to 'normal' in that period.

In 2000 a urine test for EPO was developed, but the health checks remain and the UCI – whose blood testers were inevitably christened 'vampires' when they began paying their early morning visits – carry out a vast number. On the opening morning of the track world championships they tested sixty-six riders. Two showed 'anomalies' and were forced to withdraw. One was the British rider Rob Hayles. BANG! CLATTER! PANIC!

Brailsford had just spent an hour riding his bike on the treadmill next to his office – a ritual he does at 7 a.m. every day. He felt fantastic that morning. But minutes later, when he strolled into the track centre to observe the last minute preparations for the championships, he was accosted by the British team doctor, Roger Palfreeman. 'I knew all the riders had been screened,' recalled Brailsford later. 'I didn't think anything of it. But Rog comes up to me and says, "Dave, we've got a problem." My heart sank. Within ten minutes, the whole world collapsed around me.'

For Brailsford it was the worst case scenario. Only, it wasn't. With 'the red light flashing', he tried to cling onto one important fact: Hayles, who had been due that first day to ride the individual pursuit, had not tested positive. His haematocrit had measured

50.3 per cent – 0.3 per cent over the limit set by the UCI, something for which there could – as there have been in previous cases
– be a perfectly logical, innocent explanation. But the explanations would have to come later. In the short term, there was confusion and, inevitably, suspicion. Brailsford's fear was that the
suspicion would engulf not only Hayles, but the entire British
team. His first task, however, was to break the news to the thirty-
five-year-old rider, a mainstay of the track team for more than a
decade.

'I went and got Rob out of his room. I told him, "Right Rob,
you're not riding." He was distraught. Then I had to ask him the
question: "Have you taken anything?" He looked me in the eye
and told me he hadn't. Then I had to take him to do the urine test
[for EPO], as is the procedure. As we were driving down to the
velodrome for him to do that he phoned his wife, and said: "Look,
don't bother coming to the velodrome today. I've gone over 50
per cent." 'I heard her ask, "Rob, have you done anything?" and
he said: "No."

'I didn't want to hear that conversation, to be honest; it felt
like an invasion of privacy. But at the same time, I was glad I did
hear it. If he's going to tell anyone the truth, he's going to tell his
wife. The way he spoke gave me strength; he didn't sound like
someone who was lying. But at the same time I'm thinking, if
he is lying, if this is a doping situation, there won't be a lot of
sympathy.'

Next, Brailsford delegated to Shane Sutton the task of keeping the rest of the team focused on the job in hand, while he fought
the flames, spending the day answering the media's questions,
trying to explain the nuances of the blood tests, constantly reiter-
ating that Hayles' test was 'an anomaly' rather than a positive drugs
test, while also leaving open the possibility that his rider had in
fact used drugs. Brailsford's instinct was to believe Hayles, but, on

the other hand, he was aware of the risk of aligning himself too closely with his rider until he could be sure of the facts. He had been burned once before, after all. 'I was sat in a bloody restaurant in Biarritz when two guys from the drugs police in Paris appeared with guns,' he recalled of the time, almost four years earlier, when he sat discussing future plans with David Millar, hours before the Scot confessed, during an interrogation by the drugs police, that he had used EPO.

Now, having only the previous day featured in a big interview in *The Times* newspaper, in which he espoused his team's clean ethos, Brailsford admitted he 'felt a bit of an idiot ... all the emotion of what happened with Dave Millar came flooding back. I felt beside myself. I kept saying to myself: look at the facts, look at the facts, look at the facts. But it seemed like the worst thing that could happen, on the worst day ... it was difficult to keep it in perspective, particularly because as an organization we try to be very open and transparent and we pride ourselves on the fact that we do this properly and clean.'

Later, more details emerged of Hayles' 'failed' test. Information was gleaned from the follow-up blood tests, ordered by Brailsford to be carried out every two days for four weeks. These suggested that Hayles' red blood cell count hadn't suddenly increased; rather, the volume of blood plasma had decreased, thus increasing the concentration – rather than the actual number – of red blood cells. Although Hayles hadn't previously gone over the 50 per cent limit, he later revealed that he had been close, registering 48 per cent on the eve of the 2006 Commonwealth Games in Melbourne. His natural level, it appeared, was somewhere in the high forties, ranging typically from forty-five to forty-eight. What had caused it to suddenly lurch over fifty remains unknown for sure, but it is thought that a heavy workload of training, followed by an 'extreme taper' – amounting almost to complete rest – can affect the blood plasma (within a few days of Hayles' anomaly, with the rider having resumed training, his haematocrit had dropped to 45 per cent).

Medical opinion, including that of the UCI doctor Chris Jarvis, backs up the theory that heavy training, followed by rest, can result in such fluctuations. 'I have come across athletes who have recorded plus-fifty haematocrit and are not guilty of doping – absolutely,' explains Jarvis. 'There are various physiological factors that can affect it. Training hard and then tapering off can have a significant effect. One colleague told me of an individual who, at the end of a long stage race, had a haematocrit of forty. After resting for a week he was above fifty. There are other possible factors – dehydration, even moving around. The best time to do the test is when an athlete is in bed, which is why they're done first thing in the morning. I understand, though, that [Hayles] had been up and about for a couple of hours. That could have an effect.'

(Incidentally, the other rider forced to withdraw on the same day as Hayles, Pim Ligthart, a nineteen-year-old Dutchman about to ride his first world championships, was subsequently cleared. In his case, a stomach virus had stimulated the production of new red blood cells; Ligthart's haematocrit, in fact, measured only 43 per cent, but the high concentration of new red cells alerted the suspicions of the UCI blood testers, and caused his 'failed' test. As Hayles noted, that was 'good news for him, but it was too late – he missed the championship'. Hayles also observed, in relation to his own fate, that: 'It's a bit ironic that I was stood down on health grounds – the stress it caused me has probably knocked a few months off my life.')

In time, the evidence available to Brailsford and the doctors who studied the case appeared to suggest that Hayles' anomaly was just that – an anomaly. But on the opening day of the championships it was a disaster, stirring up suspicion around the British team, and forcing Brailsford to seriously consider his position. 'For twenty-four hours I was going to quit. I thought, we're pushing too hard, we're too good, everybody's gonna think it's being done under false pretences. I don't want to be in a situation where out of the blue it all disappears, and I've got no control. I haven't lied, my integrity's intact; if I do something ridiculous, I pay the consequences. But if all of a sudden everything I've got is gone on the basis of what someone else has done … I thought, I'll go and sell cars instead. That first night [after Hayles' withdrawal] Shane and I were rocked. Seriously rocked. Shane and I live on the energy of it all. Neither of us are good sleepers at the best of times, but we were texting each other at all hours that first night. Just saying, "Fucking hell, this is shit."'

If ever Brailsford needed his British team to produce a performance, to reaffirm his faith, rekindle his enthusiasm, reignite his passion, it was at the world championships in Manchester at the end of March, 2008. But could he ever have foreseen what would unfold over the course of five nights, in front of 5,000-capacity crowds? Could anyone?

The opening night, against the backdrop of the Hayles case, is played out to a slightly surreal atmosphere – perhaps not sensed by the crowd, but infecting many of those involved with the British team like a mild virus. Bradley Wiggins, the defending world and Olympic pursuit champion, qualifies second to a virtually unknown Dutchman – this after vomiting shortly before his qualifying ride. Later, he puts his sickness and the puzzle surrounding his friend and fellow team pursuiter Hayles behind him, to roar to victory, pulverizing his Dutch opponent in the final.

In the team sprint Hoy is going for a new record: a remarkable tenth consecutive medal in the discipline. With Jamie Staff and Ross Edgar the line-up is a little unfamiliar, but they qualify second, in a British record time, to set up a meeting, inevitably, with the French in the final. For this, the French pull a surprise – they reinstate Arnaud Tournant, who replaces Mickael Bourgain for the anchor leg. So the final will conclude with Hoy and Tournant, racing head-to-head yet again.

In the event, Hoy, taking over from Staff and then Edgar, has too big a gap to close – the French are untouchable. Their winning time, 43.271 seconds, is their second world record of the evening. But the British trio are pleased: despite Edgar, by his own admission, not being at his best, their 43.777 seconds is a British best, albeit the margin between the two top teams has stretched in the twelve months since Palma from two-thousandths of a second to more than half a second. 'The French have raised the bar,' concedes Hoy. 'You can't be disappointed to finish second to a performance like that. I think they are beatable, but it'll take a perfect ride. It needs all three of us to be at our absolute best.'

On the podium, with the French on the top step, what happens next seems to sum up a curious, at times surreal, first day. As the three teams stand to attention, awaiting the French anthem, they do so in silence. The silence lingers. Still they wait; the crowd, too. But the silence lingers on, until it begins to be interrupted by embarrassed shuffling. Glances and puzzled expressions are exchanged; faces redden. Oh Christ. Has the velodrome's notoriously tinny public address system broken? Even more embarrassingly, has someone forgotten the CD with the French national anthem?

Still there is silence. And then, from a corner of the packed stands, a lone voice strikes up ...

Allons enfants de la Patrie
Le jour de gloire est arrivé!
Contre nous de la tyrannie ...

Almost simultaneously, the opening lines of 'La Marseillaise' become audible in another part of the stand, and, like a 'Mexican Wave', it spreads. Though the various choirs are in pockets, and might not be in perfect sync, the arena is soon resounding to a rendition of the French anthem. On the podium, Tournant, Grégory Baugé and Kevin Sireau join in, smiling broadly. The other riders sing – or mouth the words – and clap in time. It is rousing and strangely moving. At the end of a traumatic day perhaps even Brailsford can, finally, manage a smile – so long as he ignores any unfortunate associations conjured up by the line about *sang impur* (tainted blood).

'Thirty years of hurt' they sang in 1996, when the European Football Championships were held in England and the home team was one of the favourites to win a first major trophy since 1966. It didn't happen, of course. But thirty years is nothing. Thirty years is inconsequential. Try fifty-four.

In Cologne in 1954, Reg Harris – arguably the most famous cyclist Britain has ever produced – won his fourth world sprint title. In those days, there were separate titles for the amateur and professional ranks; Harris won his final pro' crown, and, bizarrely, Britain also provided the amateur winner – one Cyril Peacock. Britain can honestly say, then, that in 1954 it ruled the world of match sprinting – arguably the blue riband of the track cycling disciplines, with its quirky but very identifiable traditions of cat-and-mouse tactics, stationary track stands and so on.

But since 1954 there had been zilch, nothing. Racing *mano a mano*, rather than against the clock, is something the British don't appear to have mastered, even in the ten years of the British track cycling revolution. Since 1954, British riders have, with the notable exceptions of Craig MacLean's silver medal in Bordeaux in 2006, and Dave Handley's bronze in the amateur title race in 1960, failed to win a medal in the event. Yet, for many track cycling aficionados, match sprinting is the purest form of racing – it is the event that gets the blood pumping.

Which goes some way to explaining why, when the Manchester Velodrome was constructed, there was one outstanding candidate to be immortalized in bronze: Reg Harris. The statue, depicting him in bike-bending racing pose, out of the saddle and sprinting for home, his thick, muscular legs rendered in bronze, looms over the third and final bend, as the riders enter the home straight.

Harris would have marvelled at the match sprinting on display over the two days of the 2008 world championships. And he would have rejoiced, surely, at the performance of a British rider making his world championship sprint debut, whose previous credentials as a specialist sprinter were, to put it mildly, rather modest.

A sight that summed up the surprising turn of events was that of Grégory Baugé, the great Frenchman, leaning over the barriers in the track centre, head buried in his arms, at the conclusion to the two-day sprint competition. He was weeping. And no wonder: he was one of three Frenchmen to pack the first three positions in the 200 m time trial that serves as qualifying for the sprint. The World Cup winner Kevin Sireau was first; Mickael Bourgain was second; Baugé was third. Sireau's time – 9.992 seconds – sent shockwaves: it was the fastest ever recorded in Manchester; it established him as one of very few to have broken the magic ten-second barrier.

Hoy qualified fourth, with a personal best of 10.032 seconds. Having suffered a scare in the second round, when German Maximilian Levy crossed the line first, only to be relegated for an illegal move, he progressed to the quarter-final. But here he faced what looked on paper an almost impossible task. He was up against Theo Bos, unbeaten in a match sprint since 2005, world champion in 2006 and 2007, whose 9.772 seconds 200 m record, set in Moscow in 2006, is considered one of the outstanding world records in cycling. The Dutchman – the Boss – was the favourite, certainly. And then, in the first of their best-of-three heats, Hoy goes and gives him a head start.

He simply switched off. Those in the stands were paying more attention, and could scarcely believe it when Hoy appeared not to notice Bos attacking. By the time he did realize, Bos had fifteen metres' advantage. He chased, but it was futile, and, realizing there was no way he could catch him, Hoy sat up and Bos rolled through the final 200 m for perhaps the easiest win of his career. One–nil.

It meant Hoy's margin for error in heat two was nil. He paid attention this time, reacting quickly to any moves Bos made, but the two were inseparable as they raced towards the line. In the final centimetres Hoy lunged – so powerfully that his front wheel lifted off the ground as he crossed the line – but it was enough, just, to gain him the verdict. A decider was required. And this was a typical cat-and-mouse affair: Hoy leading, Bos feinting, then diving down the inside, and Hoy reacting; round the final bend and the tall, lean Dutchman leads, but Hoy draws level as they go elbow-to-elbow, and in the final metres he inches ahead. Hoy is through. 'In the first ride I gave him the race,' he says. 'I looked away and he pounced; he'd gone. It was an unforgivable mistake. I was so pissed off with myself, so angry, to make such a blatant error. I just wanted to make amends for that in the second round. When I got that one I knew I could beat him in the third. To beat Bos feels great. I've got nothing to lose now.'

In the semi-final Hoy met Roberto Chiappa, the veteran Italian enjoying something of an Indian summer. The draw could have been less kind. In the other semi, Bourgain met Sireau, who had knocked out Baugé in the quarter-final. The French, in other words, were taking care of each other: it augured well. But this was no quirk of the draw; rather, it was noticeable that, while the French were clearly the fastest on paper – witness their domination of the qualifying time trial – they were making hard work of the man-against-man duels of match sprinting, where pure speed is useful – clearly – but isn't everything. Tactics also come into it. Sireau, indeed, could be said to be fortunate to make it this far – he had been beaten in the second round by Chiappa, and had only managed to progress through the repêchage – effectively the last chance saloon that allows knocked out riders a final shot at redemption.

In his semi-final, Sireau, the twenty year old with an awesome turn of speed, beat Bourgain over two straight – but hard-fought – rides. Hoy, meanwhile, dispatched Chiappa with relative ease. He was through to the sprint final, something which exercised the statisticians. It was his first ever crack at the world sprint title – had anyone won the world sprint title at a first attempt? It also appeared that there was now the possibility of Hoy becoming the first cyclist ever to win the grand slam of all four sprint titles – kilo, team sprint, keirin … sprint? And even more impressively, he could become the first cyclist ever to win world titles in four different disciplines. From the domestic point of view, there was also the chance of the wait for a British rider to win the sprint title coming to a stunning conclusion … could fifty-four years of hurt finally be about to end?

And so to the final. Seconds out, round one. These two riders met a month earlier, in the World Cup final in Copenhagen. Sireau won 2–0. In fact, Hoy has never beaten the Frenchman in 'meaningful competition'. The baby-faced Sireau, resplendent in his all-white World Cup winner's outfit, eyes hidden behind dark glasses, is the outstanding favourite. The gun goes off and Hoy leads it out,

riding slowly around the bottom of the track, craning his neck to
check his opponent. Sireau keeps his distance, stalking him, waiting for the moment to pounce. Perhaps hoping that, as in his quarter-final against Bos, Hoy's attention will wander – he only needs
a split second.

With one-and-a-half laps to go, Sireau makes his move. He
surges past Hoy, a gap opens, it stretches, and, on the final lap,
as they enter the back straight, Hoy appears to be struggling to
close it. He is fighting his bike, his style unusually ragged, but,
surprisingly, given the speed Sireau is capable of, he seems to find
an extra gear: the gap narrows, Hoy is on to his back wheel. He
has to come the long way, around the outside, but on the final
bend he draws level, and on the home straight the two riders are
side-by-side, and on the line, with a photograph needed to separate them, Hoy gets the verdict. One–nil. He doesn't acknowledge
the victory.

Round two. A reverse of the first: Sireau leads, very slowly.
Hoy follows, his gaze not wandering from the Frenchman. He is
a little higher up the track, like an animal about to pounce on its
prey. Sireau gradually increases the pace but Hoy doesn't move.
And as they cross the line with a lap to go, the clanging bell adding
to a charged, frenzied atmosphere, they are moving fast, almost
sprinting flat out. Hoy, the bulkier of the two, still in Sireau's
shadow, still a little higher up the banking than his opponent,
looks menacing. Sireau looks slight by comparison, and vulnerable. Then Sireau dives for the bottom of the track – the sprinters'
line, they call it – and Hoy responds. Sireau is sprinting flat out
now; he can't afford to look round. But he knows Hoy is approaching; he can sense him. On the back straight he flicks out – not
dramatically, not enough to incur a penalty, just a subtle devia-
tion in his line, enough to make Hoy wary, perhaps force him to
check his effort, alter his line.

It doesn't work: Hoy is onto him, alongside him, and narrowly ahead as they come out of the final bend – where Reg Harris has the best view – and there are no doubts as he thunders along the finishing straight. Long before the line Sireau appears defeated; he looks like he's hit reverse. Hoy crosses the line first, hands on the drops, head nodding up and down three times in quiet celebration, which is more than can be said for the 5,000 people in the crowd. 'The personification of class and dedication,' says the BBC commentator Hugh Porter as Hoy milks the applause and finally rolls to a halt at the point in the stand where his parents, Carol and David, sister Carrie and girlfriend Sarra, are sitting.

Meanwhile, the person wearing the broadest smile in track centre is Jan van Eijden, the specialist sprint coach hired by British Cycling to help Hoy master the transition from powerful kilo rider to tactically astute sprinter. 'I'm a bit surprised,' admits Van Eijden. 'I didn't expect it, but we've seen the whole season that he has the potential, and we all know what a classy bike rider he is, and a classy guy. He gives me a lot of credit but it's everyone: Iain Dyer, Shane Sutton, Scott Gardner … the whole team that's behind him. We all back each other up. But Chris is the one on the line.'

There seem to be tears in Van Eijden's eyes. 'I am a bit emotional,' he admits. Could that be because, the last time the world championships were held in Manchester, in 2000, he was the winner? 'No – it's for Chris,' he says. 'I go through the emotions of the race too much, but it's just my way. I still live every race. I really enjoyed that! I knew he was capable but it was a question of how long it would take him to make the transition … now he goes to the Olympics as one of the fastest. And as the world champion! He has everything. It's nice of him to give me credit, but, you know, I have to give *him* the credit. He gave me the chance to work with him. He was already many times a world champion, but he sucked it in; he sucked up all I had to tell him, any help I could give him. Now he can go to the Olympics and win three gold medals. I really believe that.'

It was late when they got back to the hotel – after 11 p.m. – but Brailsford called a team meeting. 'I got everyone in the team into a room and said: "Anyone who's over fifty-four, stick your hand up." Only two did, and I said: "What was done tonight has never been done in any of our lifetimes – apart from you two old fellas." That brought it home. We've been winning so many medals it gets a bit diluted, but no one had won that title since Reg Harris. Think about how many world championships have been held since then. Chris's ride was nothing short of phenomenal. It was the win against Bos that did it for me: that was the turning point. That was incredible.'

And so, indeed, was the collective performance of Brailsford's team. With two days left, the gold medal tally stood at six – just one short of the record-breaking total in Palma. The unthinkable looked on: they could surpass that. It presented Brailsford with a problem: 'I had to get the thesaurus out to look for new superlatives.'

You could see his point as he reeled off his highlights. 'Bradley Wiggins in the pursuit – that was a massive performance. Then the next night, the team pursuit; for Bradley and the boys to come out and break the world record – that was something special. Chris beating Bos – unbelievable. Rebecca [Romero] in the women's pursuit – incredible. Vicky [Pendleton] stepping up with two more gold medals – incredible.'

There was a sense of inevitability, next day, in Hoy's march to the final of the keirin. Yet the semi-final looked, on paper, like it could pose a problem. For one thing, the six-man field included three Australians – Shane Perkins, Shane Kelly and the reigning Olympic champion, Ryan Bayley. Ordinarily, or traditionally, that would be enough to instil fear in the rest of the field, which, as well as Hoy, included 2005 world champion Teun Mulder of the Netherlands. The keirin is an event in which team tactics can be deployed, and there was a time when you'd have fancied the Aussies, with such overwhelming numerical advantage, to stitch up this semi-final.

But there was an intriguing subplot to this race, giving rise to suspicions that the Aussies might not be a unified force. According to reports in the Australian press, Perkins and Bayley are sworn enemies and can barely stand to be in the same room as each other, never mind work together in a race situation. Theirs is a feud that has been intensified by the former becoming engaged to the latter's sister, though Bayley has insisted that that has little to do with it. 'It's not because he's engaged to my sister,' Bayley explained. 'I didn't like him a long time before that.'

In the semi-final, Hoy, though he is boxed in and surrounded by Australians for the early part of the race, hits the front just inside two laps to go, and executes his normal race plan: he rides so fast that no one can get near him, never mind come past him. He wins. For the three Australians it is a disaster. They occupy the last three places: fourth, fifth and sixth. Earlier, Hoy had also won the qualifying round, meaning that – if you discount the invitational Japanese keirin in Copenhagen – his run of successive wins in international – or official UCI – keirins now stands at twenty-four.

The final, though it includes Arnaud Tournant and Mulder, is arguably weaker than the semi. Again making his surge with two laps to go, taking the lead and holding it, Hoy makes it look ridiculously easy. Mulder fights back in the closing straight, but Hoy begins his celebrations before he has even crossed the line. It is not a victory – it is utter domination, the likes of which keirin racing has never witnessed. For the record, that is twenty-five successive wins. He is 'the Tiger Woods of keirin racing', suggests Hugh

Porter, adding, 'I really hope that, when Chris does retire, he is given a very important position in sport. They've given the rowers knighthoods … I'd be the first to support it if they said, "Arise, Sir Chris."'

Brailsford's verdict? 'Just … un … believable.' And by the end of it all, with his team having won nine gold medals? 'We've crushed everybody. I don't think there's any other word for it.' Which might sound triumphalist, but Brailsford's expression speaks of surprise more than anything. He really can't believe it.

And Martin Barras, the Australian coach who had so memorably asserted in Palma, twelve months ago, that his team had received 'a righteous kick up the arse', what did he make of it? 'It's like the house is on fire, and we're just trying to save the furniture.'

'I don't think we've peaked yet,' says the now nine-time world champion Hoy as he reflects on a glorious individual and team performance. 'In terms of performance, and equipment, I honestly believe there's more to come.'

Brailsford expands on this. Sitting on a chair in Shane Sutton's office – behind him, on a white board, a scrawled message reads: 'Note to self: Relax' – the British performance director reflects on the championships, from the low of Rob Hayles' exclusion, to the 'phenomenal … unbelievable … incredible' performances of his leading athletes; 'so many great, great sporting moments', as Brailsford puts it. Yet it has been, he admits, 'an emotional rollercoaster, tainted by what happened at the start with Rob. It's just as well that we have a very good psychiatrist on the team. He's earned his corn this week, I can tell you.'

The dust is settling now on what will, a few days later, be described on the cover of one magazine as the best performance by any British team in any sport. Ever. Inside, it poses what is now a reasonable question: 'Is Chris Hoy Britain's greatest ever cyclist?' And next day, the achievement receives the April Fool's Day treatment, with the *Cycling News* website reporting that the UCI is investigating whether the interaction of the stripes on the British team's skinsuits with mystical ley lines – connecting Stonehenge with Rosslyn Chapel and running directly through the Manchester Velodrome – could have given them an unfair advantage. It must be some kind of measure of the team's dominance that some believed it.

Brailsford exudes satisfaction – and enthusiasm. As he talks about coming into work every morning at 7 a.m., riding for an hour on the treadmill, to set himself up for the day; and as he reveals that Shane Sutton, his office separated from Brailsford's by very thin walls, 'hasn't mastered the art of not shouting – even when he's having conversations about me, about the things I don't do well ...' it is clear that his enthusiasm has returned. And sheer, undiluted, unrestrained enthusiasm – from Brailsford to Hoy to the coaches, mechanics and masseurs – seems to be a crucial element in the chemistry of the British team, perhaps *the* crucial element, permeating the entire squad like damp – or liquid sunshine.

It isn't all wide-eyed enthusiasm, however. As Brailsford talks, there is a mischievous glint in his eye. 'Neither you, nor any of the teams here, have seen the full range of what we have,' he says. 'We have a team of people, boffins basically, headed up by Chris [Boardman], and what they've produced is ... miraculous. But timing is everything. We haven't used everything here, but we've used everything at some point – in World Cups and other events. We have someone photographing us using it; photographing the commissaries inspecting it, and passing it as legal. We've got all this photographic evidence in a portfolio; it's a file of pictures, proving that we've used all this stuff in competition, and proving it's been passed as okay. If we are challenged at the Olympics in Beijing, we produce that and say: there you are.'

Now Brailsford is on a roll. 'One of the major, major things has happened here – a really major innovation, here in Manchester. And no one's noticed it. But we've got it on film. It's in the file. It's in the file of the Secret Squirrel Club, which Chris is in charge of. I'm not in it, in fact. I'm not allowed in the Secret Squirrel Club, because I blab. I'm too keen to tell everybody. So I better shut up.

'All I will say is that there's more to come.'

CHAPTER 15

'This Is Your Everest'

Beijing, August 2008

'There's more to come.' Chris Hoy and Dave Brailsford echoed each other when they said this at the conclusion to the world championships in Manchester in March. *More* to come? Both sounded so certain, but ... really?

The build-up to Beijing was strange, not least because the momentum established by the British team in Manchester was lost, for the simple reason that there was no racing. It was the track cyclists' off-season. So there was a hiatus; they disappeared from view; they went into hibernation. Some hibernation this, though: it was one that would entail nothing but clean living and hard work.

In mid-June, six weeks out from the Olympics, I met Hoy in Manchester. He was chirpy and radiated good health. He had just done a personal best in the weights room, squat-lifting 227.5 kg: more than double his bodyweight. It meant ... well, what did it mean? That he can lift heavy weights? But does it mean he can ride a bike faster? 'It's a component,' he said. 'And my aim is to do a personal best in every component before Beijing.'

Hoy is confident, bullish in the run-up to Beijing – strikingly, almost scarily, so. There are no setbacks, no blips, not even the traditional pre-major event crash. Could that be a bad omen? Hoy doesn't think so; he says he 'doesn't believe' in superstition. 'To me,' he says, 'it's a sign of weakness. Some athletes have lucky socks or teddy bears, but I don't believe in that. What happens if you forget your lucky sock, or something happens to your teddy? It would affect you mentally, which is crazy. So I definitely regard superstition as a weakness.'

What he does believe in is good coffee. So he does order one special item for Beijing which he has seen on a gadget show on TV. The prospect of being the owner of a hand-pump espresso machine, and being able to enjoy his usual two double espressos a day, fills him with excitement. 'Everyone is taking the piss out of my hand-pump espresso machine,' he complains in Newport, where the British team has its final pre-Beijing training camp. 'But we'll see who's laughing when we get to the athletes' village and they find out the coffee is terrible.'

Details, details.

In Newport, personal bests in the other 'components' are ticked off. 'Things have been going very well,' says an even chirpier Hoy three days before leaving for Beijing. 'In one session this week I did six personal bests over 100 m and 200 m. For the 200, I did a 9 ... actually, I'd rather not say what I did. Just that I did two sub-tens.'

This is significant: he has never been below ten seconds over 200 m before. The world record, 9.772 seconds, set by Theo Bos on the ultra-quick track in Moscow, is an awesome mark, but sub-ten-second times for the 200 m are still rare; in track and field, they are probably equivalent to a sub-9.9-second 100 m. 'It didn't feel particularly special though,' says Hoy. 'It just felt normal. I just carried on with my session. I didn't get carried away, partly because everyone else in the team – the team pursuiters, for example – are also doing incredible times in every session. It's quite frightening how everyone is going. It's a sign that it's all falling into place. Everything's flowing nicely, I'm not chasing my form. Training sessions just happen. And your confidence grows as you train better and rest more. At the moment I'm happy that I'll be going to Beijing in the form of my life. I can't do anything about the other guys, only myself. And from that point of view I'm in a nice position.'

He didn't want to reveal his actual time, incidentally, for fear that the information would leak out to some of his rivals. It was interesting that he was so guarded. It was a consequence, no doubt, of the 'hibernation' – the fact that all the track cyclists were preparing in splendid isolation, without the regular feedback on their form and fitness that is provided by racing. Hoy did race twice in minor races in Germany, winning the sprint competitions in both, which suggested he was in decent form but proved little. None of his rivals, other than Theo Bos, were racing there, and while Bos looked a shadow of the rider who'd dominated this event up to 2007, and who still holds that outstanding world record, there could be all kinds of reasons for his indifferent form – Hoy knew 'The Boss' couldn't be discounted. More alarming was the news that filtered through from the French championships. Mickaël Bourgain had, according to reports, recorded a 9.8-second 200 m – the second-fastest time ever recorded in competition. As Hoy predicted in Manchester, it appeared that the French would arrive in Beijing having 'upped their game'.

And so to Beijing, the twenty-five-strong British team – 2 BMX, 6 road, 2 mountain bike, 15 track – arriving with a couple of new faces and without a couple of familiar ones, since Craig MacLean and Jason Queally have missed out. At the beginning of July both had taken on 20-year-old Jason Kenny in a specially arranged trial in Manchester, the outcome of which presented the selectors – for all that MacLean and Queally have been such stalwarts of the team – with no great dilemma.

Kenny, the triple world junior champion in 2006, produced times that weren't just impressive, they were phenomenal. 'We witnessed an unbelievable trial, with all the riders posting world-class times,' said Brailsford, 'and I want to pay tribute to Craig and Jason for the way they approached it. They are true champions in the way they conducted themselves when they learned they had not made the cut.'

'I can't be disappointed,' said MacLean, sounding, inevitably, disappointed. 'Jason Kenny proved that he deserves to go. I just want to wish them the best of luck.'

Queally is also disappointed, and announces his retirement. But liberated from the ban on gambling imposed on Olympic athletes, he visits the bookies, places a substantial long-odds bet on one of his old team-mates, and settles back to watch the Games unfold on television, betting slip stored in a very safe place. He doesn't mention the bet to the team-mate in question.

When the cyclists arrive at the athletes' village in Beijing they are taken into a studio, and shown a film, put together by Sir Clive Woodward, coach to England's Rugby World Cup winning team in 2003, now the British Olympic Association's performance director. It is intended as a motivational film, featuring British Olympic heroes, and asking the question, 'How do you want to be remembered?' But when it finishes the cyclists, unlike some athletes from other sports, respond with silence. They don't burst into applause, or wipe away tears, as others do. They appear unmoved.

Two days before the track cycling programme begins, they are shown another film, this one put together by the team's own performance analysts. This one splices together images of their opponents with some of themselves, and it is set to an unusual soundtrack: the rousing, confrontational, highly charged speech delivered by Jim Telfer on the Lions Tour of South Africa in 1997. As Telfer, in his gruff Borders tones, put it:

> This is your fucking Everest boys ... the top of Everest. Defeat doesn't worry me. They've had it often and so have you. It's performance that matters. If you put in the performance, you'll get what you deserve ... No luck attached to it. You have to find your own solace. Your own drive, your own ambition. Your own inner strength. The moment has arrived. The greatest game of your fucking life. They are better than you have played against so far. They are better individually. Or they wouldn't be there. So it's an awesome task you have. So it will only be done, as I say, if everyone commits themselves.

This one has the desired effect. Hoy says it is 'spine-tingling'. Ross Edgar is in tears. Most importantly, it leaves them itching to compete. As Hoy says, it's not just him, the entire team has been flying in training. Consequently, they exude supreme self-belief. It is arguably as focused, as confident – and therefore as happy – a team as any in Beijing.

The team's psychiatrist, Steve Peters, is with them, of course. Peters is an essential member of the team, as much for the staff as for the riders. 'Recently a mechanic remained very calm under pressure,' says Peters, 'and he was delighted to achieve this, and it helped the team. He was pleased, and so were we.

'Everyone is important,' he continues. 'We function as a whole. We are not the Waltons – we keep getting called that. I believe it is more like the Waltons with a touch of EastEnders. Okay, we have our moments; we have differences of opinion and sometimes we have clashes – the way you do, healthy arguments – just like any team does. [But] I try hard to give respect to everybody's opinion.'

Ahead of Beijing, Peters developed a new model. 'I call it the CORE principle, to drive home some key points for success: Commitment, Ownership, Responsibility and Excellence. It's actually "Personal Excellence", but the reason I didn't put that in was that it would then spell "CORPE" – which is too close to "corpse" so I dropped it. I only invented the term to give the idea that we actually do have a structure, because that's what I've worked hard to do: to bring structure to mental skills training. But it's not just mental skills training – it's really our approach to life.'

Has Peters told his charges how to play – and win – mind games? Possibly, because a couple of days before the Beijing Opening Ceremony, Kevin Sireau, the French sprinter who won silver behind Hoy at the world championships, fires the opening salvo, confidently predicting that the British team will 'not be as good as they were in Manchester, where they were on their home track'.

Hoy, in his 'bubble' in the athletes' village, is oblivious to Sireau's comments, so, in the interests of stirring up trouble, he has to be told. 'Did he really say that?' asks Hoy. 'Ha, excellent! He's in for a shock then, because we're going better.'

Sunday, 10 August 2008

Day two of the Games and the women's road race features 25-year-old Welshwoman Nicole Cooke, supported by British teammates Emma Pooley and Sharon Laws. The day before, it had been the men's race, and all three British men failed to finish, prompting one Sunday newspaper to suggest that the team had got its preparation wrong. So much had been expected of the cycling team, they note, and yet here, at the first hurdle, they had flopped.

Would this, they ask, be the story of the Games? One of British failures, and excuses ...

The women's event is different: Cooke is one of the favourites. And she rides a tactically perfect race, with Pooley sacrificing her own chances to help her. It works a treat, and Brailsford's 'twelve-month project' to help Cooke become Olympic champion – and win a first Olympic or world championship gold medal in a road event – is realized. On a rain-lashed day, Cooke sprints in at the head of a small break, yelling as she crosses the line, and throwing herself into Brailsford's arms. It is a sweet, sweet victory. It has also got the British cycling team up and running. Three days later, Pooley wins silver in the time trial.

Friday, 15 August

Day one in the Laoshan Velodrome, a silvery, space-age building around thirty minutes from the 'Olympic Village' – and therefore out on something of a limb in the Beijing suburbs. Inside, it is modest, its 6,000 seats making it a little bigger than the Manchester Velodrome, but not by much. It makes it initially hard to comprehend that here, in this arena, is where careers will be defined and legends created.

The only indication is the ubiquity of the five rings, the Olympic trademark; and, when the racing starts, the intensity of the athletes. It is the most marked difference in those sports in which the Olympics represent the absolute pinnacle – track and field, swimming, gymnastics, track cycling. While the atmosphere around the football and tennis competitions is flat, in these events there is a palpable intensity; what happens here, in this arena, means everything to the athletes. It is the culmination of years of preparation, and provokes a range of emotional responses, from elation to despair; extremes which are inevitably transmitted to the audience, and infuse the atmosphere with nervous tension and excitement.

One Olympic title will be awarded on the first of five nights: the team sprint. The big question is, will the British trio bridge that half-second gap to the French? On a night of shocks, the first is the GB line-up. Gone is Ross Edgar, who, as reserve, cuts a forlorn figure as he goes through a warm-up that will in all probability be for nothing. The new boy is Jason Kenny, who thus adds Edgar's scalp to those of MacLean and Queally. Again, his times in training had given the British management a relatively easy decision – the only doubts surround Kenny's lack of experience, and the fact the new British trio of Jamie Staff, Kenny and Hoy has never raced together.

It is a fact that makes their time in qualifying all the more remarkable. As Jamie Staff blasts off and thunders through the first lap in the fastest time the world has ever seen, and Kenny maintains that ripping pace through lap two, recording the fastest second lap the world has ever seen, and finally Hoy takes over, and records the fastest third lap the world has ever seen, their time flashes up on the scoreboard: 42.95 seconds, the first-ever sub-43-second team sprint. Not only have they bridged the half-second gap to the French, they have gone almost a third of a second faster again. On the night, the French, second fastest qualifiers, find *themselves* adrift this time, by half a second.

Later, much later, Brailsford will reveal the significance of that performance. 'As soon as the team sprint boys got up and broke the world record with their first ride, Shane Sutton and I looked at each other and went: "Shit, we're going to get a lot of medals." We knew, at that moment, that our calibration was right.'

There is no stopping the British trio on their march to gold, which inevitably involves a meeting in the final with their old foes the French, and a final lap head-to-head between Hoy and Arnaud Tournant, who will retire after Beijing. The British start fast, and they are up, but there appears to be a problem ... they are not the compact unit they have been in their first two rides (in the second they had gone a little slower than their first) ... Staff blasts off, Kenny is tucked in behind him, but Hoy is struggling to hold Kenny's wheel. Halfway around lap two he is a length or two off the back; it looks bad. Yet Hoy summons everything he has; by the start of the final lap he is back up to Kenny's back wheel, and then comes the surge. It is Hoy v Tournant again, and as both flash across their respective lines, on opposite sides of the track, GB have it: 43.128 seconds, 0.523 seconds faster than the French. Gold for Britain, and tears on the podium from Hoy, the first British cyclist ever to win two Olympic gold medals.

'I think our first ride battered the others into submission,' says Hoy. But what about the gap in the final between him and Kenny? Had there been a problem? Hoy shrugs and smiles. 'Yeah, I struggled – but with the speed these two guys go over the first two laps, you've got a choice: you can either give it everything to close the gap and use up a lot of energy doing that, or you pace it, and try to close it down on the home straight so that you're finishing level with the second rider at the end of his lap. It's not the ideal way to do it, it's bloody hard, but the important thing is not to panic. And I didn't.

'We have been dreaming about winning,' he continues, 'but when your dream actually comes to fruition, with the three of us all hitting top form at the same time, it's an incredible feeling. Tonight also means so much more to me because my family are here: my mum [Carol], father [David], my sister Carrie, who is six months pregnant, and her fiancé Garry, and my girlfriend Sarra – quite a big entourage.' But there will be no celebrations tonight, says David. 'We're postponing the party until Tuesday,' he says, holding up crossed fingers.

For Brailsford, the team sprint success carries enormous significance, and not just in proving that his team is 'calibrated'. 'The

French were really, really sure that they were going to win this,'
he says. 'If I'm honest, I thought we were coming here for silver;
that gold would be a step too far.

'But this,' he adds with some relish, 'will be a real kick in the
goolies for them.'

Saturday, 16 August

Day two, and blue is the colour. Yesterday, every staff member
of the British team – the coaches, mechanics, sports scientists,
physiotherapists, soigneurs, performance analysts – had been
turned out in red. Today they are all dressed in blue. You don't
need to be Nostradamus to predict that tomorrow will be white.
But what then? Whatever: they look impressive in their coordi-
nated uniforms, and stand out a mile from the others. It is a statement. It says: 'We are professional; we are a team.'

Details, details.

Today is the keirin, with an interesting sub-plot supplied by a
BBC report on the eve of the Games, alleging that the Japanese
Keirin Association (JKA) effectively bought their event a place in
the Olympics with a $3 million payment to the UCI. 'It's been done
in total transparency,' the former UCI president – and now big
cheese in the IOC – Hein Verbruggen tells the BBC. 'This was done
for the development of track cycling around the world.' Still, the
report is enough to cast my mind back to my visit to the UCI's
headquarters in Switzerland; could the Japanese 'bung' explain
the plush building? Surely not. And as Verbruggen says, the money
was used to develop track cycling worldwide, not to build fancy
headquarters.

But back to Beijing. In heat one Hoy is drawn against Grégory
Baugé among four others, but he rides it in his usual way, going
early, and winning easily. Heat two is a tougher proposition: it
includes Tournant, Shane Kelly and the reigning Olympic cham-

pion, Ryan Bayley. Yet it is the same script: Hoy goes early, and wins easily to make the final, in a field that contains another rider with a one hundred per cent record: his British team-mate Ross Edgar.

As the race starts Edgar wins a tussle with Tournant for the spot behind the derny; Hoy settles behind Edgar, then draws level and Edgar eases slightly, allowing him to claim the spot behind the bike. Clever. Now the British riders are one and two. And when Hoy makes his move, Edgar again subtly eases off. Hoy gets the gap, never looks back, and wins by several lengths, while Edgar emerges from the melee to take silver. A one-two; a second gold medal for Hoy in Beijing, and an astonishing night for British cycling, with Bradley Wiggins winning gold in the pursuit and Steven Burke taking bronze; Rebecca Romero and Wendy Houvenaghel guaranteeing another one-two by both reaching the women's pursuit final; and Chris Newton claiming bronze in the points race. 'That keirin win just means everything to me,' says Hoy. 'After the kilo was dropped I thought it might be the end of my individual career. But to come back and win a different event is just fantastic.'

Sunday, 17 August

Sprint qualifying in the morning. This, says Hoy's coach Iain Dyer, is the 'pinch point'. It was a long night last night, after the keirin, and a lengthy visit to dope control, and Hoy returned to the athletes' village late, tired and hungry. He couldn't sleep. 'I was buzzing,' he says. The dope control process had been complicated by convoluted form filling and bungling officials. Today, the inside of Hoy's right arm is covered in bruises from cack-handed attempts to extract blood.

Not that the lack of sleep seems to affect him in sprint qualifying. He is fastest, in 9.815 seconds – an Olympic record and his first sub-ten in competition – to usurp none other than Jason Kenny, whose 9.857 also broke the Olympic record. And a further interesting factoid: Hoy now holds every Olympic record in the sprint disciplines, for the 200 m, kilometre and team sprint.

Monday, 18 August

The story today is that Britain's team pursuit squad smashes the world record, reducing it to a scarcely believable 3 minutes, 53.314 seconds, in the process slicing two seconds off the old mark – which they'd set the previous day. Bradley Wiggins, Paul Manning, Ed Clancy and Geraint Thomas comprise the foursome for an event that is sublime to watch. They are fast, slick, precise – poetry in motion. And for Wiggins it means a second gold medal, with a third possibility in tomorrow's Madison.

But Hoy also has a third in his sights: he and Kenny both progress to the semi-final of the sprint. And neither loses a single heat along the way. Bos is a casualty, and so, at the hands of the wunderkind Kenny, is Sireau.

Tuesday, 19 August

Victoria Pendleton, whose shattering experience in Athens four years ago almost persuaded her to give up, fulfils her promise and her dream by dominating the women's sprint and winning Britain's seventh cycling gold medal. But there is a first disappointment: Wiggins's and Mark Cavendish's bid to follow their world Madison title with Olympic gold fails. Wiggins, with an Olympic record in the pursuit, and world record in the team pursuit, appears to run out of steam. His personal ambition of three gold medals is foiled. But one cyclist can still do it, and thus become the first British athlete to do so since Henry Taylor, a swimmer, in 1908. Chris Hoy.

In the sprint semi-final Hoy is drawn against Mickaël Bourgain of France, Kenny against Maximilian Levy of Germany. Hoy toys with Bourgain, keeping the Frenchman in front, then coming around him on the final lap to win heat one. Against Levy, Kenny is cunning, dummy attacking, playing with his rival, and finally beating him easily. The second heats see more skirmishes, but Bourgain and Levy can't compete and throw in the towel, allowing the British riders easy victories. They will meet each other in the final.

This poses an interesting challenge for the sprint coaches, Iain Dyer and Jan van Eijden, whose job, ordinarily, entails talking tactics, and sussing out opponents. Here, there is clearly a dilemma. Do they tell Kenny how to beat Hoy? Or do they tell Hoy how to beat Kenny?

'We spoke about it briefly last night,' says Dyer. 'We dared to dream that they both might be in the final together, so Jan and I said to each other, "If both make it, we'll take turns taking them to the line." We weren't going to say anything, just shake hands, wish them the best of luck, and that was it.'

Hoy rolls off first in heat one, but forces Kenny into the lead, meaning that the young sprinter leads it out. Hoy stalks him around the track, and when he hits the gas, he closes the gap easily, coming over the top of Kenny to take round one. Round two is similar: Kenny leads, Hoy waits, leaving it a little longer, but finally drawing alongside on the final bend, clashing elbows, and emerging in front on the home straight, punching the air as he crosses the line. The three gold medals are his. But it is another statistic that attests to his dominance here: he has raced eighteen times, including all heats, and won each and every one of them. In none has he even looked like being challenged.

Kenny is beaten, but smiling. A silver medal, to add to his team sprint gold, is not a bad haul for a 20-year-old. 'If you'd said six months ago I'd get silver, I wouldn't have believed you,' he says. 'Chris is unbelievable. If you get up on the track and do a really good time, he'll step up and go even faster. I mean, I see him training every day, so I know his strengths and weaknesses ... '

His weaknesses? 'Well, maybe not weaknesses,' smiles Kenny, 'just weaker strengths.'

For Brailsford, Hoy 'does genuinely embody those Olympic values of fair play and working hard. He is the real deal. His standing within the squad is massive. He is the leader of the pack. Whenever there's a wobble in our team, people stop and you can see all the heads look at Chris. Like a pack of wolves, when something spooks them, they all stop and turn and look at the leader. That's Chris Hoy.'

Pendleton, standing waiting for Hoy's victory ceremony, with her own gold medal hanging around her neck, is similarly effusive. 'Chris is a legend,' she says. 'Everyone asks me, "Who is my sporting hero?" thinking I'd choose someone from history. And I say, "It's Chris Hoy." He's an inspiration. He's a real role model and someone to whom we in the UK should pay more attention.' Edgar, meanwhile, puts his team-mate's success down simply to 'years and years of hideously hard training'.

Today is the culmination of all that; of thousands of hours of work, adding layer upon layer of meticulous preparation. Yet as Hoy said in 2005, upon learning that his event, the kilo, was to be axed from the Olympics, even his wildest dreams couldn't have conjured up what has just happened. Three gold medals mean he is Britain's most successful Olympian in a century and Scotland's greatest Olympian of all time. But now, here in Beijing, there is a final irony – stepping forward to present his third gold medal is none other than the president of the UCI, Pat McQuaid. As Hoy leans forward a smiling McQuaid tells him: 'You have to forgive me now. There's no way you'd have won three golds if the kilo had still been on the programme.'

Hoy replies: 'Yeah, fair enough.'

A few moments earlier, after beating Kenny in their second heat, and the customary pumped fist celebrations, Hoy had rolled slowly around the track to where his family were camped, embracing first his father, burying his face in his chest, before working his way along the line. There are tears all round, especially from Hoy himself. He struggles to hold himself together, though not too hard; if now isn't a time for emotion, when is? He explains that he has been keeping such a tight lid on it all, suppressing all those emotional thoughts with logical ones, just as Steve Peters has advised – and he has taken this to such an extreme that whenever team-mates won gold, as they did in the velodrome on four occasions, Hoy insisted on standing with his back towards proceedings. This, he explains, was so that he couldn't see his team-mates' emotional reactions. He didn't want to risk getting caught up in it himself.

'We try to act like robots,' he says, 'to keep our emotions capped throughout the whole process. That's why it all came out afterwards.' The sight of Hoy dissolving into tears – 'The Great Bawl of China' will be one headline; most others focus on the medals, or 'Great Haul of China' – is one that resonates with many, including David Beckham, who, when asked for his favourite moment of the Olympics, says that it was when Hoy won the sprint and went to see his dad in the stand. 'It reminded me of when I was starting out and my own dad was there supporting me in the stands.'

David Hoy, meanwhile, can uncross his fingers now, and start planning the celebrations.

Six hours later, Hoy and I are sitting in a taxi outside Bar Bud, an Olympic party venue in the centre of Beijing. Tonight's party has been truncated: Hoy is knackered. It has all caught up with him, and for the last couple of hours he has dreamed not of champagne, but of a double cheeseburger and fries and a McChicken sandwich (which, at 4 a.m., he will be seen scoffing in the athletes' village).

He slumps in the taxi, clearly drained, but also struggling to comprehend what he has done, and how his life might change. He has no idea, none at all, how it is playing back home, even though there are some 'tasty offers' already trickling in, for photoshoots in glossy magazines, that kind of thing. He is a little shocked that photographs of him at home should be deemed to be so valuable. But what has tickled him most is Jason Queally's revelation that he placed a bet on him winning three gold medals. As a consequence, Queally is £4,500 better off. 'I can't believe he did that,' says Hoy. 'It's so flattering that he had the faith and confidence in me to do that.'

Just as our taxi is about to pull away, a large set of knuckles raps on the window. The door swings open, and a huge figure looms in the darkness. 'You going to the athletes' village?' asks a Canadian accent. 'Yeah, sure,' says Hoy, vacating the front seat and moving into the back.

On the way to the village we chat. He is a wrestler from Calgary and his name is Ari Taub. Which class is he in? 'The heaviest one,' he says. You don't say. He is 19 stone. How did he get on? 'I got beat. First round.'

When I look him up later I see that his Olympics lasted just four minutes – 'One and done for Ari Taub' as one headline put it, before describing him as 'Canada's least likely Olympian'. He is a 37-year-old father of two sets of identical twins, a Greco-Roman wrestler who self-funded his Olympic adventure, having tried for twenty years to get to the Games. After his bout he told journalists that he doesn't regret a thing, that the sacrifices, and the $100,000 he says it cost him, have all been worthwhile. 'I'm having a great time just being here and talking to people,' he had told them. Now, a little surreally, he is sharing a cab with one of the most decorated athletes of the Beijing Games, whose three gold medals are currently stuffed into his jeans pockets. And the truly wonderful thing is that Taub is completely oblivious.

Taub is friendly. 'What's your sport?' he asks, turning, with some difficulty, to face Hoy.

'I'm a cyclist,' says Hoy.

'Oh yeah?' says Taub. 'You ride the Tour de France?'

'No,' says Hoy, 'I'm a sprinter – I do the short distances, in the velodrome.'

'Oh,' says Taub, a little disappointed. 'I love the Tour de France. One day I want to ride the whole Tour, in front of the race.' (Crikey, we think.)

'One guy in our team, Mark Cavendish, won four stages this year,' says Hoy.

'Yeah, I know!' says Taub. 'How about that? I watched it all. That guy's awesome, eh?'

The taxi arrives at my hotel, and I leave them chatting about Mark Cavendish, though not before informing Taub that Cavendish happens to be the only member of the British track cycling team not to have won a medal in Beijing. At that he swivels his considerable bulk ninety degrees to look a little more closely at Hoy, who has kept resolutely quiet about his success.

'This guy made history yesterday,' I tell Taub, and leave them to it.

CHAPTER 16

Foot to the Floor Time

Melbourne, 8 April 2012

It's the final of the keirin at the world championships in Melbourne, and Hoy is well positioned with three laps to go. Maximilian Levy of Germany leads, Simon van Velthooven of New Zealand is second, Jason Kenny is third. And then there's Hoy, an ominous, brooding presence, gripping the hooks of his handlebars, twisting his hands, as though ready to turn the throttle.

Since Beijing, Hoy has been playing around with different approaches to the keirin. No longer a one-trick pony, he has proved that he can win races from the front, the back and the middle. But here in Melbourne he is about to be faced with his biggest test. On the back straight, inside two laps to go, Kenny lets a small gap open to Levy and Van Velthooven. Hoy remains behind him. He thinks about coming around the outside, but as he makes his move, Kenny speeds up. They are rivals here, not teammates. Hoy drops back again as Kenny continues his acceleration, going over the top of the leading pair. But they, too, speed up. They become a leading trio, fanning across the track, confronting Hoy with a virtual wall of human bodies.

There is nowhere for him to go. He is boxed in. Hopelessly boxed in. It is too late to attack around the outside. He dives back down the track, as though seeking sanctuary behind the wall. Levy leads on the inside, Van Velthooven follows in the middle, and Kenny is on the outside, half-way up the banking. Hoy moves up the inside of Van Velthooven. He is now directly behind Levy. And as they come out of the final bend, Hoy flicks out, just enough to let Van Velthooven know he's there; the New Zealander in turn wobbles, altering his line a fraction, forcing Kenny to go even wider; and, into the small gap that opens up between Levy and Van Velthooven, goes Hoy. The biggest man on the track dives into the gap and emerges like a mouse popping out of a hole. Now there is clear track ahead of him. He presses hard. And just before the line, he inches past Levy.

It's Hoy's fourth world keirin title. His eleventh world championship gold medal. And it has almost certainly been the most astonishing of all of them.

As was clear in Melbourne, Hoy was not finished. In fact, as the London Olympics approached, it seemed that history was repeating itself. He was once again hitting top form when it mattered. He was improving. In the autumn before London there was a personal best in the gym. Déjà vu all over again.

In all honesty, I didn't imagine that I would be revisiting and updating this book for the London Games. It wasn't for the same reason that Shane Sutton questioned whether Hoy would appear at his fourth Olympics. 'If Chris Hoy makes the team for London us coaches won't have been doing our jobs properly,' said Sutton in the immediate aftermath of Beijing. How that wound Hoy up!

But while Sutton reasoned that his age and the emergence of a new generation of sprinters would rule him out, my uncertainty owed nothing to his ability. Instead, I questioned whether he could sustain his hunger. While Hoy always said that he would not miss the opportunity to compete in a home Olympics – 'As soon as the announcement was made in 2005, I knew I'd be going, there was never any question,' he insisted – I wondered if the opportunities that would flow his way after Beijing would prove too much of a distraction, and eventually overcome him, or gradually wear him down. Even in the course of our taxi ride in Beijing it had been apparent that the interest back home was enormous – and so it proved.

And there were other distractions: he settled down and moved into a nice big house in Cheshire; he was knighted in the 2009 New Year Honours list; he married Sarra the following year; and he became the face of products from Kellogg's Bran Flakes to Gillette razors – all very pleasant, but new priorities, or 'distractions' (recall what Sutton had said: 'You think he'd be settled now, right, married and all the rest of it? Nah, he's not willing to share the moment. It's all about him, and that is one *really* good to trait to have when you want to reach the top.').

Yet Hoy made his most important decision within months of Beijing. He was offered a choice: do you want to be a celebrity who capitalizes on his fame, or an athlete? It was a choice that boiled down to this: rest on your laurels, or try to add new ones. He chose to remain an athlete.

As I re-read the first edition of this book on the eve of the London Olympics, I was struck by several passages. Some brought a wry smile, such as David Hoy claiming that he regretted not buying his son a set of golf clubs instead of a bike. It was a joke, but the implication was that, if Chris was going to pursue a sporting career, golf clubs seemed a more sensible, less demanding and potentially more lucrative choice. Cycling wasn't a career choice. It was little more than a hobby, and the idea that you could earn a living as a track cyclist in Britain was fanciful. The notion that you could ever become wealthy was ludicrous. The suggestion that you could ever have a 'Sir' in front of your name for your efforts in a velodrome was utterly ridiculous.

The second passage I was struck by – and which links to the above point – concerned Jason Queally. He struggled after winning a gold medal at the Sydney Olympics in 2000 because he had to maximize the commercial opportunities available to him. They were not connected to track cycling; they were extra-curricular activities that he was forced to juggle with his cycling career, and which proved detrimental to it. Recall that the day after the 2001 world championships in Antwerp, Queally flew off to America to make an attempt at the world land speed record. It is reminiscent of Jesse Owens or other Olympic champions who were constrained by the rules on amateurism, and compelled to take on horses in exhibition races or become virtual circus acts in order to earn a living. But it is yet another sign of how things have changed in less than a decade that Hoy could remain an athlete, with his main focus still on training and racing, without having to worry about lost commercial opportunities, or becoming a glorified circus act. The choice was his to make: he could be an athlete and perhaps miss out on appearances on *I'm a Celebrity, Get Me Out of Here*, or similar, but still make a good living. It had become viable.

The one thing that hasn't changed, perhaps, is Hoy himself. In this respect, I was struck, too, by a quote from Martin Barras, the coach who worked with the British sprinters briefly in the early 2000s. For a coach, said Barras, Hoy was 'a dream come true … I show my riders a video of Chris because I want them to copy him. There's an honesty about what he does, in training and racing. No foxing or bluffing. And he does it consistently.'

Barras noted that Hoy was 'getting older'. He was speaking in 2007. Hoy's age became an issue as the Beijing Olympics closed, when Sutton made his infamous comment. Yet, after a post-Beijing year that he tackled with less intensity – albeit he suffered a hip injury after a horrendous crash during the keirin at the Copenhagen World Cup, ruling him out of the 2009 world championships – he returned in 2010 with the bit back between his teeth. The nature of the Olympic cycle means that this half-way point feels, for the athlete, a lot closer to the next Games than the previous ones. Indeed, the previous Olympics were by now receding so rapidly in the rear-view mirror that they were all but forgotten, along with the performances and any 'credit' accrued. And, looming, was London, with the pressure to effectively start from scratch, and prove yourself all over again.

Hoy didn't really have to prove himself all over again. But, if he was to aspire to matching what he had done in Beijing, he had to believe that he needed to. He had to imagine he was starting from zero; that every training session, every day, was the most important one he'd ever done. It meant maintaining the consistency that Barras mentioned, into his sixteenth and seventeenth years as an international athlete.

There were two significant changes between Beijing and London, one concerning the Olympics, the other a little closer to home. As they did after Athens, the UCI tinkered with the track programme. This time it was in the interests of gender balance: it meant there would be the same number of medals for men and women. While that could only be applauded, less welcome was the news that, once again, events would be dropped. Gone were the individual pursuit, the points race and Madison. And in, instead, was the omnium: an event of six different disciplines, sprint and endurance, designed to reward the best all-rounder. To most observers, it seemed a poor exchange.

For Hoy, the change to the programme made no difference. The sprint, keirin and team sprint remained. But another change did affect him. Under the new rules – all of them intended to keep the number of track cyclists to a minimum, as the IOC struggle to control the total number of competing athletes – each event would feature only one rider per nation. For some of the world's best riders, this was a disaster. With only one in the sprint and keirin, for example, there can be no repeat of the British one-twos in Beijing, when Jason Kenny and Ross Edgar won silver medals behind Hoy. The French, Germans and Australians could feel similarly aggrieved; it would mean leaving some potential Olympic medallists at home, or sitting on the sidelines. And it means that the Olympics stand to be less competitive than the world championships. 'You could get to the semi-final without being overly tested,' notes Hoy. 'The best athletes deserve the chance to compete at the highest level. I think it's bad for the sport.'

The other change that affected the British set-up was the birth of a professional road team, Team Sky. When Dave Brailsford first talked about his long-term plan to set up a road team, and compete in the Tour de France, it was during the 2007 Tour. He would get the London Olympics out the way, he said, and the team would take to the road in 2013. But the plans were accelerated by two developments. The first was the acquisition of an ambitious sponsor: Sky. The second was the emergence of two top-class road riders: Mark Cavendish and Bradley Wiggins.

Both were well known to Brailsford and his team, of course, but there was surprise, nevertheless, at the speed of their progress. By 2008, when Cavendish won his four stages at the Tour, he was well on his way, and he confirmed himself as the fastest sprinter in the world with six stage wins the following year. At the same time, Wiggins proved a revelation. After switching his focus from track to road after Beijing he lost weight, trained more seriously than he had ever done before, and focused his sights on the holy grail: the general classification of the Tour de France. Publicly, he said at the start of the 2009 Tour that he was aiming for top twenty. Privately, he was thinking top ten. In the end, he finished just off the podium in fourth.

Brailsford, who had talked breezily of one day winning the Tour with a British rider, was by now working to get his road team off the ground. He signed Wiggins and the squad was launched with great fanfare in central London in January 2010. From there it was off to Australia and the Tour Down Under; and from there to the Middle East for the tours of Qatar and Oman; and then to Europe, as the relentless programme of races continued. Team Sky had 26 riders, with a core of British riders but with other nationalities, too. They raced a total of 262 days in their debut season.

Brailsford was, as he tends to be, fairly hands-on. And by April 2010, when they dispensed with their senior sports director, Scott Sunderland, so was Sutton. Back in Manchester, Steve Peters over-saw the other squads – not just track, but BMX and mountain biking as well. Inevitably, there were some who wondered whether the all-consuming nature of Team Sky – of which Brailsford was team principal, while also remaining performance director of British Cycling – would detract from efforts elsewhere. The success of the track team, for example, was the culmination of a process that had depended on attention to detail, absolute focus, and day-in, day-out commitment. Some openly questioned whether that could be maintained, among them one of the Beijing gold medallists, Jamie Staff.

Having retired as an athlete, and become coach to the American sprinters, Staff said: 'Dave Brailsford's attention turned to the road [and] I think it's having an effect on the track team. You need a leader. If your leader goes off and leads something else, you get consequences. At the end of the day it comes down to the riders, obviously, but having someone to lead the army is the key. It gives the riders the belief they have the backing. If you remove that and the riders feel like they are on their own, then cracks can appear. I see some cracks appearing.'

Brailsford responded by saying that, after Athens, he had also been distracted by another project, to set up the British Cycling Academy. It was on a smaller scale, and it was less intense. But he was insistent that he hadn't taken his eye off the ball; that his focus would return to the track programme when required, and certainly in time for London. He also said he would step back from a day-to-day role with Team Sky in 2011, delegating more responsibility to his team of coaches and sports directors.

Whether Brailsford's absences mattered to the track riders is an interesting point. Although named coach of the year at the BBC Sports Personality of the Year ceremony in 2008, Brailsford was not – and never has been – a coach. He manages the staff, including the coaches. And the coaches in charge of the sprint team remained the same: principally Iain Dyer and Jan van Eijden, with Sutton maintaining a keen interest. 'I'll never abandon Vicky Pendleton or Sir Chris,' said Sutton (who, since Hoy's knighthood, always insists on the 'Sir').

For Hoy, little changed. The main change was brought out by Staff's retirement. It left a vacancy in the team sprint, one they struggled to fill. Otherwise, he trained with London firmly in mind. That didn't mean 'backing off', he said, but it meant training differently. 'There are certain types of sessions that take such a toll on the body – that are so demanding physically – that if I'd done them every day for four years I probably wouldn't make it to London. I've been simmering the last couple of years, but now I feel the intensity and focus coming back.' He was speaking in October 2011, after a European championships that proved a disappointment: he fell ill and came home early. Five months earlier he had also suffered a fractured rib. Apart from these hiccups, everything felt 'perfect'.

There was also the vague sense that it was all coming to an end; maybe a feeling of being 'demob happy' about his approach to the 'final' season, the 'final' Olympics? 'I'm 99.9 per cent sure it's my last Olympics,' he said, 'so I'm really going to throw everything I've got at it; really commit everything. Actually, I'm really enjoying training. I'm conscious of the fact that I'll be calling an end to my career at some point, but I want to look back and feel that I did enjoy it; that it wasn't just hard work and worrying about form. After the world championships in March [2012] I'll have a little break then start up and I'll think, the gloves are off now, and I'll throw all I've got at London. It's foot to the floor time. Time to commit everything.'

'99.9 per cent'? 'Calling an end to my career at *some* point'? The only thing Hoy seemed unable to commit to was retirement. Perhaps that was necessary in order to *avoid* becoming demob happy before demobilization.

Hoy's keirin win at the world championships in Melbourne established him, once again, as the man to beat in this event. In Australia the news was not quite so good in the other two sprint disciplines. With Kenny and a new man one, Philip Hindes, they were disqualified for a technical infringement in the team sprint. In the sprint he won a bronze medal, having suffered defeat to Kenny in the semi-final.

Yet the keirin rescued Hoy's championships. Not just the victory itself, but the manner of it. How did he come from so far back? How did he squeeze through that gap? And, for that matter, *why*? In fact, the more pertinent questions concerned what it said about his desire – and the answers to these questions might haunt his opponents in the build-up to the Olympics. Because that was the point: this was not the Olympics; he could surely live with losing; and yet, even when he found himself hopelessly boxed in, Hoy had quite simply refused to concede defeat.

He seemed to struggle to explain it himself. Speaking a month after returning home, as he entered the final phase of his training for London, he told me: 'I've watched it a few times on YouTube. People have been raving about it, but if you watch, you notice that I was almost apologetic with my celebrations. The thing is, I didn't feel that I necessarily deserved to win. It was an instinctive move and it worked out, but I'd rather not have been in the position where I had to make that move.'

It was dangerous, too. Had Levy or Van Velthooven closed the door to him, he would have crashed. It might have ended his Olympics. 'But you haven't got time to think,' he said. 'It was purely an instinctive reaction; conscious thought takes longer. You expect a bit of a ripple on the last bend; you flick out a little bit to make it further for the guy on the outside. But still …'

Hoy returned from Melbourne, to his 'blueprint' for success – the training programme he had drawn up the previous autumn – trying not to relate everything back to Beijing. 'It's important to remind yourself that it's new. You can't replicate what you did in the past. Every challenge has to be new.' Things had changed. Gears, for one thing. 'Gear sizes have changed dramatically since Beijing; they're massive now. That suits me, suits my style.'

There was still work to be done. Sutton spoke to Hoy the night after the worlds. 'There are a few things we need to change, mate,' he told him. Sutton had been 'sitting back, taking an overall view', said Hoy, 'and he sees things we don't see, and the coaches don't see. He sees our body language on the bike; there are little things he picks up on.'

Hoy sounded enthusiastic, excited. 'It's not about stepping stones any more. Or interim targets. You get a bit tired of talking about this thing on the horizon. You go to other races and don't get a chance to celebrate properly because it's all about the Olympics. Even when you win a world title, the response is: "You're world champion – that must give you confidence for the Olympics."

'Everything is related to that bigger picture. But it's so massive now, there's no avoiding it.'

EPILOGUE

Hot Pants and Magic Wheels

*'If you look back on history, when it comes down to that
really important ride, when it really matters, he steps up
and smokes it.'*   Jason Kenny

London Velodrome, 2 August 2012

On the eve of the London Olympics the cycling team is buzzing.
The atmosphere and sense of mounting expectation are uncan-
nily similar to Beijing, four years ago, when Nicole Cooke's gold
medal in the road race on the second day of the Games seemed
to act as a catalyst. Here, too, the riders have been galvanised by
a couple of performances by one man: Bradley Wiggins.

On the day that Wiggins became the first British cyclist to win
the Tour de France, just five days before the London Games began,
the track squad huddled around a television in the track centre at
the Newport Velodrome. They had done the same in the athletes'
village in Beijing, watching Cooke kick for home in the rain against
the backdrop of the Great Wall of China. Four years on, it's an indication of the improved standing of the cycling team – thanks,

largely, to Beijing – that Wiggins and Hoy enjoy starting roles in the Opening Ceremony, Wiggins ringing the bell to get them underway, Hoy leading in the British team as flagbearer.

Then the medals come. Lizzie Armitstead claims silver in the women's road race on day two, then Wiggins – 'putting the hundreds and thousands' on his Tour de France-shaped cake – wins gold in the time trial, with Chris Froome taking bronze. The track racing begins the next day. 'They can't wait to get into the velodrome,' says Wiggins. 'They're raring to go. And, from what I hear, they're flying.'

On day one, Hoy is riding the team sprint with Philip Hindes and Jason Kenny. At their training camp in Newport, the signs – and the times – were more than encouraging, but there's still an element of the unknown, especially after their disqualification for an 'irregular changeover' at the world championships in Melbourne. Yet, compared with 2008, this was a settled squad. There, remember, Kenny had come into the line-up at the last minute. Before the Beijing Olympics they had never raced in a major event together.

Still, there are nerves as they line up. There always are. At 19, there's a lot riding on Hindes, the German-born sprinter who is now required to be the new Jamie Staff. No pressure, then.

And in the first ride, as the gun goes off, and they burst out of the gate to an ear-splitting roar, disaster. Hindes' wheel slips. Kenny and Hoy get off to a clean start and are going faster than him, and begin to come over the top of him as they reach the bend, when Hindes goes down. He had been out of control since leaving the gate, fighting his bike as though he had suddenly found himself on one too big for him, and so the crash looks inevitable. And yet, later, when interviewed by Jill Douglas for the BBC, Hindes admits: 'We were saying if we have a bad start we need to crash to get a restart. I just crashed, I did it on purpose to get a restart, just to have the fastest ride. I did it. So it was all planned, really.'

'So you were trying to pull a fast one there?' asks Douglas. Hindes, who grew up in Germany, obviously isn't familiar with the expression, and replies: 'Yes, I was trying to get a fast start and get everything perfect.'

A debate will begin afterwards: was Hindes guilty of cheating? The rules state that a mechanical problem or crash entitles you to a re-start, but a slipping wheel would not count as a mechanical. It's possible that the slip was caused by a problem with the start gate, or grease on the track, but appealing to the commissaires on these grounds would probably have been futile. The only way to get the re-start that would keep them in the competition was for Hindes to crash. And crash he did.

Sections of the sporting world reacted with outrage to the suggestion that he might have crashed deliberately, even comparing it to the badminton players who had been sent home from the Olympics earlier in the week for throwing group games. Yet all sports have their black arts or tricks of the trade; and if the officials have always turned a blind eye, can the athlete be blamed for exploiting the rules? And Hindes, if he did crash deliberately, was not seeking an advantage: it was to stay in the competition.

I was reminded of an incident at the 1994 national track championships, when Hoy rode the kilometre time trial. With his starting effort, he pulled his foot out of the pedal. Again, this is not a 'mechanical', but, when it happened, experienced riders – and it used to happen a lot before the introduction of more secure clipless pedals – would tumble to the track and gain a re-start. Doing so would come as naturally to a track cyclist as a footballer kicking the ball out of play if a teammate is injured. But on that occasion in 1994, when Hoy pulled his foot out, his mentor Ray Harris recalled, 'The commissaire looked at me, saying, "Push him over!" It's an old trick, that, the trick of falling off your bike if your foot comes out. But Chris didn't realise.'

Whatever the rights or wrongs of what Hindes might or might not have done, the British trio are allowed a re-start. An anxious hush descends for the second attempt. Is Hindes distracted by the incident, or nervous about fluffing his opening lines once again? No. He blasts out of the start gate, doing his opening lap in 17.5 before Kenny takes it up on lap two, and Hoy finishes it off on lap three in a time of 43.065: their fastest time since Beijing, and marginally quicker than their old rivals from France.

These two teams progress to the final, with the GB trio going faster and faster. Come the final, the raucous atmosphere is that of a football match, and then, as they are called to the start, another hush falls, similar to the sense of anticipation that precedes the showpiece of any Olympic Games, the men's 100 metres final. Hindes rockets out of the gate, Kenny follows and Hoy threatens to break his bike sprinting after him. In Beijing, recall, Hoy fell several lengths behind Kenny, and both struggled to stay with Jamie Staff; here they are a tighter unit, but the effort is clear as Hindes roars around in 17.2. They are up on the French. And they don't look back. Kenny zips around the track, his effort a perfect demonstration of pure speed, while Hoy, when he takes over, is all raw power. They finish in 42.60: a new world record.

It's Beijing all over again.

The effort takes its toll, with Kenny unable to join the celebrations and the victory laps because he is trying not to throw up his lunch. Hoy has suffered, too. 'I was hanging on, digging deep. I put every ounce of effort into that last ride. I've never suffered like I did on the final lap. It was horrible.' But his fifth gold medal, he says, is 'my most memorable. With the home crowd, it was incredible.'

* * *

The next day Hoy went for a gentle recovery ride. He hadn't slept well, partly because he was still buzzing from the track and the gold medal and the remarkable atmosphere, but also because he was slightly troubled by the questions over Hindes' crash. His fifth gold medal saw him draw level with Sir Steve Redgrave as his country's most decorated Olympic athlete. Yet in some people's eyes there was a small stain, where the others were spotless.

He did some video analysis of the keirin with his sprint coach, Jan van Eijden, studying and discussing different strategies and tactics. He got back on the track during the training sessions, when the velodrome wasn't being used for competition. The one thing he wasn't worried about was his form. 'I'm confident I've got close to, if not the best form of my life,' he said.

He was not the only one. The astonishing thing, as events in the velodrome unfold over the following days, is that every British cyclist seems to have arrived at the London Games in the form of their life. The team pursuiters break the world record to defeat their Australian rivals in the final. It was expected to be a close race; the Australians had beaten them at the World Cup meeting on the London track, but since then, two of the squad, Jack Bobridge and Michael Hepburn, had been involved in a drink-driving incident in Spain, raising questions about how focused they were on winning in London. 'Our lads got a massive boost when they heard about that,' as one member of the GB backroom staff said.

In London the Australians are never in contention, and the extraordinary spectacle of the British squad, in such perfect sync that the four members appear to be parts of a single machine, creates arguably the most frenzied atmosphere of the six days in the velodrome, the noise following them around the arena, keeping dizzying pace, like a Mexican Wave in fast motion. They average 62.16 kph (38.62 mph) for the 4,000 metres.

What are the secrets this time? What have Chris Boardman and his secret squirrels come up with? There are two items that catch the media's attention: hot pants and magic wheels. But when told about the hot pants, a common reaction is: why did no one think of this before?

They are what the name suggests: heated trousers, baggy in design, resembling salopettes, which the British riders were spotted wearing in the track centre in between training efforts in the days before the London Games. But they come into their own in competition, when there can be a period of several minutes between finishing the warm down and being called to race. They had been developed in conjunction with Loughborough University and Adidas, after three years of study and development. Steve Faulkner, a PhD student at Loughborough, told the Press Association: 'By keeping the cyclists' muscles warmer we found a substantial increase in sprinting power that would be of practical benefit to the Team GB cyclists.'

'They haven't necessarily made a significant difference on their own,' explained Hoy after the team sprint, 'but they're a tiny piece in the jigsaw. The clothing, the equipment, the training analysis: every detail we're trying to optimise. But the hot pants came after we looked at previous events, when you warm down and then your muscles cool. I have no idea if they helped tonight. But they certainly didn't harm our chances. And we broke two world records …'

Then there were the magic wheels. Isabelle Gautheron, head of the French team, began to ask questions about the GB equipment on the fourth day. 'We are looking at the kit they use,' she told *L'Equipe*. 'We are asking a lot of questions: how have they gained so many tenths of seconds? Have they found a new training process based on certain energy pathways? I am not talking about any illicit product, because anti-doping tests are so strong.

Honestly, we are looking a lot at the kit they use.' In particular, she said, the wheels: 'They hide their wheels a lot. The ones for the bikes they race on are put in wheel covers at the finish [of a race].'

It was reported in the British media that the suspicion over the wheels owed to a misunderstanding. 'I told them we had some special wheels because we had made them specially round,' said Brailsford. 'The French seem to have taken it seriously, but I was joking.'

Yet Brailsford had been speaking to a *L'Equipe* reporter who insisted he knew the British performance director had been joking. The paper even made its own joke about the fact that the wheels were labelled 'Mavic' – a French company, ironically – and its similarity to 'magic'. In fact, the journalist was on to something. Although the wheels were labelled Mavic, and appeared similar to the wheels most other teams were using, the British team's wheels were not made by Mavic. They were their own wheels. Special wheels; secret wheels. But no more *round* than any other team's.

One of the remarkable aspects of the track cycling programme in London is that the velodrome becomes the place to see and be seen. It's hailed as the 'hottest' venue, and not only on account of the constant 28°C temperature. The Duke and Duchess of Cambridge appear, as do Prince Harry, the Prime Minister David Cameron, the Chancellor George Osborne, the ex-PM Tony Blair, basketball star Kobe Bryant, Stella McCartney, her father Paul … And the man who gets the biggest cheer of them all, Bradley Wiggins. It's a gold medal factory, with, apart from the men winning the team pursuit, Victoria Pendleton dominating the keirin and the women's team pursuit squad setting a new world record every time they step on the track, then demolishing the USA in the final.

In the men's sprint, which Kenny rides, having been selected instead of Hoy, the Bolton Bullet – as he is christened by *The Times* – is flying. But the question is, and has always been, whether he can beat Grégory Baugé. Baugé has dominated the sprint and always beaten Kenny, winning the world title four years in a row – though he was stripped of his 2011 title for missing doping tests, which also earned him a backdated 12-month ban. There seems no question that, on recent form, Baugé has the edge – he is the Goliath of sprinting, and they make for a contrasting pair: the relatively small Kenny up against the man mountain Baugé, and they have contrasting strengths, with Kenny's electrifying speed and Baugé's strength and power.

Yet Kenny wins. For the first time he beats Baugé. And afterwards Baugé appears frustrated, and puzzled. He simply cannot understand how he can be the best in the world for three years – and still the best now, he insists – but be beaten when it matters most. He makes for a brooding presence in the press conference that follows the race. And then he sticks his hand up. 'I would like to ask Jason a question.'

The room stirs. This is unprecedented. 'You were the silver medallist in 2008 and you have prepared for four years for the objective today, but how did you prepare?' he asks.

'It's not like we do anything different,' replies Kenny. 'The Olympics is our main goal ...'

'But you remember in Pruszkow in 2009,' Baugé persists, 'in the quarter-final, I beat you ...'

'That's because I went into the reps [repechages],' Kenny says with a laugh.

Baugé sits back and lets the journalists ask a few more questions, then sticks his hand up again. 'If I understand you well, for the next four years you will just relax and in Rio you'll be on top again?'

'No, the Olympics is the main one,' says Kenny. 'I still want to win world championships, they mean a lot to me as a rider.'

Baugé, whose tone is only slightly humorous, and more probing, explains that he is simply 'curious' to find out how Kenny had prepared. But the inference is clear: like his team director, he appears to think that the British team must have some trick up their sleeve, some secret, that gives them an advantage when it comes to the Olympics. And they are not the only ones. As the track cycling programme closes, *L'Equipe* runs a poll, asking the question: 'Are the British cyclists' performances in the velodrome cheating?' The manner of their 'cheating' is not specified, but 72 per cent respond: 'Oui.'

London Velodrome, 7 August 2012

There's one event left in the velodrome. By now the British team has won six gold medals on the track, one fewer than in Beijing, with the precocious and vivacious Laura Trott winning her second Olympic title in the omnium. But that is followed by Victoria Pendleton falling in the women's sprint to her old rival, and the woman she had beaten in Beijing, Anna Meares. Pendleton is relegated in the first heat, when she appears to buckle under the pressure applied by the Australian, who bears down on her as they come around the final bend, and drifts out of the sprinters' lane. Her defeat in that first round seems to destroy her; she hardly puts up a fight in round two. When Meares jumps for home, Pendleton's legs fail to respond and her head drops, and the mood in the velodrome changes.

It's as though the oxygen has been sucked out of the place. Nobody had seen it coming. Of all the stories set to be written at these Olympics, in this velodrome, there seemed one certainty:

that the Games would witness the coronation of Victoria, Queen of the Track. Her defeat, in what she says is the final race of her career, serves as a reminder that, for all that it might seem otherwise, there are no certainties. 'It's sport,' as Hoy says later. 'Anything can happen.'

And speaking of unpredictable, the keirin is the final event in the velodrome, the final event of Chris Hoy's Olympic career – he is 99.9 per cent certain of that – the final chance to equal the gold medals tally of Beijing, and Hoy's final chance to move ahead of Sir Steve Redgrave as his country's greatest Olympian.

Something that Jason Kenny said the previous evening seems to resonate as Hoy lines up for the final. It was as he prepared for his second, decisive match with Baugé that it hit the Bolton Bullet: he had been selected over Hoy for the sprint. Suddenly he felt the pressure and the responsibility. 'If Chris was in my shoes now,' Kenny told himself, 'there's no way he'd lose this. It made me want to justify myself, I suppose. Because if you look back on history, when it comes down to that really important ride, when it really matters, he steps up and smokes it.'

The keirin gets underway and Hoy takes up a position in the middle of the string. He grips his bars tight, crouches down low, stretches his back, twists his hands as though gently turning the throttle – just to check it's working – and glances back, at the pocket rocket, Azizulhasni Awang of Malaysia. Awang and Maximilian Levy are the riders he fears: Levy for his power, Awang for his acceleration and ability to burst through small gaps. When the derny swings off, with two-and-a-half laps to go, Levy, who had been sitting directly behnd the bike, makes a move, and Awang goes over the top. Hoy responds, shadowing this pair. Then Awang takes over from Levy at the front, and Hoy follows him. He decides to take no chances: as they come round for two laps to go, he passes Awang and hits the front. Two laps. It's a long way to be towing the others.

He is doing enough to stay at the front, but not too much; just 'feathering the throttle', as he puts it later, leaving something in the tank for that final lap. But coming round the bend and back into the home straight for the bell, he spots, on the inside of the track, Jan van Eijden, 'two feet in the air, jumping up and down … going mental. And I knew I had to go now.'

Van Eijden is worried about Levy, who is coming up fast on the outside, travelling faster than Hoy, and drawing level on the penultimate bend. His momentum is carrying him, he moves ahead, and Hoy's shoulders begin to rock violently as he tries to peg Levy back: to not let him get a length ahead. Going into the last bend Levy has almost a length – *almost*. 'If he got a full length on me he would have shut it down and I would have been nowhere. But I knew that if I dug deep, really deep, and I kept him on the outside of me, there was a chance. He was coming with a lot of speed and I thought for a moment that the dream's over.'

So did most people in the velodrome. So did Levy. So did van Eijden. So did Hoy's mother, Carol, who turned away, covered her eyes and wouldn't turn towards the track again until it was all over.

Then Hoy seems to access a new reservoir of power: he surges, drawing back level with Levy. It's like a rowing race, watching two boats nudging forward, edging back, nudging forward. But Hoy has the inside line and, as they enter the home straight, and Levy trails him by half-a-length, there seems no doubt; it all appears crushingly inevitable, as Kenny had said. 'When it comes down to that really important ride, when it really matters, he steps up and smokes it.'

It had really mattered on the back straight, coming round the final bend, and hurtling up the finishing straight. Then, says Hoy, 'I shut my eyes as I lunged, and I drove all the way to the line, threw the bike and heard this massive roar. I thought, that must be for me. Well, I hoped it was for me …'

The crowd rises as one, the sound reaches its climax, as Hoy circles the track waving, and then rides up through the middle of a guard of honour organised by the team's staff, including van Eijden, Iain Dyer, Brailsford and Sutton. He stops beside Sutton and hugs him. What does he feel? Joy? Happiness? Fulfilment? 'Relief,' he says. 'Relief and delight. Because it's the end. The last Olympics I'll do.'

He may go to the Commonwealth Games in Glasgow in 2014, he reflects later. 'It would be the perfect scenario, the dream swan-song.' But in the next breath he admits that London might have been it, the last we will see of him in competitive action in a velodrome, with the image of him digging deep and holding off Levy on that final lap the defining and apposite one.

'Two more years; it sounds nothing,' he says. 'But it's 35 hours a week for two years, and I want to have a normal life, to enjoy a drink or two, play golf, go shopping without worrying about being on my feet too long. Not walk up stairs and think: my legs are killing me.'

He pauses, then adds: 'It's monotonous and it sounds like I'm moaning, but I'm not. I love it.'

To Glasgow, then. And there's that 0.1 per cent chance of Rio.

Chris Hoy Palmarès

1999
First Gold – World Cup, Mexico, team sprint
Gold – European Championships, Italy, team sprint
Silver – World Championships, Berlin, team sprint

2000
Silver – World Championships, Manchester, team sprint
Silver – Olympic Games, Sydney, team sprint

2001
Bronze – World Championships, Antwerp, team sprint

2002
Gold – Commonwealth Games, Manchester, kilometre time trial
Bronze – Commonwealth Games, Manchester, team sprint
Gold – World Championships, Copenhagen, kilometre time trial
Gold – World Championships, Copenhagen, team sprint

2003
Bronze – World Championships, Stuttgart, team sprint
Scottish Sportsman of the Year, Commonwealth Games Council for Scotland
BBC Scotland Sports Personality of the Year

2004
Gold – World Championships, Melbourne, kilometre time trial
Bronze – World Championships, Melbourne, team sprint
Gold – Olympic Games, Athens, kilometre time trial
Awarded MBE

2005
Gold – World Championships, Los Angeles, team sprint
Cycling News Track Rider of the Year

2006
Gold – World Championships, Bordeaux, kilometre time trial
Silver – World Championships, Bordeaux, team sprint
Gold – Commonwealth Games, Melbourne, team sprint
Bronze – Commonwealth Games, Melbourne, kilometre time trial

2007
Gold – World Championships, Palma, kilometre time trial
Gold – World Championships, Palma, keirin
Silver – World Championships, Palma, team sprint
World record, 500 m flying start, La Paz, Bolivia
Scottish Sportsman of the Year (for the fourth time)

2008
Gold – World Championships, Manchester, individual sprint
Gold – World Championships, Manchester, keirin
Silver – World Championships, Manchester, team sprint
Gold – World Cup, Copenhagen, keirin (26th World Cup gold)
Gold – Olympic Games, Beijing, team sprint
Gold – Olympic Games, Beijing, keirin
Gold – Olympic Games, Beijing, individual sprint

2009
Gold – World Cup, Copenhagen, team sprint
Gold – World Cup, Manchester, keirin
Gold – World Cup, Manchester, sprint
Gold – World Cup, Manchester, team sprint

2010
Gold – World Championships, Copenhagen, keirin
Bronze – World Championships, Copenhagen, team sprint
Gold – World Cup, Melbourne, keirin
Gold – World Cup, Melbourne, team sprint

Silver – World Cup, Cali, team sprint
Silver – World Cup, Cali, sprint

2011
Silver – World Championships, Apeldoorn, keirin
Silver – World Championships, Apeldoorn, team sprint
Silver – World Championships, Apeldoorn, sprint
Gold – World Cup, Astana, sprint
Silver – World Cup, Astana, keirin

2012
Gold – World Cup, London, keirin
Gold – World Cup, London, sprint
Bronze – World Cup, London, team sprint
Gold – World Championships, Melbourne, keirin
Bronze – World Championships, Melbourne, sprint
Gold – Olympic Games, London, team sprint
Gold – Olympic Games, London, keirin

Track Cycling Glossary

Keirin Between six and nine riders start a keirin, riding the early laps behind a 'derny' motorcycle, which cranks up the pace and then swings off two-and-a-half laps from the end. There follows a mass sprint for the line, which is not for the faint-hearted – collisions and crashes are fairly common. Keirin racing originated in Japan where it is at the centre of a betting industry worth annually around $7.5 billion.

Derny A motorized bicycle designed and built for motor-paced track cycling events. The first dernys were built by Roger Derny of Paris in 1938.

Team sprint Three riders, three laps. The first rider leads out and swings up the banking after one lap, allowing the second rider to take over for lap two, when he swings off to allow man three to finish the job. Usually the team sprint involves two teams on opposite sides of the track; fastest wins.

Individual sprint Also known as the 'match sprint' this is the oldest track discipline, and for many the blue riband event. Run over four laps, the riders are only timed over the final 200 m. The early stages tend to be highly tactical, with each rider seeking to gain the most advantageous position – often, but not always, at the rear. Match sprinting often features 'cat and mouse' antics, the riders sometimes coming to a complete standstill with what is known as a 'track stand'.

Track Stand Seen in the individual sprint, this means a rider comes to a standstill, rocking gently back and forth on the bike in an attempt to manoeuvre his rival into a disadvantageous position.

Kilometre Time Trial ('Kilo') The simplest track event: a kilometre against the clock. For women the discipline is set over 500 m. The kilo was controversially dropped from the Olympic programme in 2005.

Pursuit Two riders start on opposite sides of the track, one in the home straight, one in the back straight. If one catches the other then the race is over; otherwise, it is the fastest over 4,000 m (for men) or 3,000 m (for women).

Team pursuit Four-man (or three-woman) teams start on opposite sides of the track and attempt to catch the other. One of the most visually spectacular of the track disciplines, since it requires inch-perfect precision. Each rider takes a turn at the front then swings up the banking and re-joins the string at the rear. The men race over 4,000 m, the women over 3,000 m.

Madison Has its origins at the New York Six-Day race in Madison Square Garden, where it was introduced to lessen the workload for the six-day racer who raced, literally, for six days (and nights). Two-man (or Madison) racing was introduced in 1899; it is a group (or bunch) race contested by teams of two, with only one racing at a time, while the other slowly circles the track. When his team-mate catches him, he drops down and is brought up to race speed – and re-introduced to the fray – with a 'hand sling.'

Six-Day Racing First held in London in 1878, and hugely popular in the USA until the 1930s, the early six-day races saw riders race almost non-stop for six days. These days the sport is big in Europe in winter, in places like Ghent, Munich, Grenoble and Rotterdam, where the riders race evening sessions, usually from around 7pm to 2am.

Devil Take the Hindmost Bunch race where the action is at the back rather than the front, with the last rider across the line on specific laps eliminated.

Points race Bunch race with points awarded on specific laps – rider with the most points at the end wins. Riders who lap the field can either be awarded bonus points or, being a lap up, are automatically declared winner – the rules vary.

Scratch race Straightforward: bunch race usually over 20 km; first across the line at the end wins.

Index

you need [from] the diary of the poor guy who is one of the many riders being dismantled daily by Chris Hoy and the Brits.' Sadly, Ray Harris, who was Chris's first coach and an inspiration to many hundreds of young cyclists, died in 2009.

A big thank you to Arnaud Tournant, who, for all that he is a legend, is also a very nice guy. Happy retirement at the end of 2008, Arnaud – you deserve it. And that world kilo record of yours is safe – for the moment.

Speaking of which, from the great Bolivia adventure, thanks to Ruben Martinez, Kenneth Baillie, Andy Buckley, Brendan Gallagher, Jill Douglas, John Graham, Michael Steele, Ken Farnes, Martin Bruin, Guy Elliott, Mirna Zapata and Chyang Hwang. Unfortunately there was sad news a few months after our return from Bolivia. Jesus Jr Bernardo Lujan Veneros, who was such a help during our stay, died in late 2007, aged fifty. As David Hoy explained: 'Bernardo was at the velodrome every day at 6 a.m., already well into his list of things to do, and was still working away at 9 p.m. when we were heading back to our hotel. He lived for his cycling. He and his family lived in the flat high above the grand-stand. Although we had tremendous help from many people in Bolivia, Bernardo's practical help – just looking for things to do, taking photographs, dealing with problems so that we had none – was invaluable. The success of our trip and many of the best memories are, to a great degree, down to Bernardo.'

I am grateful to Moray McLeish, Alan Pattullo, Kirsten Speirs, to the Brydie family, to Morag Aitken, David 'Spook' Munro, and their kids Meg and Fin; and to Graeme Herd, who knows Chris Hoy and Craig MacLean better than most, and whose wit and wisdom appears almost subliminally in this book (especially the 'Sliding Doors' chapter). Thank you also to colleagues William Fotheringham, Brian Palmer, Donald Walker and Colin Leslie of *The Scotsman*, Graham Bean and Richard Bath of *Scotland on*

Sunday, and all on *The Guardian* sports desk. Thanks, too, to my agent, Mark 'Stan' Stanton, and to Tom Whiting and everyone at HarperCollins.

Finally, for all their help, support, feedback and tolerance, a very big thank you to my father, Brian, brothers Robin and Peter, and thanks also to Laurie Traynor.

The following books provided essential reading: Chris Boardman, *The Complete Book of Cycling* (Partridge); William Fotheringham, *Roule Britannia* (Yellow Jersey Press); Tommy Godwin, *It Wasn't That Easy* (John Pinkerton Memorial Publishing Fund); Peter Joffre Nye with Jeff Groman and Mark Tyson, *The Six-Day Bicycle Races: America's Jazz Age Sport* (Van Der Plas Publications/Cycle Publishing); Geoffrey Nicholson, *Tony Doyle: Six-Day Rider* (Springfield Books Ltd); Les Woodland, *The Crooked Path to Victory* (Cycle Publishing); and *Dope: The Use of Drugs in Sport* (David & Charles).

Richard Moore
Edinburgh
April 2008